BEYOND THE CALL OF DUTY

SUNY SERIES IN ETHICAL THEORY
ROBERT B. LOUDEN, EDITOR

Recent years have seen a proliferation of work in applied and professional ethics. At the same time, however, serious questions have been raised concerning the very status of morality in contemporary culture and the future of moral theory efforts. Volumes within the SUNY Press Ethical Theory series address the present need for sustained investigations into basic philosophical questions about ethics.

BEYOND THE CALL OF DUTY

Supererogation,
Obligation, and Offence

GREGORY MELLEMA

STATE UNIVERSITY OF NEW YORK PRESS

Published by
State University of New York Press, Albany

© 1991 State University of New York

All rights reserved

Printed in the United States of America

No part of this book may be used or reproduced
in any manner whatsoever without written permission
except in the case of brief quotations embodied in
critical articles and reviews.

For information, address State University of New York
Press, State University Plaza, Albany, N.Y., 12246

Production by E. Moore
Marketing by Dana E. Yanulavich

Library of Congress Cataloging-in-Publication Data

Mellema, Gregory, 1948–
    Beyond the call of duty : supererogation, obligation, and offence
/ Gregory Mellema.
      p. cm. — (SUNY series in ethical theory)
    Includes bibliographical references and index.
    ISBN 0-7914-0737-3 (ch : acid-free). — ISBN 0-7914-0738-1 (pb : acid-free)
    1. Supererogation. I. Title. II. Series.
BJ1451.M455 1991
170—dc20   90-45680
                                                              CIP

10 9 8 7 6 5 4 3 2 1

To my father

Contents

Acknowledgments — ix

Chapter One — 1
  Introduction

Chapter Two — 13
  Good Consequences, Altruism, and
  Continuity with Duty

Chapter Three — 43
  Theism and Supererogation

Chapter Four — 69
  Other Contemporary Anti-Supererogationists

Chapter Five — 105
  Quasi-Supererogation

Chapter Six — 131
  Supererogation, Virtue, and Vocation

Chapter Seven — 161
  A Cost-Benefit Analysis

viii   Contents

Chapter Eight   181
    Supererogation and Offence

    Notes   211

    Index   221

Acknowledgments

Some of the material in chapters two and five is based upon previously published work. An earlier version of section four of chapter two appears in *The Journal of Value Inquiry,* April, 1991 (25:2), in an article entitled "Supererogation and the Fulfillment of Duty." And section one of chapter five is based upon my article, "Quasi-Supererogation," published in *Philosophical Studies,* LII (1987), pages 141–150. I am grateful to the editors of these journals for permission to make use of this material.

I am indebted to my colleagues in the Calvin College Philosophy Department who provided me, in the context of many sessions of our Tuesday colloquium, with comments and criticisms over a period of several years. My appreciation for this help extends to former colleagues Alvin Plantinga and David Snyder. In addition I wish to to thank Victor Anderson, Fred Feldman, John Schneider, Douglas Schuurman, and Mark Williams for helpful advice regarding various portions of the discussion. Most of all I am grateful to Michael Stocker and Michael J. Zimmerman for their detailed criticisms of a nearly final version of the manuscript.

Chapter 1

INTRODUCTION

In February, 1988 the Vienna daily newspaper *Die Presse* interviewed Austrian President Kurt Waldheim about the report of a commission concerning his conduct as a Wehrmacht officer from 1942 to 1945. While the report found no proof that Waldheim had committed war crimes, it nevertheless noted that he was "excellently informed" of atrocities committed by German army units in Greece and Yugoslavia and made no attempt to stop them. Waldheim's response in the interview included these remarks: "Yes, I admit I wanted to survive [by following orders]. . . . I have the deepest respect for all those who resisted. But I ask understanding for all the hundreds of thousands who didn't do that, but nonetheless did not become personally guilty."[1]

With these words Waldheim is making two important claims about the moral status of his involvement in the atrocities, claims which in many ways seem to reflect the way in which people commonly think about their failures to act. First, he is conceding that his desire to survive led him to follow orders rather than to resist. Thus, he appears to be conceding that he might have followed a course of action morally superior to that which he in fact followed. Second, by asking for the understanding of the readers of *Die Presse*, Waldheim appears to be claiming that his failure to resist is not deserving of moral condemnation. Although those who resisted deserve great respect, those who did not resist deserve understanding. Presumably, then, moral condemnation is not what they deserve, and he concludes that those who did not resist are not personally guilty.

No doubt it might be debated at great length whether those who did not resist are personally guilty. One might very well wish to dispute Waldheim's claim that those who failed to speak out against the atrocities which they knew were taking place manage to escape being personally guilty for what happened. Rather than focusing upon the difficult question of personal guilt, however, I suggest concentrating upon Waldheim's plea for understanding. Those who resisted deserve praise, as he sees it, but those who failed to resist deserve understanding.

Is it possible to be understanding toward those who failed to resist? Generally speaking, is it possible to be understanding to those who fail to do that which is good or praiseworthy? One avenue of approach to answering this question is to begin by asking whether those who fail to do that which is good or praiseworthy have thereby violated any duties or obligations. It is one thing to fail to perform a good act, but it is another thing to fail to perform a good act which it is one's duty or obligation to perform. Hence it is one thing to be understanding toward one who fails to do the former, and it is another thing to be understanding toward one who fails to do the latter. And, other things being equal, it is surely more difficult to be understanding toward one who fails to do the latter.

Clearly Waldheim's request for understanding is based upon the presupposition that his failure to resist did not constitute a failure to fulfil a duty or obligation. He concedes that resisting is an action which would have been preferable to following orders, but his request for understanding seems undeniably to be based upon the belief that he had no moral duty or obligation to resist. Thus, his position regarding those who resisted can perhaps be stated by affirming, on the one hand, that what they did was good or praiseworthy, and denying, on the other hand, that what they did fulfilled a duty or obligation. Consequently, Waldheim's position regarding his own involvement can perhaps be stated by affirming, on the one hand, that what he did was neither good nor praiseworthy, and denying, on the other hand, that he thereby failed to fulfil a duty or obligation.

There is one further element which seems to characterize Waldheim's view of his own moral status. As pointed out already, he appears to believe that his failure to resist is not deserving of blame or moral condemnation. Not only can one not justifiably accuse him of failing to fulfil a duty, on his view, but one cannot even justifiably blame or condemn him for failing to resist. One can justifiably praise those who did resist, but from this it does not automatically follow that one can justifiably blame those who did not resist. In Waldheim's view, therefore, his failure to resist appears to be neither the failure to fulfil a duty nor does it appear to be something which can be justifiably blamed or condemned on moral grounds.

Given this characterization of the situation, it is now possible to identify the acts of those who resisted as (on Waldheim's view) what have come to be known as acts of supererogation. It will be my contention throughout the course of this discussion that an act of supererogation can be identified by its possession of three characteristics. First, it is an act whose performance fulfils no moral duty or obligation. Second, it is an act whose performance is morally praiseworthy or meritorious. Third, it is an act whose omission is not morally blameworthy.

While a great deal more will be said about this definition and each of the three conditions, for present purposes it can be seen that each of the conditions is satisfied by the actions of those who resisted, as Waldheim evidently views the matter. First, those who resisted did what they were under no moral obligation to do. Second, those who resisted did something morally praiseworthy or meritorious. Third, those who resisted would not have acted in a morally blameworthy manner if they had not resisted. Accordingly, those who elected not to resist did not thereby act in a blameworthy manner.

It is often said that works of supererogation involve going beyond the call of duty, doing good in a way which transcends the requirements of moral obligation. While not all accounts of supererogation yield the consequence that every act of supererogation can be construed as an instance of going beyond the call of duty, it is reasonable to judge that Waldheim is thinking of the actions of those who resisted in this manner. Those who resisted were taking a risk of significant proportions, and they chose to act according to the higher calling of what they believed to be right and good. Duty did not require them to act in this manner, but they nevertheless did so. Hence they acted over and above the requirements of duty. Duty often requires moral agents to pursue what is right and good, but in this instance what they pursued went beyond such requirements.

In the context of these considerations it is now clearer why Waldheim believes it is reasonable to ask for the understanding of the readers of *Die Presse*. There are some individuals who, by taking risks of significant proportions, transcend the requirements of moral obligation. These individuals deserve high respect; they go beyond the requirements of duty to pursue what they believe to be an important good. But not everyone acts in this meritorious manner. Some decline to follow this exemplary course of action, choosing instead not to take the required risk or to pay the required cost. Of them it can truthfully be said that they have not done all that they might have, morally speaking. But, nevertheless, they have neither violated a moral duty nor done anything which deserves moral blame or condemnation. They have simply failed to perform an act of supererogation. Those who perform acts of supererogation deserve praise, but those who forbear to perform such acts cannot be faulted, at least on moral grounds, for what they have failed to do.

Naturally, the foregoing is an imaginative re-creation of the considerations leading up to the statements made by Waldheim in his interview. Certainly there is room for disagreement as to whether these ideas are an accurate reflection of his views. And certainly there is room for disagreement as to whether the act of resisting can be legitimately characterized as an act of supererogation. Perhaps some of Waldheim's critics will feel that the third condition is not satisfied. In other words, some may remain skeptical as to whether Waldheim's failure to resist is not something worthy of moral blame or condemnation (and I find myself inclined to share this skepticism; in this regard one might compare Waldheim's words with sentiments expressed by Richard Nixon in his memoirs).[2] Others may even feel that the first condition is not satisfied, that the officers knowing of the atrocities had a moral duty or obligation to resist. According to this point of view, Waldheim can be condemned for having violated his moral duty, having failed to do what he was morally obliged to do.

Yet it is not totally implausible to consider the act of resisting as a candidate for the status of a supererogatory act. And here it might be instructive to compare the act of resisting with another candidate for the status of a supererogatory act described in a now famous example by J.O. Urmson, "Saints and Heroes":

> We may imagine a squad of soldiers to be practising the throwing of live hand grenades; a grenade slips from the hand of one of them and rolls on the ground near the squad; one of them sacrifices his life by throwing himself on the grenade and protecting his comrades with his own body. It is quite unreasonable

to suppose that such a man must be impelled by the sort of emotion that he might be impelled by if his best friend were in the squad.[3]

In order to protect the lives of his comrades, a soldier throws himself upon the live grenade. In doing so he sacrifices his own life. Can this act be rightly judged as an act of supererogation?

In order to satisfy the first condition to qualify as an act of supererogation, the soldier's act cannot fulfil a duty or obligation. Concerning the satisfaction of this condition Urmson writes:

> But if the soldier had not thrown himself on the grenade, would he have failed in his duty? Though clearly he is superior in some way to his comrades, can we possibly say that they failed in their duty by not trying to be the one who sacrificed himself? If he had not done so, could anyone have said to him, 'You ought to have thrown yourself on that grenade'? . . . The answer to all these questions is plainly negative.[4]

Urmson argues emphatically that the soldier has not fulfilled a duty by throwing himself upon the grenade. Thus, he could not reasonably be charged with the failure to do his duty if he had not thrown himself upon the grenade. And those around him who did not act as he did cannot reasonably be charged with the failure to fulfil their duty.

According to the second condition, the performance of an act must be morally praiseworthy or meritorious to qualify as supererogatory. Clearly the soldier's act fulfils this condition. Indeed, it is hard to think of a clearer example of an act whose performance is worthy of praise from a moral point of view. If there are any truly praiseworthy acts in human life, what the soldier does seems to be a paradigm example. It is an act which Urmson describes as 'heroic'.

The third condition of an act of supererogation is that its omission is not blameworthy. Just as one who omits to perform an act of supererogation cannot rightly be charged with the failure to fulfil a duty, so one who omits such an act of supererogation cannot rightly be condemned for the omission on moral grounds. Here too the soldier's act seems to qualify. While the performance of the act is praiseworthy, the omission of the act would by no means be morally blameworthy. The soldier would not have been open to moral blame or condemnation if he had not thrown himself upon the grenade. Similarly, there are no grounds for ascribing moral blame or condemnation to the other soldiers in the example for their failure to act in a sacrificial manner.

It is reasonable to conclude that the soldier in Urmson's example performs an act of supererogation. Urmson is correct in arguing that the soldier has no moral duty to sacrifice his life. Moreover, it is clear that what the soldier does is morally praiseworthy, and there would have been nothing morally blameworthy had he failed to throw himself on the grenade. Thus, all three conditions required to qualify as an act of supererogation appear to be satisfied.

In addition, it is plausible to describe the soldier's act as an instance of going beyond the call of duty. While there are various duties which are binding upon the soldier, throwing himself upon the grenade is not one of them. By sacrificing his life for the sake of his comrades, he transcends the requirements of duty by pursuing what he believes to be what is good and right.

Two candidates for the status of supererogation have now been examined, the resistance of the officers knowledgeable of the atrocities during World War II and the sacrifice of his life by the soldier in Urmson's example. Many might have doubts about describing the officers' resistance as acts of supererogation, particularly those with vivid memories of the War (if this were not so, it is hard to explain the widespread agitation over Waldheim's own involvement). It seems much less controversial to claim that the soldier in Urmson's example performs an act of supererogation. If it is denied that the soldier performs an act of supererogation, it is hard to see which of the three conditions fails to be satisfied.

Both of these examples revolve around courses of action involving elements of heroism, and examples similar to these have figured heavily in discussions of supererogation. However, there are many other types of acts which have been claimed to be acts of supererogation. As the title of his essay implies, Urmson suggests that the behavior of saints is comparable with the behavior of heroes in the conditions under consideration. One who conducts one's life in a saintly fashion does not fulfil any moral duties; to conduct one's life in a saintly manner is to do that which is beyond the call of duty. Moreover, those of us who do not live as saints cannot reasonably be blamed for the failure to do so (any more than we can thereby be charged with a failure to do our duty). Hence, given that saintly behavior is undisputedly morally praiseworthy, one can rightly conclude that it is supererogatory to conduct one's life in a saintly manner.

David Heyd has argued that, in addition to heroism and saintliness, there are five other identifiable categories of acts which are capable of qualifying as supererogatory.[5] First, there are acts of beneficence, such as acts of charity, generosity, and gift giving. In due course it will be seen that not all acts of beneficence qualify as acts of supererogation. But Heyd believes that for the most part beneficent behavior satisfies the required conditions. Performing these acts is praiseworthy but not morally required, and failing to perform them does not render one open to moral blame.

Second, doing favors can be acts of supererogation. Under most circumstances the favor done by one person for another person is both praiseworthy and non-obligatory, and it would not be blameworthy for the person to refrain from doing the favor. Heyd believes that by its very nature a favor is never obligatory; one never fulfils a moral duty by doing a favor. However, it is often difficult to tell whether a given service is a favor or a moral requirement. When one sees a stranger in need of a particular thing—such as a man with a physical disability unable to operate a drinking fountain—it is sometimes hard to know whether assisting the person counts as a favor or the discharge of a moral duty. And even when such an act fulfils no duty, it is possible that one's failure to perform it is blameworthy. But there are nevertheless occasions on which one succeeds in performing an act of supererogation when one performs a favor.

Third, volunteering is an activity which Heyd regards as a paradigmatic example of supererogation. When a person promises to perform or refrain from an act, the very act of promising or volunteering can qualify as an act of supererogation. Although the act of volunteering is ordinarily not something which itself fulfils a moral duty, it is nevertheless often praiseworthy, and one who fails to volunteer does not normally warrant blame or moral condemnation. An ironic feature of volunteering is that it often creates an obligation to do that which one volunteers or promises to do. Thus, the act which one volunteers to perform cannot in typical situations qualify as an act of supererogation. I might volunteer to perform an act of great self-sacrifice, and by doing so I might transcend the bounds of duty. But having done this, other things being equal, I am arguably duty bound to perform the act. At the very least, other things being equal, my subsequent failure is morally blameworthy.

Fourth, forbearing to do what is within one's rights can qualify as supererogatory. A person who declines to exercise particular rights to certain goods can under normal circumstances qualify for having performed an act of supererogation. Heyd cautions that this forbearance cannot be based upon simple neglect; permitting others to have what one is entitled to through sheer neglect is in all probability not sufficiently praiseworthy to satisfy the second condition. Merit does not accrue to the performance of these acts of forbearance when a person simply forgets to exercise the rights to the goods in question. But, in many cases where one's forbearance is deliberate or purposeful, all of the conditions are satisifed for the act of forbearance to qualify as supererogatory.

Fifth, forgiving, pardoning, and mercy qualify as supererogatory. Heyd's discussion of this area is lengthy, for many writers have been inclined to think that we have obligations (or "quasi-obligations") to be forgiving or merciful; on their view being forgiving or merciful is something which moral agents are obliged to be. Heyd, however, plausibly defends the view that many particular instances of forgiveness, mercy, and pardon clearly satisfy the conditions for being acts of supererogation. Thus, while it is reasonable to suppose that one has a moral obligation to be a forgiving person, it is still possible that a particular act of forgiveness can qualify as an act of supererogation.

Counting acts of heroism and saintliness, then, Heyd distinguishes six categories of acts which can qualify as acts of supererogation. He does not regard this classification as exhaustive; he is willing to grant that there are acts of supererogation which do not comfortably fit under any of the six headings. Whether or not this is the case will not be a particular concern of the subsequent treatment of supererogation. In fact, one can easily think of examples of supererogatory acts which seem to resist the six-fold classification (several will emerge in the course of the discussion); however, this six-fold grouping is a useful place to begin one's thinking about the different ways in which supererogation manifests itself.

Up to this point I have proceeded on the assumption that there are three features or characteristics which are necessary and sufficient for an act's being supererogatory: Its performance fulfils no duty; Its performance is praiseworthy; Its omission is not blameworthy. It might be noted by those with any familiarity with the literature on supererogation that the characterization I have offered, though fairly standard, is not universally accepted as the correct account. In the next chapter I consider an alternative account which requires that an act of supererogation must be intended to bring about good consequences, that it be altruistic in spirit, and that acts of supererogation be continuous with duty in the sense that there is a common scale of value between supererogation and duty. I argue that the first two of these requirements are too strong. I then propose a sense in which some type of continuity requirement is perhaps desirable in an account of supererogation, and I amend my own account in a way which embodies such a requirement. So amended, acts of supererogation never fail on my account to qualify as acts in which one goes beyond the call of duty.

Up to this point I have also proceeded on the assumption that there are acts of supererogation. While it may be a matter of considerable controversy whether the resistance of the officers who were knowledgeable of the atrocities of the German army qualifies as supererogatory, I have defended the view that the soldier falling upon a live grenade to save the lives of his comrades is an act of supererogation. Moreover, I have indicated approval of Heyd's contention that there can be acts of supererogation in each of his six categories.

A surprisingly large number of people, however, resist the idea that there are any acts of supererogation at all. To them it does not seem possible that any human act simultaneously meets all of the conditions required to be an act of supererogation. Some of this resistance is based upon theological considerations. Chapter three surveys some of this resistance and the theological ideas motivating it. During the time of the Reformation this anti-supererogationist sentiment arose in the form of a reaction to some of the more objectionable practices and beliefs of the Holy Catholic Church. In this context certain views of Luther, Calvin, and Melanchthon are examined. But I shall argue that twentieth-century theology has seen a resurgence of the anti-supererogationist sentiment, and I shall make an attempt to understand what is motivating these contemporary writers. I argue that it is difficult to see how their arguments succeed in showing that there can be no acts of supererogation. However, it is also my suggestion that there are some important lessons to be learned by philosophical ethicists in what they have to say.

Chapter four examines a number of other contemporary writers who, for a variety of reasons, have embraced positions which leave little or no room for supererogation. These writers do not appeal to theological concepts or categories to support their position. Rather, what they appear to have in common is an understanding of the nature of duty or obligation sufficiently robust that it tends to leave no room for the realm of the morally praiseworthy outside the boundaries of duty. The literature on supererogation is filled with detailed discussions of the anti-supererogationist tendencies of Kantian ethics and (for almost entirely opposite reasons) consequentialist ethics. It is not my attempt to speak directly to these issues. Nevertheless, it will be clear from the discussion which follows that the views of most of these contemporary writers surveyed in chapter four reject supererogation for reasons which, broadly speaking, are either Kantian or consequentialist in orientation.

Chapters five and six attempt to address some of the underlying concerns of those who are reluctant to acknowledge that acts of supererogation are possible. In chapter five I introduce the concept of 'quasi-supererogation'. An act of quasi-supererogation is similar to an act of supererogation, except that one is blameworthy for the failure to perform an act of quasi-supererogation. I argue that the recognition that acts of quasi-supererogation are possible has the potential for alleviating some of the fears of those with anti-supererogationist proclivities. For there are many who are inclined to regard supererogation as the invention of those who wish to justify the practice of seldom going out of one's way to help others. I argue that an acknowledgement of quasi-supererogatory acts makes the justification of this practice far more difficult than it would otherwise be. Accordingly, my suggestion is that some of the anti-supererogationist's worst fears concerning supererogation may be largely groundless.

The relation between supererogation and virtue is examined in chapter six. Based upon some work of Gregory Trianosky, one of few writers to have profitably explored this area, I develop some additional considerations designed to alleviate the fears of those skeptical of supererogation. The same is true when one examines the notion of vocation and its implications for the role of duty in one's life. Those who are fearful of acknowledging supererogation can take comfort in knowing that enlightened advocates of supererogation are willing to grant that within the scope of one's vocation the possibility of supererogation is greatly curtailed. And, based upon an insight by Kierkegaard, the concept of 'vocation' can be seen to shed additional light on the relevance of virtue to supererogation.

Chapter seven concentrates upon the cost or risk involved in performing acts of supererogation. I examine an influential thesis propounded by Barry Curtis which characterizes supererogation in terms of a balance between the cost or risk which is involved and the moral value of performing the act in question. This thesis calls attention to some important ways in which one's judgments as to whether a given act is supererogatory involves something along the lines of a cost-benefit analysis. Nevertheless, I conclude that Curtis's analysis treats supererogation in a manner which is overly simplistic.

The concept of 'offence' is explored in chapter eight. Acts of offence are the mirror image counterparts of acts of supererogation in the following sense: the performance of an act of offence is not forbidden, it is nevertheless blameworthy, and its omission is not praiseworthy. Roderick Chisholm, Ernest Sosa, and others have argued that acts of offence are possible in human life, but, as in the case of supererogation, there is room for skepticism. Interestingly, there may be more reason to be skeptical of acts of offence than acts of supererogation. The concepts of supererogation and offence appear to be neatly symmetrical with respect to what is obligatory versus what is forbidden, on the one hand, and what is praiseworthy versus what is blameworthy on the other. But it will be argued that there is in reality no neat logical symmetry between the two. And on the basis of this demonstration it will be shown that there is nothing surprising in one's being more reluctant to grant that acts of offence are possible than to grant that acts of supererogation are possible.

In the end I endorse the idea that acts of supererogation are possible (without, of course, thereby endorsing all of the alleged examples of supererogatory acts offered in the literature). There are higher courses of action in life we might have pursued, nobler sacrifices we might have made, more significant benefits to others we might have brought about. In many diverse ways we have failed to realize the good that is within our power, and to the extent that others are aware of these failures it is our desire that they be understanding. There are many of an anti-supererogationist persuasion who would hold that these failures are inevitably the violation of moral duty, and if this were true it would be difficult to ask others to be understanding of our failures. I do not know of any argument that would serve as a final and convincing refutation of the views of the anti-supererogationist. But it will be my attempt to suggest in what follows that, all things considered, it is more reasonable to hold that these failures are not inevitably the violation of moral duty, and I believe that, given the way human beings are constituted, it is indeed reasonable to expect others to be understanding of these failures.

Chapter 2

GOOD CONSEQUENCES, ALTRUISM,
AND CONTINUITY WITH DUTY

The concept of supererogation has so far been characterized in terms of satisfying three conditions. According to this characterization, the performance of an act qualifies as supererogatory if and only if: (1) The performance of the act fulfils no moral duty or obligation; (2) The performance of the act is morally praiseworthy; and (3) The omission of the act is not morally blameworthy.[1]

Other writers have offered characterizations of supererogation which differ in various ways from that which I am proposing, and in this chapter I shall examine some of these differences. The point of this examination is not simply an exercise in arguing over minute points of disagreement. Rather, there are three issues of substance which I believe ought to be addressed before proceeding to the anti-supererogationist controversies treated in subsequent chapters. First, must acts of supererogation have, or be intended to have, good consequences? Second, must acts of supererogation serve to, or be intended to, benefit others? Third, are acts of supererogation continuous with duty in the sense that they realize more of the same kind of value than is realized in the fulfillment of duty?

I will argue that the first and second questions ought to be answered in the negative. The third question is more difficult to answer, and I tentatively conclude that some type of continuity requirement is desirable. I then go on in section four to describe how a form of the continuity requirement can be built into the account I have offered. (This final section is somewhat technical and can be omitted without losing track of the main themes of the discussion.) In an appendix to this chapter I examine the objection that many standard accounts of supererogation contain at least one redundant clause, and I argue that this objection does not affect the account defended here.

1. Etymological Background

Before examining these issues, I believe it will be useful to begin with some brief remarks about the etymology of the term 'supererogation'. The term derives from the Latin verb *supererogare*, to overexpend or spend in addition. This verb can be found in the Vulgate account of the Good Samaritan parable (Luke 10:35): "He tooke forth two pence, and gave to the host, and said, 'Have care of him, and whatsoever thou shalt supererogate, I at my returne will repay thee.'"[2] In this scenario the innkeeper is given two pence by the Samaritan for the care of the wounded victim, and the Samaritan promises to reimburse the innkeeper for what it costs to care for the victim in excess of two pence.

The story of the Good Samaritan is frequently cited in discussions of supererogation, for it is commonly alleged that the Samaritan is performing an act of supererogation by delivering the victim to the inn. Interestingly, however, the Latin verb is used here in connection with the efforts of the innkeeper, not the efforts of the Samaritan. It would be possible to imagine the innkeeper willing to cooperate with the Samaritan's request only until such time as the initial payment covers the victim's costs. Having been paid in advance, the innkeeper is required to provide the victim's lodging. Beyond the point covered by the initial payment, however, the innkeeper is being asked to subsidize the remainder of the victim's lodging costs, at least temporarily. In addition, the innkeeper is being asked to care for the victim, and it is possible to think of this care as an additional cost or burden. But the Latin verb is evidently being employed only in connection with the monetary cost of caring for the victim. And the idea, once again, is that the innkeeper is being asked to provide for the victim's lodging beyond what is required by the advance payment.

One might observe that the idea conveyed here bears only superficial resemblance to what is understood by the term 'supererogation' in contemporary discourse. It is highly questionable whether the innkeeper is being asked to do something which satisfies the three conditions proposed above. Under the circumstances described in the parable, it is plausible to judge that the innkeeper has a moral obligation to comply with the Samaritan's request to supererogate. After all, the victim's physical survival is apparently at stake (the victim is described in verse 30 as being left "half dead" by the thieves). At the very least, it would seem unreasonable for the innkeeper to refuse to comply, especially when the lodging costs which are not provided for by the advance payment will eventually be covered. Thus, a refusal under the terms offered by the Samaritan would leave the innkeeper open to moral blame. In terms of what 'supererogation' means in contemporary discourse, it seems plausible to judge that the Samaritan acts in a supererogatory manner, but it is doubtful that the same is true of the innkeeper's compliance with the Samaritan's request.

Aside from the Luke passage, there is one other occurrence in ancient literature of the verb from which 'supererogation' has evolved (or, in this case, its Greek counterpart). It appears in paragraph thirty-nine of Lucian's *Saturnalia*

> But if they were able to make an agreement with you to be moderate in their demands, as they now say they are, and refrain from bad behavior during banquets, then let them join us and dine with us, and good luck to them! Furthermore we shall send some of our clothing, as you direct, and spend as much gold as we can as well, and altogether we shan't be found wanting in anything.[3]

The verb occurs in the phrase which is translated, ". . . spend as much gold as we can. . . . " The speaker, Cronus, emphasizes that one can guarantee not being found wanting in anything by spending as much as possible.

It is clear that spending gold in this manner constitutes overexpending or spending beyond what the situation requires, even if the requirements of the situation are construed in terms of not being found wanting in anything. Just as the innkeeper is being asked to spend what is required for the victim's care over and above what the Samaritan pays in advance, so in this passage Cronus is recommending the expenditure of gold in a manner which has no limits or boundaries imposed upon it. He is recommending the expenditure of as much gold as possible, and there is no doubt that over-expending is precisely what one who follows his recommendation will do. However, it is also obvious that the behavior he is recommending does not qualify for the status of supererogatory in the contemporary sense. A great expenditure of gold in the circumstances described by Cronus is surely not the type of behavior which fits contemporary usage. Thus, just as the innkeeper is being asked to do something which falls short of what a contemporary speaker would describe as supererogatory, what Cronus is recommending (showering oneself in luxuries) is scarcely the kind of behavior which would impress a contemporary as an act of supererogation.

To summarize, the Latin verb *supererogare*, to overexpend or spend in addition, does not nearly capture the meaning of the term 'supererogation' in modern discourse; its modern usage, after all, is the product of a considerable evolutionary development. When the Latin verb is used in connection with what the innkeeper is being asked to do, it comes as no surprise that the innkeeper is being asked to do something which falls short of what a contemporary person would describe as supererogatory. A similar situation prevails when its Greek counterpart occurs in Lucian; what Cronus recommends—spending as much gold as possible—is a far cry from acting in a supererogatory manner.

Still, it is evident that the modern concept of supererogation bears some important connections to the concept of over-expending. There is a sense in which people who perform acts of supererogation typically make expenditures of their goods or energy over and above what is required of them. The basic idea of spending more than what the situation requires, suitably broadened to contexts in which one is spending more than just money, does appear to be at the heart of the modern concept of supererogation. At later stages of the discussion this point will become evident in various ways, and how this idea becomes suitably broadened to contexts other than the expenditure of money is precisely what the concept of continuity (discussed in section three) is designed to elucidate. For now the point to be noted is that the modern concept of supererogation is a considerably more refined notion than that from which it has evolved, but one can clearly see that the crude notion of over-expending is at the core of the modern concept.

2. GOOD CONSEQUENCES AND BENEFITING OTHERS

The concept of supererogation is standardly defined in the literature in a way roughly similar to the following: The performance of an act qualifies as supererogatory if and only if (1) The agent has no moral duty or obligation to perform it; (2) The performance of the act is morally praiseworthy; and (3) The omission of the act is not morally blameworthy. In what follows I shall refer to this account as the "standard account." The account I have offered differs from the standard account in the formulation of the first condition. In section four of this chapter I shall explain my reasons for stating the first condition in terms of an agent's not fulfilling a duty rather than in terms of an agent's not having a duty to perform the act in question. But for the present I shall simply note that my account differs from the standard account in this one respect.

Two influential philosophers who subscribe to the standard account are Sheldon Peterfreund and Robin Attfield. In his essay, "On the Relation between Supererogation and Basic Duty," Peterfreund states that an act of supererogation cannot be required or even expected of anyone; it is not a person's duty to perform it. Second, an act of supererogation is a "praiseworthy and meritorious" kind of act. Third, regarding a person who fails to perform these acts, Peterfreund states, ". . . no one can reproach him."[4]

Peterfreund does not state explicitly that the omission of an act of supererogation cannot be blameworthy, but I believe that the idea he is attempting to convey with "cannot be reproached" agrees with the idea that the omission is not blameworthy. For in a subsequent sentence he goes on to state, "By contrast, the man who does not fulfill his duties under certain conditions is blameworthy."[5] The omission referred to here is judged morally blameworthy, and if this situation is contrasted with that of a person performing an act of supererogation, it would certainly appear that in Peterfreund's opinion the omission of an act of supererogation is not blameworthy.

Attfield likewise characterizes acts of supererogation as acts which a moral agent has no duty or obligation to perform but which are nevertheless praiseworthy to perform. In addition, acts of supererogation are ". . . morally desirable without its being wrong not to perform them."[6] As is the case with Peterfreund, Attfield does not state explicitly that the omission of an act of supererogation cannot be blameworthy. However, given the reasonable assumption that he is understanding behavior which is morally wrong as behavior for which one could rightly be blamed, his account can be classified as an instance of the standard account.

What is important to notice about the account of Peterfreund and Attfield for the purposes of the present discussion is that neither lays down the requirement that acts of supererogation serve to bring about, or are intended to bring about, good consequences. And neither lays down the requirement that acts of supererogation serve to, or are intended to, benefit others. Typically acts of supererogation are performed with the intent of generating good consequences or benefiting others. But the accounts of supererogation examined so far decline to incorporate these as elements which must be present in order for an act to qualify as supererogatory.

In what is perhaps one of the most authoritative works on supererogation, David Heyd offers the following definition. An act is supererogatory if and only if: (1) It is neither obligatory nor forbidden; (2) Its omission is not wrong, and does not deserve sanction; (3) It is morally good, both by virtue of its (intended) consequences and by virtue of its intrinsic value (being beyond duty); and (4) It is done voluntarily for someone else's good, and is thus meritorious.[7] Clearly, Heyd's account goes far beyond what is required in the standard account. More specifically, Heyd's third condition requires that an act of supererogation is good by virtue of its (intended) consequences, and Heyd's fourth condition requires that an act of supererogation is performed for the benefit of others.

Conditions (3) and (4) in Heyd's definition form what is easily the most elaborate account in the literature of the idea that the performance of an act of supererogation is morally good, praiseworthy, or meritorious. Condition (3) concerns the morally good (intended) effects or consequences of the act and its intrinsic value, while condition (4) requires the intention of another's good.

A curious feature of condition (3) is Heyd's placement of parentheses around the word "intended": an act of supererogation is morally good by virtue of its (intended) consequences. Here one might be unclear as to what Heyd has in mind. In one passage he seems to speak as if an act of supererogation is good by virtue of its actual consequences:

> Supererogatory actions according to condition (3) must, therefore, bring about some good. They must result in the promotion

Good Consequences   19

of some value be it pleasure, happiness, welfare, friendship, or other values that enjoy a less wide consensus.[8]

From this passage it is natural to conclude that these good consequences are a necessary condition for the act which produces them to qualify as supererogatory.

This impression is misleading, however, for in a later passage Heyd declares that the act's value is derived from its intended consequences. And to say that its value is derived from its intended consequences means two things:

> First, that the agent must have the intention of promoting good by his action . . . and secondly, that the act *may* be supererogatory even if the good consequences in fact fail to ensue—as long as they were sincerely intended. The last point means that success is not essential to supererogatory action.[9]

Here the clear message is that the intended consequences must be good for an act to qualify as supererogatory, but it is not an absolute requirement that the actual consequences of an act of supererogation be good.

I shall proceed on the understanding that this latter passage is the authoritative statement of what Heyd intends by condition (3) because it would be most unreasonable to restrict the class of supererogatory acts to those bringing about good actual consequences. Sometimes it is through sheer accident that a person's good intentions bring about no good consequences in reality, as when someone makes a heroic effort to save a drowning man but is thwarted by the sudden appearance of a shark. Thus, it is important to understand that this condition requires that the intended consequences of an act be good in order for the act to qualify as an act of supererogation, not that the act's actual consequences be good for it to qualify.

Still, there are questions that can be raised about condition (3). Should one make it an ironclad requirement that every act of supererogation has good intended consequences? Is it impossible to conceive of an act of supererogation which does not involve the intent to produce good consequences? The following example purports to show that it is indeed possible to perform acts of supererogation in situations where there are no good results or consequences intended.

Suppose a man is held prisoner by political terrorists. He is commanded to swear allegiance to the leader of the terrorists and to renounce allegiance to his own government. The prisoner knows that a refusal to cooperate will result only in bad consequences. He will be beaten, and the angered terrorists will only stiffen their resolve to eradicate all opposition to their cause. Moreover, no one but the terrorists will ever know if he refuses. Nevertheless, the man is willing to endure these bad consequences. As a man of high principle, he is simply unwilling to renounce allegiance to his own government. He is willing to endure pain rather than cooperate.

In this example one might well judge that the man performs an act of supererogation by refusing to cooperate. In heroic fashion he stands up for what he believes to be the good and the right thing to do, and he does so in a manner which certainly appears to exceed the requirements of moral obligation. Yet the act he performs does not seem to have any good intended consequences. He does what he considers to be good and right, but there is no good result which he intends to bring about through his refusal. In this way one might argue that Heyd's condition (3) is too strong. There are acts which one would intuitively wish to classify as acts of supererogation which fail to satisfy that condition.

In response, one might argue that the man's refusal brings about good consequences after all. For example, there is the peace of mind which is brought about by one's doing what one believes is right. The man's refusal spares him the unpleasant feelings of having taken the easy way out, and it is hard to deny that the peace of mind he will be enabled to experience is a type of good consequence.

Nevertheless, it is here that one must distinguish once again between the actual and intended consequences of a person's acts. It is one thing to resist the terrorists' demands with the end result that one attains peace of mind, but it is another thing to resist with the intent that one attain peace of mind. And surely it is possible to imagine the man in the example refusing the demands with no other objective in mind than to abide by his principles, with the prospect of being haunted by pangs of conscience playing no role whatsoever. He will in fact experience peace of mind as the result of resisting the terrorists' demands, but he does not resist the terrorists' demands with the intent of experiencing this peace of mind. If so, there is no guarantee that condition three is satisfied.

I conclude that examples such as these seem to show that condition (3) is too strong a requirement for an act to qualify as an act of supererogation. Perhaps it is true in most typical instances that acts of supererogation are performed with the intent of bringing about good consequences. However, there can be acts of supererogation even when the act is performed by a person with no intent of bringing about good consequences.

According to condition (4), an act of supererogation must be done voluntarily for someone else's good. Clearly the example of the prisoner refusing to renounce his country shows that condition (4) is likewise too strong. The prisoner in the previous example can do no good for any other person by refusing to cooperate. Were it possible for other prisoners to be inspired by his bravery, the situation would be different. But there is no possibility of this bravery being known by others in addition to the terrorists themselves. Thus, it seems reasonable to conclude that his refusal to cooperate constitutes an act of supererogation, even though he does not act voluntarily for someone else's good.

Of course, one can be skeptical as to whether the prisoner performs an act of supererogation. As will be seen in subsequent chapters, there are some who call into question whether there are any acts of supererogation at all. Thus, there is a sense in which the success of my argument that Heyd's conditions (3) and (4) are too strong presupposes that these opponents of supererogation are mistaken. But on the supposition that acts of supererogation are possible, the heroism of the prisoner who refuses to cooperate appears to be a paradigm example of an act of supererogation. At the very least, it seems clear that its failure to satisfy condition (3) or condition (4) is not by itself reasonable grounds for denying it the status of supererogation.

Another feature of condition (4) worth noting is that a person removed from society will have virtually no opportunity to perform an act of supererogation. According to this condition, it is essential to acts of supererogation that they be performed in the context of a social setting or situation. Unless one actively seeks to promote someone else's good, one cannot be said to act in a supererogatory manner. Apart from the presence of others, one is in no position to satisfy this requirement. "Only other regarding duties," according to Heyd, "can be surpassed supererogatorily."[10]

It is unfortunate that Heyd offers no argument in support of this view. After presenting his definition, he declares that the rest of the chapter will be devoted to the explanation and elaboration of this definition and to critical comments regarding alternative definitions. But it is evidently not a part of his project to argue in favor of the various conditions which comprise the definition he offers. As I have argued, the example of the prisoner held by terrorists appears to show that condition (4) is too strong. It is not essential for an act's qualifying as supererogatory that it be performed voluntarily for someone else's good, and it is by no means evident in the absence of an argument to the contrary that a person entirely removed from society will find it impossible to perform acts of supererogation.

The standard account and the definition I have proposed require neither that an act have good intended consequences nor that it be performed voluntarily for someone else's good in order to qualify as an act of supererogation. They merely require that the performance of the act is morally praiseworthy. The prisoner's refusal to cooperate with the terrorists is clearly an act which satisfies this condition; there is no question that what he does is worthy of praise or approbation. But it is not an act performed for the sake of good intended consequences, nor is it an act performed voluntarily for the sake of someone else's good. It is simply performed without regard for good consequences, for there does not appear to be any possibility of bringing about good consequences.

I conclude that Heyd's definition makes an admirable attempt to spell out some of the particulars by which the performance of an act comes to attain the status of being meritorious or praiseworthy. In many ordinary situations the performance of an act becomes praiseworthy by virtue of its good intended consequences or its being for someone else's good. But there are other ways for the performance of an act to become praiseworthy, and I have attempted to show that an act of supererogation can be performed in such a manner that intended good consequences or benefits to others play no role whatsoever. One can act in accord with an awareness of principle and have no regard for the good consequences of one's act or the benefits which will accrue to others. To the extent that Heyd's definition makes no provision for such acts qualifying for the status of supererogatory, there is a sense in which it appears to assign too central a role to these elements.

3. THE CONTINUITY REQUIREMENT

David Heyd's discussion of the continuity requirement arises in the context of commenting upon the account of supererogation proposed by Roderick Chisholm. Thus, I will begin this section with a brief summary of Chisholm's account. Roderick Chisholm has written about supererogation in at least three articles. In his 1963 paper, "Supererogation and Offence: A Conceptual Scheme for Ethics," he characterizes the supererogatory as that which is good but not obligatory to do, or, as he later puts it, 'non-obligatory well-doing'.[11] In his 1964 paper, "The Ethics of Requirement," acts of supererogation are again described as acts of non-obligatory well-doing, and Chisholm notes that one can say of acts of supererogation that, "You ought to perform them, but you don't have to."[12]

In a 1966 essay coauthored by Chisholm and Ernest Sosa, "Intrinsic Preferability and the Problem of Supererogation," supererogation is once again described as non-obligatory well-doing.[13] However, at a later point in the essay the authors construct a conceptual scheme based upon the idea that there are five mutually exclusive categories in which any human act can fall. These are the obligatory, the forbidden, the indifferent, the supererogatory, and the offensive. According to this scheme, an act is obligatory just in case its performance is morally good and its nonperformance morally bad. An act is forbidden just in case its performance is morally bad and its nonperformance morally good. An act is indifferent just in case its performance is neither morally good nor morally bad. An act is supererogatory just in case its performance is morally good and its nonperformance is not morally bad. And an act is offensive just in case its performance is morally bad and its nonperformance is not morally good.

Here supererogation turns out to be one of five moral categories of action, and the scheme introduced by the authors makes clear the precise logical relationships between the five categories. A superficial examination of these three essays might lead one to believe that Chisholm has proposed two distinct accounts of supererogation. On the one hand, supererogation is described as non-obligatory well-doing, and on the other hand it is designated as the class of acts whose performance is morally good and whose nonperformance is not morally bad. By saying that an act is supererogatory if and only if its performance is morally good and its nonperformance is not morally bad, one seems to be saying nothing about the non-obligatory status of the act. Thus, it might appear that the characterization of supererogation which emerges from the five-fold scheme of Chisholm and Sosa is grossly deficient. It fails to bring out perhaps the most crucial feature of supererogation, that an act of supererogation is never obligatory to perform.

Nevertheless, a careful examination of the facts reveals that an act of supererogation is indeed non-obligatory in the system proposed by Chisholm and Sosa. For an act is obligatory in this system if and only if its performance is morally good and its nonperformance is morally bad. It is common to acts of supererogation and acts of obligation that their performance is morally good. However, the nonperformance of acts of supererogation is not morally bad, while the nonperformance of acts of obligation is morally bad. Hence an act of supererogation can never qualify as an act of obligation, for otherwise its nonperformance would be morally bad. But, by hypothesis, the nonperformance of an act of supererogation is never morally bad. Therefore, while Chisholm and Sosa make no explicit statement to the effect that acts of supererogation are non-obligatory, it is clearly a logical consequence of the scheme that this is the case.

In conclusion, the characterization of supererogation offered by Chisholm is not far removed from the standard characterization. First, the performance of an act of supererogation is non-obligatory. Second, its performance is morally good and constitutes moral welldoing. Third, its nonperformance is not morally bad. The differences between Chisholm's characterization and the standard characterization are these: Where the standard characterization employs the term 'praiseworthy', Chisholm speaks of 'good' or 'well-doing', and what the standard characterization describes as 'blameworthy' Chisholm describes as 'bad'. To the extent that one believes that a good act is one that is praiseworthy, and vice versa, or that a bad act is one that is blameworthy, and vice versa, one will find Chisholm's view in rough agreement with the standard characterization.

Chisholm's characterization of supererogation is criticized by Heyd (although he does not mention Chisholm by name) on the grounds that it includes too much.[14] To see why Heyd believes that it includes too much, the reader is directed to some preceding paragraphs in which he stipulates that the relation between supererogation and duty ought to be characterized by what he calls "continuity":

> Yet whichever definition [of morally good] is adopted, supererogation should be characterized as realizing *more* of the same type of value attached to obligatory action. That is to say: there is a common and continuous scale of values shared by supererogation and duty. How supererogatory acts that consist of over-subscription (like paying more than is owed) display this feature of continuity can easily be seen; other cases of supererogation (like mercy or volunteering) contain this feature too, but not in such a clear manner as in the former case. This logical

condition of continuity is necessary if a Nietzschean morality, for instance, is to be excluded from what is covered from the definition of supererogation.[15]

Here the main idea is that the goodness of an act of supererogation must be a goodness of a type shared by acts of obligation, while at the same time the goodness of the former must exceed (in some manner which is difficult to spell out precisely) that of the latter. If one exceeds the requirements of duty in performing an act of supererogation, then it is reasonable to believe that there is a scale according to which—with reference to a particular type of goodness—the goodness achieved by performing an act of supererogation exceeds the goodness achieved by the fulfillment of the duty.

If Heyd is correct that this continuity requirement ought to be operative, it is not sufficient to define acts of supererogation in terms of its being morally good to perform them. For the possession of not just any type of goodness suffices to distinguish supererogatory acts from many non-supererogatory acts. One might, for instance, attempt to argue that living in accord with a Nietzschean type of morality qualifies as supererogation (though Heyd does not explain exactly how such an argument would proceed), and hence one cannot rest content with saying simply that a supererogatory act is one which is good to do. One must specify a certain type of goodness of the sort stipulated by the continuity requirement. Chisholm's definition fails to make any stipulation about the type of goodness which is involved in performing acts of supererogation, and hence it is charged with allowing too much.

It is hard to make clear sense of everything Heyd is claiming in this passage, but Heyd is certainly correct in charging that Chisholm has failed to specify a sense of goodness which will guarantee that the continuity requirement is satisfied. Given the characterization proposed by Chisholm, it is possible that this requirement will frequently be violated. If so, Heyd believes, Chisholm's account will allow acts to qualify as supererogatory which (because there fails to be a continuous scale of values between them and acts which are obligatory to perform) ought not. Nevertheless, it is important to note that if this is a weakness of Chisholm's characterization, it appears to be no less a weakness of the other definitions so far examined. The standard characterization specifies that an act of supererogation must be praiseworthy to perform, but there is no guarantee that a common and continuous scale of values is secured as the result of its being praiseworthy.

By stipulating that an act of supererogation be praiseworthy to perform, there is no greater guarantee that continuity is preserved than by simply stipulating that an act of supererogation be good to do.

It is here that Heyd's own definition emerges as the only definition which makes clear provisions for satisfying the continuity requirement. Heyd's third condition requires that an act of supererogation be morally good, both by virtue of its intended consequences and by virtue of its intrinsic value (being beyond duty). Apparently an act cannot qualify as being good by virtue of its intrinsic value, according to Heyd's formulation, unless it is beyond duty. But to say this of an act seems to imply that there is a common and continuous scale of value according to which the value of the act exceeds the value of fulfilling duty. Thus, it appears that an act can meet condition (3) of Heyd's definition only if it satisfies the continuity requirement. Every act of supererogation is stipulated to be beyond duty by Heyd's condition (3), and this stipulation succeeds in setting Heyd's definition apart from the others so far examined and establishing it as the only definition which appears to satisfy the continuity requirement.

The core idea, once again, is that an act of supererogation realizes more of the same type of value which attaches to the performance of an obligatory act. In some cases this phenomenon is easily seen, says Heyd, and he offers as an example paying more to someone than what is owed. There is a certain value which attaches to my paying a man that which is owed to him; this is the value which attaches to the fulfillment of a moral obligation. But there is a greater value which attaches to paying the man more than what is owed to him. By transcending the requirements of duty I have realized a greater degree of value than by merely fulfilling my duty.

It is essential to this notion that it is the same value which is realized in the case of fulfilling my duty and in the case of transcending my duty. There is a common and continuous scale of value shared by supererogation and duty, and the difference between supererogation and duty is reflected in the degree to which the value is realized in each. The value is realized to a greater degree in supererogation than in obligation. By transcending the requirements of duty I realize a higher degree of the same value than I realize by merely acting in accord with duty. Later Heyd describes the situation in terms of " . . . the achievement of an ideal which is 'higher' than the end of those acts which are obligatory. Yet this ideal is higher on the same *scale* as the one on which the end of the obligatory act is situated."[16]

On such a scale supererogation achieves an ideal which is higher than that of fulfilling obligation.

Heyd concedes that there are cases, such as volunteering, in which continuity is present but not in such a clear and obvious manner as in cases of over-subscription. Suppose a swimmer calls for help, and several of us standing on the shore are capable of rescuing the swimmer. The water temperature is very cold, and the rescue effort promises to be considerable. Nevertheless, I volunteer to perform the rescue, and the others standing on the shore are spared from having to do so.

If I were the only person standing on the shore, then it is plausible to judge that it is my obligation to take action with the result that the swimmer is rescued. Here there is no opportunity for me to be the member of the group who volunteers, for no one else is present. Still, I perform the same act of rescuing the swimmer in distress, and by rescuing the swimmer I succeed in realizing a certain value. However, by the continuity principle I realize a greater degree of value in the scenario where I am a member of a group and volunteer to perform the rescue. In the group scenario there is the possibility of waiting to see whether someone else volunteers, and hence I might escape the admittedly unpleasant prospect of the rescue effort. But I volunteer, and I thereby realize a greater degree of value than if I had merely been discharging an obligation to rescue the swimmer. This appears to be the basic idea Heyd has in mind.

Perhaps a discussion of the continuity requirement can be clarified by stating a 'continuity principle' as follows: If an agent performs an act of supererogation, then the performance of the act realizes a higher degree of value than if the agent had simply fulfilled a moral obligation through the performance of the act. In the case of paying a man more than what is owed to him, I realize a higher degree of value than if this were the very sum I owe to him and I pay it to him. (In addition, of course, I realize a higher degree of value than if I pay him what I in fact owe him.) And in the case of the swimmer in distress, I realize a higher degree of value than if it had been my obligation to rescue the swimmer and I fulfilled this obligation by performing the rescue. (Here it might be argued that the group really does have an obligation to rescue the swimmer, but from this it does not follow that each member of the group has an obligation to perform the rescue.)

The notion of a continuous scale of value between acts of supererogation and acts which fulfil moral obligation might strike some as dubious. What exactly is the value which is realized more fully when I pay a man more than what is owed to him, as compared to paying him this same amount by virtue of fulfilling a moral obligation? And what value is realized more fully when I volunteer to rescue a swimmer in distress, as compared to when I rescue a swimmer to fulfil a moral obligation? The idea that some particular scale of value is operative in each and every instance of performing an act of supererogation might strike some as an article of faith whose truth in fact is highly questionable. Alternatively, a commitment to the existence of such a scale of value might lead some to the conclusion that acts of supererogation are quite rare.

It is my belief that the continuity principle can be made somewhat more attractive by appealing to some overall scale of value such as the presence of goodness in the universe. Suppose that the continuity principle be understood simply as the proposition that if an agent performs an act of supererogation, then, other things being equal, there is more good realized in the universe than if the agent had fulfilled a moral obligation through its performance. More good is realized in the universe if I pay a man more than what I owe, other things being equal, than if I pay him exactly what I owe. And more good is realized in the universe if I volunteer to rescue the swimmer in distress and subsequently do so than if I rescue the swimmer out of sheer obligation, other things being equal.

What exactly is the excess good realized in the performance of these acts of supererogation? Presumably the answer depends in part upon the state of mind leading up to their performance. In the case of paying a man more than what I owe, the underlying motive might be either gratitude, generosity, a desire for the man's well being, or a combination of these. To the extent that one agrees that these are good motives and that their existence promotes or enhances the overall level of good in the universe, one will perhaps agree that the continuity principle is operative in this example. In the case of volunteering to rescue the swimmer in distress, the underlying motive might be the desire to give assistance to another human being, a readiness to make a sacrifice for the sake of another, the desire to spare others from having to rescue the swimmer, or a combination of these. Again, these are good motives, and it is reasonable to judge that the overall level of good in the universe is increased when one acts on them. And if one were to perform these same acts out of evil motives, the continuity principle would not be satisfied, and the act could no longer be described as an act of supererogation.

While there might be reluctance among some to embrace the continuity requirement in the terms Heyd describes it, making reference to a series of common scales of value between supererogation and obligation, I believe the continuity principle is basically defensible. It is sensible to require of an act of supererogation that its performance bring about a greater degree of good in the universe than if the performance of the same act had fulfilled an obligation. In the performance of every act of supererogation there is a moral good realized which would not have been realized if it fulfilled an obligation, and this good can be viewed as incremental to the good already realized in the fulfillment of the obligation. This is a point seldom raised in discussions of supererogation, and it is to Heyd's credit that it is given a central emphasis throughout his book.

In this section I have stated a version of the continuity requirement which does not appeal to the dubious concept of a scale of values. Although I have stopped short of offering a forthright endorsement of this requirement, it is a requirement which strikes me as reasonable. Indeed, in the next section I adjust my own account of supererogation in such a way that it embodies the continuity requirement. It might be thought that the continuity requirement vindicates Heyd's condition (3), in that one is forced to admit that the prisoner refusing to renounce his country is realizing more good in the universe than if he did so out of moral obligation. But, once again, one must remember that condition (3) is framed in terms of good intended consequences. The good that is realized in what the prisoner does stems from a courageous frame of mind, but this courage is obviously not the intended outcome of his refusal. I conclude that it is reasonable to conceive of the relation between duty and supererogation in terms of the continuity requirement, and in the next section I will reveal the manner in which I incorporate this requirement in my own account.

4. SUPEREROGATION AND THE FULFILLMENT OF DUTY

The standard characterization of supererogation requires that a person have no duty or obligation to perform an act of supererogation, or, alternately, that it is not obligatory for the person to perform the act (hereafter, I shall refer to this requirement as the 'duty condition'). By contrast, the account I have proposed is framed in terms of the act's performance fulfilling no duty or obligation. In this section I shall explain this difference between the standard account and my own account, call attention to some problems which beset the standard account's formulation of the duty condition, and introduce a slight refinement in my own formulation which makes clear that the continuity principle is operative.

It is one thing to say that an agent has an obligation to perform an act, and it is quite another thing to say that the agent fulfils or discharges an obligation by performing the act. If the agent has an obligation to perform the act, then, of course, the performance of the act fulfils this particular obligation, other things being equal. But if an agent fulfils an obligation by performing the act, then it does not follow that the agent has or had an obligation to perform the act. For it might be that it is by virtue of having a different obligation, such as an obligation to perform either this act or another act, that the agent fulfils an obligation by performing it. If I have an obligation to rescue one of two drowning swimmers, and it is not in my power to rescue both of them, then I fulfil this obligation by rescuing one of them. But I do not have an obligation to rescue the particular one I rescue, for I cannot reasonably be charged with a failure to discharge my obligation in the event that I choose to rescue the other.

This distinction has long been recognized by moral philosophers, but its relevance to supererogation has not been clearly noted in the literature. In an attempt to explain its relevance to supererogation, as well as my reasons for finding the standard characterization unsatisfactory as it stands, I begin with the following observation by Michael Stocker:

> We fulfill duties by performing acts. But it is never a duty to do any act. Thus, it has never been a duty to do any of the acts we have done, and it will never be a duty to do any of the acts we will do. Nonetheless we can fulfill our duties only by performing acts. What I have just said strikes me as not only paradoxical but true.[17]

In order to see why Stocker asserts that we never have a duty to do any act, suppose I have a duty to make an appearance before my parole officer sometime during February, and I fulfil this duty by making an appearance on 9 February. I perform a particular act and thereby fulfil a duty, but I do not have a duty to perform the particular act I perform. Had I appeared the next day, thus performing a different act, I would have fulfilled the same duty. Moreover, I could not reasonably be charged with the failure to fulfil a duty to appear on 9 February, for surely that is not my duty.

The same is true of all, or virtually all, duties which are binding upon human agents. We fulfil duties by performing various acts, but we do not have duties to perform these particular acts. A duty is rarely, if ever, so specific that only one particular act could ever fulfil it. The fulfillment of every duty admits of at least some options, even the duty to press a particular button at a particular moment (where the options would include choice of finger, body posture, and so forth).

It is important to recognize that Stocker is speaking about act tokens when he asserts that we never have a duty to do any act. For if one begins to consider act types, the situation is entirely different. Consider the following act type:

1. Appearing before my parole officer during February.

An act of this type is instantiated both by my appearing on 9 February and by my appearing on 10 February. Thus, not only do I fulfil my duty by appearing on either day, but I also actually have a duty to perform an act of this type.

Assuming for the moment that duties are to be conceived in terms of act tokens rather than act types, the defender of the standard characterization is faced with a somewhat disquieting difficulty. For since one rarely, if ever, has a duty to perform a particular act token, it follows that the duty condition hardly ever fails to be satisfied. Invariably one has no duty to perform the act in question, and thus virtually every act satisfying the other conditions turns out to be supererogatory. Virtually every act which is praiseworthy to perform but not blameworthy to omit turns out to achieve the status of supererogation. Such acts might well fulfil duties, but on this account they are nevertheless classified as acts of supererogation. Clearly, then, such an account is defective. It yields a criterion which is far too generous.

This line of reasoning might naturally lead one to suppose that the concept of duty, and hence the duty condition, ought to be characterized in terms of act types rather than act tokens. According to this suggestion it would be appropriate to say that an act of a certain type is supererogatory only if the agent performing it has no duty to perform an act of that type. Thus, on this account, my appearing before my parole officer during February fails to qualify as an act of supererogation, for I have a duty to perform an act of this type. My appearing before my parole officer during February is precisely the fulfillment of my duty to perform an act of this type. Therefore, even though I have no duty with respect to the act token I perform, nevertheless the act token I perform is of a type which I have a duty to perform.

It does not require a great deal of insight, however, to see that this interpretation of the duty condition raises serious problems of its own. Clearly, an act token is not uniquely the instance of one act type. The act token I perform when I appear before my parole officer at 11:25 A.M., 9 February, wearing a three-piece suit is an instance of type (1). But it is also an instance of many other types, including the following:

2. Appearing before my parole officer during 9 February
3. Appearing before my parole officer between eleven and twelve o'clock the morning of 9 February
4. Appearing before my parole officer at 11:25 A.M., 9 February
5. Appearing before my parole officer during 9 February, wearing a three-piece suit.

While I have a duty to perform an act of type (1), I have no duty to perform an act of types (2)–(5). Thus, the act token I perform is simultaneously an instance of many types, some of which I have a duty to perform and others of which I do not. There is perhaps nothing problematic in this state of affairs as such, but problems quickly arise for the interpretation of the duty condition described above. For if the concept of supererogation is formulated in terms of act types rather than act tokens, one is forced to say that my visit to the parole officer is both supererogatory and not supererogatory, depending upon the act type one has in mind. My performing an act of type (1) is not supererogatory, and yet my performing an act of type (2) is supererogatory, even though I perform them both via the same act token. (For the sake of simplicity assume that the other conditions are satisfied in this example).

According to this approach, then, whether or not one has done something supererogatory depends upon one's perspective. If one has fulfilled a duty (and the other conditions are satisfied), then relative to some types (of which one's act is a token), one has succeeded in performing an act of supererogation and relative to other types one has failed to perform an act of supererogation. Such acts will take on the status of supererogation relative to some types and not to others. Relative to types which are sufficiently detailed, in particular, virtually every such act will eventually achieve the designation of supererogation.

It would not be impossible to adopt an account of supererogation which is relativist in this manner. Surely one could define 'supererogation' in conformity with these ideas and adjust one's manner of speaking accordingly. But clearly this is not the way people really do think or speak about supererogation. Acts are not spoken of as being supererogatory only relative to their mode of characterization. Whatever disagreement may exist regarding the concept of supererogation, there appears to be no disagreement on this score. The question of whether a person has performed an act of supererogation is one which requires an unambiguous answer. Either the performance of the act is one of supererogation or it is not. A person who has fulfilled a duty should not be allowed the luxury of claiming that, after all, it really is an act of supererogation from certain perspectives. No one who has written on the subject, so far as I know, has embraced such a position, according to which every such act qualifies as supererogatory relative to a sufficiently detailed act type.

The solution I propose (and this seems to be the direction Stocker himself ends up going in his essay, "Supererogation and Duties")[18] is that the duty condition should give way to a condition formulated in the language of fulfilling duties. Thus, my proposal is that moralists have too long been mistaken in characterizing supererogation in terms of the agent's having no duty to perform an act. There is, however, another option left to be examined for those still wishing to defend the adequacy of the standard characterization, and to this option I now turn.

According to Kant, there are certain duties which agents are free to fulfil when they choose to do so. Mill too acknowledges such duties, calling them 'duties of imperfect obligation', and remarks that, " . . . though the act is obligatory, the particular occasions of performing it are left to our choice, as in the case of charity or beneficence."[19] Charity is obligatory, according to Mill, but the choice of particular occasions for performing acts of charity is optional.

Duties of this variety are referred to by Stocker simply as 'imperfect duties', and he argues that they are best conceived as disjunctive in form. If the variables $x_1, x_2, \ldots, x_n$ range over act tokens, then an imperfect duty can be conceived as a duty to perform either x_1 or x_2 or ... or x_n. As has already been seen, my duty to appear before the parole officer is not a duty to perform an act token (it is not, one might say, a 'perfect duty'). But it can be depicted as a duty to choose one particular act out of a specified range of options and perform it. If I appear on 9 November at 11:25 A.M. wearing a three-piece suit, then I have chosen one of the available options. (Perhaps some will object to Stocker's approach on the grounds that there are non-denumerably many options and hence they are unlistable, but I shall proceed on the assumption that this is at worst a technical difficulty for which there is no doubt a technical solution.)

The relevance of imperfect duties to the project of characterizing supererogation is very straightforward. The duty condition asserts that an act of supererogation is one which the agent performing it has no duty or obligation to perform. Earlier it was observed that agents rarely if ever have a duty to perform a particular act token. However, if imperfect duties are now admitted as genuine duties, the situation is drastically changed. For while I have no duty to appear before my parole officer on 9 November at 11:25 A.M. wearing a three-piece suit, I have an imperfect duty to perform either this act or any of the other acts in a range of allowable options. Thus, it may be argued that my act fails the test of supererogation after all, which is as it should be. The duty condition can be interpreted, therefore, in such a way that the performance of an act falling within the scope of an imperfect duty cannot qualify as supererogatory.

Although I believe Kant and Mill are correct in asserting that there are duties of imperfect obligation and that Stocker is correct in depicting these as duties whose scope is disjunctive in form, nevertheless I do not believe that an appeal to imperfect duties will succeed in saving the standard formulation of the duty condition. For problems arise when one begins to consider situations in which an agent goes beyond the call of duty. Suppose that Margaret has a duty to send one hundred dollars to a local broadcast facility (because she earlier pledged to do so), but, caught up in a spirit of generosity, she instead sends a check for two hundred fifty dollars. Call the act token she thereby performs "x*." Then one can rightly observe that x* both fulfils a duty and goes beyond the fulfillment of a duty. It is an act, I believe, which deserves to be classified as an act of supererogation.

Now consider Margaret's duty to send one hundred dollars. There are a great many act tokens from which Margaret can choose to discharge this duty. These act tokens, then, can be viewed as disjuncts within the scope of her imperfect duty. And the crucial question to be asked is whether x* is identical with one of these disjuncts.

Suppose first that x* is identical with one of these disjuncts. From this it follows that by performing x* Margaret discharges her duty to send money to the public broadcast facility, which is as it should be. But if x* is identical with one of these disjuncts, it also follows that x* falls within the scope of an imperfect duty which is binding upon Margaret. And if x* falls within the scope of an imperfect duty, then, on the interpretation of the duty condition under consideration, x* cannot qualify as an act of supererogation. In the same way that my appearing before my parole officer on 9 November at 11:25 A.M. wearing a three-piece suit fails the test of supererogation because of its status as a disjunct in one of my imperfect duties, so x* fails the test of supererogation here for the same reason. It cannot both fall within the scope of an imperfect duty and qualify for the designation of supererogation. (It might be suggested that this difficulty can be overcome by revising the duty condition to read, "The agent has no duty to perform the act other than those by whose performance the agent goes beyond the call of duty." But this suggestion carries with it the rather odd consequence that a person can be in the position of actually having an imperfect duty to go beyond the call of itself. While one might conceivably have an imperfect duty to go beyond the call of another duty, as when one promises to go beyond the call of duty, there is surely something puzzling about the idea of a duty to go beyond the call of itself.)

Moving to the other horn of the dilemma, then, suppose that x* is not identical with one of the disjuncts. From this supposition it follows that x* does not fall within the scope of Margaret's imperfect duty. Consequently, the duty condition is satisfied and x* qualifies as an act of supererogation, which is as it should be. Unfortunately, however, if x* is not identical with one of the disjuncts, it also follows that Margaret has not discharged her duty to send money to the broadcast facility. There are many ways she might have discharged this duty, for there are many disjuncts from which to choose. But instead she performs an act which is by hypothesis none of these, and hence her duty remains unfulfilled.

Intuitively, it seems correct to say that by performing x* Margaret both fulfils her promise to send one hundred dollars to the broadcast facility and performs an act of supererogation. But the method under consideration does not appear capable of doing justice to this complex state of affairs. On the supposition that x^* appears as a disjunct in Margaret's imperfect duty, one can account for the fulfillment of her duty but not the element of going beyond it. And on the supposition that x^* is not such a disjunct, the reverse is true. The situation would be entirely different if Margaret had first mailed a check for one hundred dollars and later mailed a second check for one hundred fifty dollars. Then the first of these act tokens would presumably be identical with one of the disjuncts of her imperfect duty, and the second act token would qualify as an act of supererogation. But it would scarcely be plausible to maintain, as an attempt to save the duty condition, that sending a check for two hundred fifty dollars is somehow the composite of two act tokens, sending one hundred dollars and simultaneously sending one hundred fifty dollars (and thus the composite of an infinite number of distinct act tokens). Moreover, and more importantly, on this account it would still be the case that going beyond the call of duty can never qualify as supererogation in and of itself.

The defender of a virtue oriented theory of morality, moreover, might register an additional grievance regarding the interpretation of the duty condition under consideration. Not all duties, it might be argued, are duties to perform actions or refrain from performing actions. Some duties consist in simply exhibiting virtues of various sorts over extended periods of time. Thus, agents can have duties to be certain kinds of persons, duties which cannot be completely cashed out in terms of duties to perform or refrain from performing particular act tokens or disjunctions of act tokens. If there are such duties, then it is difficult to see how they can be captured within the confines of a theory of imperfect duties. On the other hand, such duties can presumably be fulfilled, and hence their existence appears to pose no obvious difficulties for the type of view I defend.[20]

Up to this point I have suggested that there are problems which beset the standard characterization of the relation between supererogation and duty. Although I do not claim to have considered all of the possible strategies which might be advanced in an effort to save the standard characterization, it is my claim that a characterization of the duty condition in the language of fulfilling duties is a more satisfactory alternative. My proposal, then, is that the duty condition consist of the stipulation that there are no duties which the performance of the act in question thereby fulfils. (The qualifier "thereby" is designed to prevent one from claiming that there can be no acts of supererogation on the grounds that every act fulfils a great many duties to refrain from forbidden acts.) Because there is a significant difference between the (standard) requirement that an agent has no duty to perform an act and the (proposed) requirement that an agent fulfils no duty through the performance of an act, it is my proposal that the relation between supererogation and duty be formulated along the lines of the latter requirement.

The account I wish to propose, however, necessitates introducing one small refinement in order to do justice to the continuity requirement. The refinement I shall introduce consists of a distinction between an act's fulfilling a duty 'directly' and an act's fulfilling a duty 'non-directly'. Suppose that an act can be said to fulfil a duty non-directly if and only if the act fulfils the duty, and the performance of the act is morally praiseworthy for reasons other than the mere fact that it fulfils a duty. An act which fulfils a duty can accordingly be said to fulfil a duty directly just in case it does not do so non-directly: its performance (if it is praiseworthy at all) is praiseworthy for no other reason than the fact that it fulfils a duty. The account I shall propose consists in the principle that by performing an act of supererogation one might thereby fulfil a duty, but by performing an act of supererogation one cannot fulfil a duty directly. An act of supererogation, therefore, fulfils duties only in which the performance of the act is praiseworthy for reasons other than the mere fact that it fulfils a duty. (The account proposed by Stocker in "Supererogation and Duties" proceeds along similar lines.)

From this characterization of the duty condition it follows that instances in which agents go beyond the call of duty can qualify as acts of supererogation. By performing x^* Margaret succeeds in fulfilling a duty, but there is no duty which x^* fulfils directly. In particular, x^* does not directly fulfil Margaret's duty to send one hundred dollars, for the performance of x^* is praiseworthy for reasons of generosity, not simply the fact that it fulfils a duty. Consequently, x^* qualifies as an act of supererogation. The underlying intuition is that the performance of a second-mile act, if praiseworthy, is praiseworthy by virtue of going beyond duty or doing something other than what duty requires; hence it is not praiseworthy merely by virtue of fulfilling a duty.

It is at this point that my account reveals its embodiment of the continuity principle, the principle that if an agent performs an act of supererogation, then, other things being equal, there is more good realized in the universe through its performance than if the agent had fulfilled a moral obligation through its performance. Imagine that

Margaret's duty had been to send two hundred fifty dollars to the broadcast facility. Then by performing x* Margaret would have fulfilled this duty directly. For her performance of x* would have been praiseworthy, if at all, for no other reason than the mere fact that it would have fulfilled a duty. Instead, Margaret's performance of x* fulfils a duty non-directly; it is praiseworthy for reasons of generosity (as well, perhaps, as the fact that it fulfils a duty). The fulfillment of a duty directly generates the good of having fulfilled a duty. The fulfillment of a duty non-directly generates the additional good which renders the performance of an act (additionally) praiseworthy.

Given the distinction I have drawn between an act's directly fulfilling a duty and its non-directly fulfilling a duty, the continuity principle operative in the account I am proposing can be stated more precisely as follows: If an agent performs an act of supererogation, then, other things being equal, there is more good realized in the universe through its performance than if the agent had *directly* fulfilled a moral obligation through its performance. It is necessary to specify that the contrast is with a moral obligation which is fulfilled directly, for it is conceivable that performing an act of supererogation generates no distinguishably greater good than if it had non-directly fulfilled a moral obligation. If I send one hundred dollars to a broadcast facility, having made no prior pledge or promise to do so, then, if my act is supererogatory, its performance realizes more good than if I send the money and thereby directly fulfil an obligation to do so (and this is perfectly compatible with the fact that my obligation has arisen from an earlier pledge which itself generates a certain amount of good). But it is not clear that its performance realizes more good than if I send the money and thereby non-directly fulfil an obligation. It is not clear that my sending the money realizes more good than if I had earlier pledged ten dollars and now write a check for one hundred.

In this section I have argued that the standard characterization of the duty condition is problematic and that the duty condition I have proposed is a more satisfactory alternative. The duty condition I propose is that an act of supererogation fulfils no moral duty or obligation directly. It can fulfil duties only in which the performance of the act is praiseworthy for reasons other than the mere fact that it fulfils a duty. I have suggested that my account is more hospitable to virtue oriented theories of morality than the standard characterization, and that it does not run afoul of the continuity principle. In what follows, to avoid tedious repetition, I will sometimes describe acts of supererogation as fulfilling no duties (without specifying the qualifier 'directly') or even as being non-obligatory. But officially, the duty condition I adopt is this: An act is supererogatory only if it fulfils no moral duty or obligation directly.

APPENDIX

It has frequently been pointed out that standard accounts of supererogation are redundant for the simple reason that if an act is not blameworthy or wrong to omit, then one cannot possibly have a duty or obligation to perform it. Thus, the standard account can be reduced from three conditions to two. It is not necessary to stipulate that one can have no duty or obligation to perform an act of supererogation if one goes on to stipulate that it is never blameworthy or wrong to omit an act of supererogation.

Heyd makes essentially this observation regarding his own account. Regarding the first two conditions, Heyd declares that condition (2) ("Its omission is not wrong, and does not deserve sanction") actually entails condition (1) ("It is neither obligatory nor forbidden"). Thus, he states that condition (1) is therefore logically speaking superfluous. Conditions (2), (3), and (4) constitute sufficient conditions for an act's qualifying as supererogatory. Nevertheless, Heyd finds it convenient on methodological and expository grounds to include condition (1), and for this reason his definition consists of all four conditions.

Is Heyd correct in asserting that condition (2) entails condition (1)? If the omission of an act is not wrong and does not deserve sanction or criticism, does it follow that the act is neither obligatory nor forbidden? Surely the truth of condition (2) implies that the act is not obligatory, as the argument just examined purports to show. For if an act is obligatory, other things being equal, it is always wrong to omit and its omission always deserves criticism. Given the assumption that the violation of duty is always blameworthy, it is always blameworthy to fail to do that which is obligatory. Hence if it is never wrong to omit an act of supererogation, it automatically follows that it is not obligatory to perform an act of supererogation.

However, it is not the case that the truth of condition (2) implies that the act is not forbidden, and hence Heyd appears to be mistaken that condition (1) is entailed by the second. There are many acts which satisfy condition (2) whose performance is nevertheless forbidden. Or, to put it another way, there are many forbidden acts whose omissions are not wrong and do not deserve sanction or criticism. If it is forbidden to torture someone, it surely does not follow that it is wrong to withhold torture from the person. Indeed, it scarcely seems possible for there to be a forbidden act whose omission is wrong and deserves sanction or criticism. But it is clear, at any rate, that there are some forbidden acts whose omission is not wrong and does not deserve sanction or criticism. Hence some acts satisfying condition (2) are clearly forbidden to perform.

On the basis of these observations, it appears that Heyd is mistaken in his contention that condition (2) entails condition (1). If the omission of an act is not wrong and does not deserve criticism or sanction, it does not follow that the act is neither obligatory nor forbidden. But what is important to note here is that Heyd is correct in concluding that the act in question is not obligatory. The truth of condition (2) does not guarantee that the act in question is not forbidden, but it does appear to guarantee that the act is not obligatory. And this point is significant for the standard account. Given the assumption that it is always morally blameworthy to violate duty—an assumption which seems difficult to deny—condition (1) of the standard account looks redundant. Condition (3) establishes that an act of supererogation is never blameworthy to omit, and given the assumption that it is always blameworthy to violate duty, it follows that one can never violate duty by omitting an act of supererogation. But this is just another way of saying that one can have no duty to perform an act of supererogation. Therefore, Heyd's point seems to show that the standard account's condition (1) is redundant.

Nevertheless, the same is not true of the account I have proposed, for condition (1) of my account is stated in the language of fulfilling no duties. Thus, it would be fallacious to argue that if my condition (3) is true, it automatically follows that the performance of the act in question fulfils no obligation. It is true that when one fails to do an obligatory act, one's failure is forbidden. But it is one thing to fail an obligation and another thing to fail to perform an act which fulfils an obligation. And one who fails to do the latter does not necessarily fail to fulfil the relevant obligation. Suppose I have an obligation to give my sandwich to someone who is in the process of starving to death. If there are twenty such people starving to death in my immediate vicinity, I can fulfil this obligation by giving my sandwich to any of the twenty. Thus, if I give my sandwich to the twentieth person, I thereby fail to give it to the nineteenth. I thereby fail, in other words, to perform an act (giving my sandwich to the nineteenth person) which, though it is not itself blameworthy to omit, nevertheless fulfils an obligation. For I have elected to fulfil this obligation by performing a different act.

From these considerations it is apparent that from the fact that one fails to perform an act which fulfils an obligation it does not follow that one's failure is morally blameworthy. For one might nevertheless fulfil the same obligation through the performance of another act. (Conversely, one's omission can fail to be blameworthy even though one would fulfil an obligation by not omitting the act in question.) Therefore, an argument purporting to show that my condition (3) entails my condition (1) is fallacious. I conclude that condition (1) of the standard account is redundant, given the assumption that it is always morally blameworthy to violate duty, but condition (1) of my account is not redundant.

Chapter 3

THEISM AND
SUPEREROGATION

Discussions of supererogation often proceed as if it were a foregone conclusion that people are capable of performing acts of supererogation. There may be disagreement over whether certain specific acts meet the qualifications for being judged acts of supererogation, just as there are disagreements over what these qualifications ought to be. But those participating in such disagreements are normally united in their assumption that there are such things as acts of supererogation and that people possess the capability to perform them.

Nevertheless, there are those who challenge this assumption. There are those who are convinced that among the categories of action which people perform, there is no category of supererogation. Perhaps there are some who are of the persuasion that human beings are simply incapable of morally praiseworthy behavior. If there are any who are of this persuasion, they will surely judge it impossible for people to perform acts of supererogation. But typically the anti-supererogationist impulse is generated by the idea that an act can never be praiseworthy to perform while at the same time failing to fulfil a duty. An act, that is to say, can be praiseworthy to perform as long as one is doing one's duty. But apart from the fulfillment of duty, it is impossible to perform an act in a manner which is praiseworthy.

In this chapter I will examine this anti-supererogationist impulse as it has developed in a theistic context. As the result of holding certain theistic views, some have arrived at the conviction that a person's behavior can be morally praiseworthy only when it occurs as the fulfillment of duty. Given the assumption that God exists, that all human beings are God's creatures, and that God has instituted certain moral requirements to be binding upon these creatures, many theists have concluded that there can be no acts of supererogation in human life. I will begin with a discussion of the role this conviction played in the thought of three Reformation figures: Martin Luther, John Calvin, and Philip Melanchthon. I will then turn to some contemporary formulations of this theistic perspective, noting similarities and differences between the concerns of contemporary theistic anti-supererogationists and the concerns of the Reformers. In conclusion, I shall raise the general question whether such a perspective is indeed an inevitable consequence of a commitment to the view that God exists, that all human beings are God's creatures, and that God's moral requirements are binding upon these creatures.

1. THE REFORMERS

Among the practices of the Holy Catholic Church which succeeded in inflaming the passions of the Protestant Reformers, the sale of indulgences holds a unique place. The purchase of an indulgence was ostensibly a means to alleviate punishments for those who transgressed God's commandments, and the interest in purchasing indulgences was considerable. Not surprisingly, the Church profited handsomely from this arrangement, and it is well known that the sale of indulgences eventually degenerated into a practice beset with corruption of the worst sort.

The principle underlying the idea that the purchase of an indulgence can lessen the penalties for sin was that Jesus Christ and the saints had, through their exemplary lives on earth, built up a treasury of good works. Since this treasury can be of no direct benefit to these individuals, the scheme of indulgences was devised to enable others to benefit. Those who fail to live saintly lives are assigned penalties (perhaps a period of confinement in purgatory), and through the purchase of indulgences it was believed possible for a measure of the accrued merit of Christ and the saints to be applied to their account. And when a measure of this merit is applied to the account of one faced with a penalty, the penalty is correspondingly lessened.

According to this picture, God exacts penalties for transgressing his commandments. But such penalties apply only to those whose lives generate a surplus of evil relative to good. A few people manage to end their lives with a surplus of good relative to evil, and these saintly individuals make possible the treasury of good works. This treasury of good works, in turn, makes possible the lessening of punishments to those facing the prospect of punishment. But God is presumably satisfied if the entire ledger is kept perfectly balanced. It is of no direct concern to God who benefits from the surplus created by whom. To the Church, then, is given the delicate task of administering these transactions in such a way that the balance sheet remains intact.

The scheme of selling indulgences presupposes that acts of supererogation are possible. While on earth, Christ did all that was required of him; but in addition to this he performed meritorious works not required of him (John 11:1–37). And to a lesser degree the saints performed meritorious works not required of them. Perhaps in a few instances these saints responsible for creating a treasury of merit failed to fulfil all of the duties required of them, but they apparently succeeded in performing enough meritorious works to compensate for these failures. These saints finished their lives with a surplus of good relative to evil, and this surplus accrued to the treasury. Subsequently, of course, it was applied to the accounts of those purchasing indulgences or those designated as beneficiaries by the purchasers of indulgences.

The original meaning of the Latin verb *supererogare,* to overspend or spend more than is required, is not altogether unrelated to the circumstances by which such a treasury is built up. For there is a clear sense in which the merit which accrues from the works of Christ and the saints is conceived as quantifiable. Each of the saints contributes a certain amount of merit, and the sale of indulgences involves the withdrawal of a certain amount from the treasury. Moreover, it is possible to think of the saints' contributions to the treasury as made possible by their expenditure of effort. It takes a great expenditure of effort and self-discipline to fulfil or discharge the obligations one is faced with, for God's demands for one's life are considerable (the Ten Commandments, for example). But the expenditure of still more effort and self-discipline makes possible the performance of meritorious works over and above the requirements of obligation. Thus, there is perhaps a sense in which, from the perspective of the Church, the saints expended more effort than was required. This over-expenditure then makes it possible for sinners to benefit through the purchase of indulgences.

The idea that it is possible for certain saints to perform meritorious works over and above the requirements God places upon them was accommodated by the scholastic distinction between the counsels of God and the commandments of God. In an often quoted passage Thomas Aquinas states this distinction as follows:

> The difference between a counsel and a commandment is that a commandment implies obligation, whereas a counsel is left to the option of the one to whom it is given. So in the New Law, which is the law of liberty, counsels are fittingly added to the commandments, but not in the Old Law, which is the law of bondage.[1]

The commandments of God are obligatory; a person is under an obligation to do what God has commanded. Such commandments are said to be associated with the Old Law, or the law of bondage. The counsels of God, on the other hand, have an optional status. One to whom a counsel of God is directed has the option of following or declining to follow the recommendations it contains. In this way the counsels of God are associated with the New Law, or the law of liberty. It is appropriate for one to exercise liberty in responding to these counsels.

The counsels of God, according to Thomas, are beneficial to those to whom they are directed. Just as counsels of a wise friend are of great use in regulating one's affairs, so the counsels of Christ, "our wisest and greatest Friend," are described by Thomas as "supremely useful and becoming."[2] Thus, it appears to be in the best interests of persons to respond positively to God's counsels, for they are designed to be useful. Of course, one can resolve to respond negatively to the counsels of God, but one is then acting contrary to one's own best interests.

There are three areas in human life to which Thomas believes all of God's counsels ultimately pertain: external wealth (concupiscence of the eyes), carnal pleasures (concupiscence of the flesh), and honors (pride of life). God's counsels encourage us to renounce riches in favor of poverty, to renounce carnal pleasures in favor of chastity, and to renounce pride in favor of obedience. It is not required of us to renounce riches, carnal pleasures, and pride altogether (at least those of us who have not made vows of poverty, chastity, and obedience); but to the extent that we follow these counsels, we will attain more speedily to eternal happiness.

> He that cleaves wholly to the things of the world, so as to make them his end . . . falls away altogether from spiritual goods. . . . Nevertheless, for man to gain the aforesaid end, he does not need to renounce the things of the world altogether, since he can, while using the things of this world, attain to eternal happiness, provided he does not place his end in them. But he will attain more speedily thereto by giving up the goods of this world entirely.[3]

The crucial point is to avoid permitting the worldly goods to become our end in life. Beyond that, it is not obligatory to give them up altogether; rather, it is the function of the counsels to lead us in the direction of giving them up.

Generally speaking, the counsels of God involve renouncing riches, carnal pleasures, and pride. But it is important to see that these counsels are directed to people in the context of their particular circumstances. A certain course of action may be a counsel for someone in one set of circumstances but not in another. Thus, in a particular case, one might have a counsel to give alms to a poor man, or to set aside carnal pleasures for the sake of a period of prayer, or to do a particular good deed on behalf of one's enemies. In the context of these particular circumstances one is encouraged to perform these acts. In another set of circumstances it is conceivable that God's counsels may direct one toward different, perhaps even opposite, courses of action (such as refraining from prayer for the time being). But the important point is that these are not the commandments of God. Again, one is not obliged to perform them, but the counsels of God always serve to provide encouragement to one in the direction of performing them.

In the same discussion Thomas qualifies his claim that God's counsels are useful to all by cautioning that some people are ill-disposed or unfit for observing certain counsels. Thus, although the counsels are expedient to all, considered in themselves, they can be inexpedient for some people to follow. When one's disposition is not inclined to the renunciation of riches, carnal pleasure, or pride, or if one is unfit for observing these counsels, they may be inexpedient to follow. It is not entirely clear what is meant by this qualification, but the general idea is illustrated in Christ's counsel of perpetual poverty. The counsel to "Go, sell all thou hast" is preceded by an important qualification, "If thou wilt be perfect" (Matthew 19:21). Only to one with a desire to be perfect is the counsel directed. One who lacks this desire is ill-disposed or unfit for observing it. Of course, some interpret these words of Christ as a commandment, not a counsel. But interpreted as a counsel, Thomas emphasizes that it is to be regarded as a counsel not directed to all persons.

In verse 12 of the same chapter Christ gives the counsel of perfect chastity: "There are eunochs who have made themselves eunochs for the kingdom of heaven." He then adds the qualification, "He that can take it, let him take it." And the Apostle Paul gives the counsel of virginity in I Corinthians 7 and adds in verse 35 the qualification, "And this I speak for your profit, not to cast a snare upon you." To those who are ill-disposed or unfit to observe these counsels of perfect chastity, they are not directed.

To summarize, Thomas distinguishes between the commandments of God and the counsels of God. The commandments of God are obligatory to obey, but the counsels are optional recommendations for the benefit of those to whom they are directed. All of God's counsels can be classified according to their connection with one of three categories: the renunciation of wealth, the renunciation of carnal pleasure, and the renunciation of pride. And the counsels are directed only to those for whom they are expedient. They are not directed to those unfit or ill-disposed to observe them.

It is not altogether clear to what extent Thomas approved of the practice of indulgences, but the Church did not hesitate to appeal to his authority in justifying the practice. Clearly, the distinction between the commandments and counsels of God opens the door for an acknowledgement that people can perform meritorious works apart from duty or obligation. One who lives in accord with God's commandments and in addition follows God's counsels is in a position to create the surplus of merit which can be transferred to others in the manner already described. The counsels of God make possible the creation of a treasury of merit, while the commandments of God do not. By virtue of obedience to God's commandments it is impossible for one to build up a treasury of merit, but the same is not true of one who both obeys God's commandments and who follows God's counsels.

It is for this reason that the distinction between the commandments and counsels of God became the focus of concern among the Reformers. Both Martin Luther and John Calvin vigorously rejected the idea that there are counsels of God, which are optional to follow distinct from the commandments of God. According to Luther, "... there are no good works except those which God has commanded."[4] Whenever a good work is performed, the person is simply carrying out what God has commanded. Thus, what Thomas calls counsels are in reality commandments. Injunctions to renounce wealth, carnal pleasure, and pride are injunctions to good works; presumably, then, they are obligatory, for there are no good works apart from that which God has commanded.

John Calvin puts the point somewhat more forcefully in the following passage:

> These commandments—"Do not take vengeance; love your enemies," which were once delivered to all Jews and then to all Christians in common—have been turned by the Schoolmen into "counsels", which we are free either to obey or not to obey. What pestilential ignorance or malice is this! ... The reason they assign for not receiving them as laws is that they seem too burdensome and heavy, especially for Christians who are under the law of grace. Do they dare thus to abolish God's eternal law that we are to love our neighbor? ... Either let them blot out these things from the law or recognize that the Lord was Lawgiver, and let them not falsely misrepresent him as a mere giver of counsel.[5]

Clearly aware that the distinction between the commandments and counsels of God opens the door to the possibility of performing meritorious works apart from duty or obligation, Calvin protests bitterly. It is a gross misunderstanding of God's law to hold that it can be divided into two portions, one of which we are obliged to honor and one of which we are free to obey or to not obey.

From Calvin's perspective the injunctions of God form a unified whole. All of God's injunctions are binding upon all of God's creatures. By introducing a distinction between the commandments and counsels of God, men have sought to escape from those laws of God which seem too burdensome or heavy. It is convenient to assign such laws the status of a mere counsel; whether one lives in accord with such counsels then becomes optional. One can regard their fulfillment as expedient or useful for one's pilgrimage to spiritual perfection, and their omission is at the same time perfectly excusable. However, for Calvin it is nothing more than a display of man's folly to divide God's law into a part which is obligatory and a part which is optional on the grounds that many of God's laws seem too burdensome or heavy.

The admonition to love one's enemy is cited by Calvin as an example of a commandment of God which the Schoolmen have turned into a mere counsel. Surely it would be less burdensome to regard this admonition as a recommendation for our spiritual perfection than as a requirement with the binding force of obligation. But from the words of Christ in the Sermon on the Mount, "Love your enemies, pray for those who persecute you" (Matthew 5:44), Calvin believes that it is undisputable that we are commanded to love our enemies: "Who will not here conclude with Chrysostom that the obligatory character of these utterances reveals them clearly to be not exhortations but imperatives?"[6]

More generally, Calvin believes we are commanded to love God with all of our heart, all our soul, and all our strength. Of all God's commandments which seem burdensome or heavy, there are few which compare to this commandment. "Compared with this law," says Calvin, "everything ought to be considered easy."[7] Calvin concedes in the same passage that many of God's commands are "indeed hard and difficult for our feebleness," but this does not change the fact that they are still God's commands. To live under the illusion that only certain of God's laws are obligatory is simply pestilential ignorance. If God commands us to love him with all of our heart, all our soul, and all our strength, then that is exactly what we are required to do.

Ironically, neither Luther nor Calvin reacts to the discussion in Thomas's writings about the need to place qualifications upon those to whom the counsels are directed. Not only are some of God's injunctions classified as mere counsels, but the counsels of God are directed only to those for whom they will be edifying or useful. Surely from the point of view of Luther and Calvin such qualifications represent a still further erosion of the binding force of God's law. Given their position, the laws of God are obligatory without exception, and they are directed to all persons without exception. There is no room in such a scheme for certain persons to be excused on the grounds that they are unfit or ill-disposed to benefit from following them.

In the minds of the Reformers the idea that God's law can be fragmented into two pieces, the one obligatory and the other optional, seemed to represent a perverse attempt to dodge the force of those laws judged most oppressive. In their minds it seemed to represent at best a misunderstanding of the requirements of God's law and at worst a justification of indulgences. Naturally, then, their inclination was to reject the possibility of supererogatory works; it is not within the power of human agents to exceed the requirements of God's laws, much less accrue merit by exceeding these requirements, and any doctrine lending support to this idea is to be regarded with suspicion.

Even the saints, according to Luther, "have done nothing which is superabundant. Therefore, they have left nothing to be allocated through indulgences. . . . "[8] The reason is that, on Luther's view, what the saints have done is obligatory; even their acts of martyrdom are obligatory. Once again, there are no good works in human life apart from what God has commanded. Thus, if acts of martyrdom are good works, it follows that the person performing them is under an obligation to perform them. And if such acts turn out to be merely the fulfillment of one's obligation, there is no possibility that a surplus of merit can be accumulated through their performance. A treasury of merit created by the superabundant works of the saints is an impossibility, for no human is capable of superabundant works. No matter how meritorious one's works, even to the point of martyrdom, a human being can never rise above the level of obligation to build a surplus of merit. Luther appears to leave open the possibility that Christ succeeded in building a treasury of merit through the life he lived while on earth, the implications of which could be pursued at great length. But, for the purposes of the present discussion, no saint has succeeded in doing so.

The anti-supererogationist position of the Reformers directly undermined the possibility of indulgences. However, it is probably misleading to conceive of the practice of indulgences as the sole motivation for their anti-supererogationist inclinations. For it was the doctrine that persons are justified by faith alone which was perhaps the deeper impulse of the Reformation, and this doctrine itself seemed to the Reformers to conflict with the idea that there are meritorious works apart from the fulfillment of God's commandments. For if persons can be justified by faith alone, never by works, then a person can presumably never be judged righteous in God's eyes solely on the basis of works. How, then, can people perform actions which are praiseworthy or meritorious outside the confines of obedience to

God's laws? Opening the door to the possibility of performing acts of supererogation, on this line of reasoning, seems to open the door to the possibility of being justified by one's works.

Of course, this line of reasoning is not perfectly airtight if it is taken as an argument to disprove the possibility of supererogation. There is no contradiction in affirming that a person can never be judged righteous in God's eyes on the basis of works alone and affirming at the same time that a person can perform acts of supererogation. For an act whose performance fulfils no duty and is yet praiseworthy may still fall short of justifying a person in God's eyes. A person can go through life performing occasional acts of supererogation and still come nowhere near being justified on the basis of these acts; such a person can still be said to be justified by faith, not works. Nevertheless, the idea that acts of supererogation are possible for human agents perhaps can be construed as contrary to the spirit of the doctrine that persons can be justified by faith alone. And the acceptance of this doctrine certainly was a contributing factor to these anti-supererogationist tendencies on the part of the Reformers.

Philip Melanchthon, a lesser-known figure of the Reformation, shares many of the same sentiments as Luther and Calvin concerning the distinction between God's commandments and God's counsels. He speaks of certain "Sophists" who have "made counsels" from Divine laws. "That is, they have taught that certain things are not necessarily demanded by God, but only recommended, so that if anyone cares to, he may obey, and they absolve the one who does not obey."[9] Melanchthon believes that in doing so these individuals have "erred shamefully and godlessly." These laws are not to be regarded as mere recommendations; they are demanded of us and are to be regarded as commandments.

Concerning the view that God's law is to be divided into commandments which are obligatory and counsels which are optional, Melanchthon asks why those holding such a view do not simply interpret the entirety of God's law as consisting of counsels. As long as they do not acknowledge that God has ordered them to do something unless it pleases them to do it, why do they not regard all of God's commandments as optional? Melanchthon's implication appears to be that the division between commandments and counsels, as standardly described, is highly arbitrary. Those laws of God which men are pleased to honor and obey retain the status of commandments, while those laws which are difficult to obey are relegated to the category of counsels.

Curiously, Melanchthon's own position is that, among the entirety of God's ordinances, all but one are commandments. "As far as I know," he says, "in the Gospels there is only one instance of counsel, that on celibacy."[10] Celibacy is not required of God's creatures, but it is nevertheless recommended as something good. He quotes Saint Paul as saying of those who are unmarried that it is well for them to remain as they are. Those who are married, of course, have not thereby sinned and should not be made to seek a divorce for the sake of attaining celibacy; but to those who are unmarried it is recommended not to look for someone to marry (I Corinthians 7:25–27).

Technically, then, Melanchthon recognizes the distinction between God's commandments and God's counsels. There are certain things God requires of all persons, but there is also room for acknowledging a place for counsels in the law of God. Unlike Luther and Calvin, he concedes that there is a distinction to be made in the manner Thomas suggests. Nevertheless, there is in his view (as far as he is aware) only one clear instance of a counsel in all of Scripture. Aside from the counsel of celibacy, all of God's injunctions must be regarded as obligatory. Thus, while Thomas identifies a multiplicity of counsels in the areas of renouncing wealth, carnal pleasures, and honor, Melanchthon sees the state of marriage as the only area in which acquiescence with the injunctions of God is purely optional. To the extent that we are admonished to renounce wealth, carnal pleasures outside the bounds of marriage, and honor, we are obligated to renounce these.

Clearly, the spirit of Melanchthon's position is much closer to that of Luther and Calvin than it is to that of Thomas. While Melanchthon acknowledges one instance of a counsel among God's ordinances and thus leaves room for supererogation in human life, the counsel of celibacy is an exception. It is pleasing to God that a person remain celibate, and a person who does so presumably does something meritorious apart from the fulfillment of duty. But in all other areas of life, the fulfillment of God's law is the fulfillment of duty. That a treasury of merit can be accumulated under such circumstances as these is scarcely conceivable. Hence, Melanchthon maintains a solidarity with Luther and Calvin with regard to the question of finding the Church's justification of the practice of indulgences intolerable.

To summarize, in its justification of the practice of indulgences, the Holy Roman Catholic Church appealed to the distinction between the commandments of God and the counsels of God. One who follows the commandments of God does what God requires one to do, but one who follows the counsels of God does what is pleasing to God over and above what is required. By following the counsels of God, then, the saints can build up a treasury or surplus of good works. And through the administration of the Church, this surplus can be allocated to the accounts of those facing the punishments of God.

Luther and Calvin vehemently object to the idea that there is a treasury of merit accumulated through the meritorious works of the saints, and they attack the problem at its source by denying that the laws of God can be divided into the categories of commandments and counsels. Their position is that all of God's laws are commandments. As such, all of God's laws are obligatory, and it is required of all of God's creatures to follow them. Consequently, all the good works of the saints constitute the fulfillment of obligation. No human creature ever performs good works over and above the requirements of God's law. Melanchthon makes an exception for the counsel of celibacy. It is pleasing to God for people to remain celibate, but those who enter marriage do not thereby violate God's law. Nevertheless, apart from the counsel of celibacy, Melanchthon stands in agreement with Luther and Calvin that God's creatures are incapable of performing good works outside the scope of what God requires and that all of God's creatures are justified by faith alone.

Before moving on to a consideration of contemporary views, I conclude this section with a brief quotation from the 1562 *Book of Common Prayer* which clearly reflects the prevailing mood of Reformational thought:

> Voluntary works besides, over and above, God's Commandments, which they call Works of Supererogation, cannot be taught without arrogancy and impiety: for by them men do declare, that they do not render unto God as much as they are bound to do, but that they do more for his sake, than of bounden duty is required: whereas Christ saith plainly, When ye have done all that are commanded to you, say, We are unprofitable servants (Article XIV).

2. Contemporary Theistic Opponents of Supererogation

Theists of the twentieth century are no longer motivated by the desire to discredit the ideas justifying the practice of selling indulgences. Yet it is common to find theologians and philosophers of religion endorsing the contention of Luther and Calvin that no human creature ever performs good works over and above the fulfillment of obligation. In fact, one can find this contention endorsed by Protestant and Roman Catholic thinkers alike. Among contemporary theists there is agreement by a significant number of thinkers from both traditions that, given a commitment to the idea that God exists and that all of us are subject to his laws, there is no room for supererogation.

In his essay, "The Theology of the Religious Life," Karl Rahner develops this point in terms of the perfection to which a person is called. (His discussion is directed to those who have embraced Christianity, but clearly his reasoning can be applied to theism in general.)

> All Christians are called to perfection. Grace constitutes a call which is the basis of moral obligation, and it calls men to love God and their neighbor with *all* their hearts and all their strength. . . . God gives us, then, the power to love him and our neighbor as well with *all* our hearts, and he imposes on us an obligation to do so. Hence, all Christians can and should attain to *that* perfection outside of which there is no other.[11]

It is frequently pointed out that one has a duty to strive for perfection, but Rahner's point is unmistakably much stronger. One has an obligation not only to strive for perfection but also to *attain* perfection. One who strives for perfection and fails to attain it has thereby failed to live up to one's obligations.

It is hard to see how there can be any room for supererogation in the scheme proposed by Rahner. For if one has an obligation to attain perfection, every praiseworthy act one performs is presumably the partial fulfillment of an obligation to attain perfection. There is no such thing as attaining perfection and then proceeding to perform a meritorious work over and above the perfection one has attained because the possibility of performing an additional praiseworthy or meritorious work suggests that such a person has not attained perfection in the first place.

Another way to state this argument is to point out that a state of perfection cannot be improved upon. If a moral agent can improve, it follows that the agent has not yet attained a state of perfection. Hence the performance of every act which is praiseworthy or meritorious draws one closer to the state of perfection, but it cannot constitute the achievement of merit over and above the attainment of perfection.

Therefore, if the state of perfection is obligatory, it appears that one cannot perform an act of supererogation. One cannot perform an act which is both praiseworthy and fails to fulfil an obligation.

The idea that all of God's creatures are required to live lives of moral perfection might be dismissed as somewhat far-fetched. It is plausible to think of God as requiring his creatures to strive for moral perfection, but how can one realistically imagine that God ordains the attainment of perfection as a moral obligation? In support of their position, those of Rahner's persuasion frequently point to various Scripture passages. In Christ's sermon on the mount, he addresses his audience with the words, "Be perfect, therefore, as your heavenly Father is perfect" (Matthew 5:48). More indirectly, James states, "Perserverance must finish its work so that you may be mature and complete, not lacking anything" (James 1:4). One must perservere to the point of moral maturity, wherein one lacks nothing which will make maturity complete. And in I Peter it is written, "But just as he who called you is holy, so be holy in all you do" (I Peter 1:15). One ought to follow Christ's example of holiness in all of one's actions. This idea is developed further in the second chapter: "To this you were called, because Christ suffered for you, leaving you as an example, that you should follow in his steps. 'He committed no sin, and no deceit was found in his mouth'" (verses 21 and 22). Since Christ committed no sin, and since persons are called to follow his example, it can be concluded that persons are called to lead sinless lives. And to the degree that leading sinless lives can be equated with a life of moral perfection, it follows that persons are called to lives of moral perfection.

A straightforward reading of these passages seems to constitute scriptural support for Rahner's contention that moral perfection is obligatory. God's creatures are directed to be perfect, to perservere to complete moral maturity, to be holy in all of their actions, and to follow Christ's example of sinlessness. It might be objected that the passage in James is a summons to strive for complete moral maturity, not a summons to attain complete moral maturity. Hence it is debatable whether this passage actually supports Rahner's claim. More significantly, however, it might be objected that these various passages are not clearly the commandments of God. One might argue, for example, that in the sermon on the mount Christ is exhorting his listeners to be perfect. It is the expressed desire of Christ that people be perfect, but it is not explicitly stated that persons are thereby obliged to be perfect. On this line of reasoning, one who fails to live a life of moral perfection is not guilty of failing to fulfil an obligation; one has only failed to do what Christ recommended. Thus, just as Thomas identifies certain of God's ordinances as counsels for the good of human beings, so it is possible to argue that these verses of scripture express recommendations. It is recommended that we follow Christ's perfect example, perservere to complete moral maturity, and consistently refrain from sin. One might observe, then, that Rahner's claims appear to be supported by several passages in scripture; however, this support depends upon a particular interpretation of these passages, and it is open for one to argue that there are alternative interpretations which fail to support Rahner's claims.

Joseph Allen adopts a somewhat different strategy in urging that a commitment to theism disallows that works of supererogation are possible. His point of departure is Urmson's example of a soldier falling upon a live grenade to save his comrades. Recall from chapter one that Urmson introduces the example to argue that certain heroic acts cannot be subsumed under the classification of duty or obligation. If the soldier had declined to throw himself upon the live grenade, according to Urmson, it would be highly implausible to maintain that the soldier had failed in his duty. One cannot plausibly maintain that the soldier has a duty or obligation to sacrifice his very life for the sake of his comrades.

Nevertheless, Allen takes issue with Urmson's conclusion:

> It is sometimes observed that we would not appropriately blame a person . . . for not being sacrificial in that way. . . . There is certainly an attraction in that way of thinking. From the standpoint of covenant love, however, there is something morally lacking, something that *ought* to be done, on the part of the soldiers who do not sacrifice their lives to save their comrades. . . . The idea that second-mile actions are not duties is a reflection of ordinary covenantal morality, not of the requirements of covenant love. . . . If by the strict requirements of covenant love a person ought to have gone the second mile—ought in the case of the grenade to have attempted to fall upon it—then that person is to be blamed for not having done so.[12]

Here Allen introduces an important distinction between ordinary conventional morality and the morality of covenant love. Ordinary conventional morality conceives of second-mile acts as acts which are optional, but from the perspective of covenant love (a love arising out of gratitude to God) such acts are required of moral agents. And those failing to fulfil such requirements have failed to do their duty. In the face of such requirements, then, there appears to be little room for the possibility of performing acts of supererogation.

Allen concedes that there is an attraction in thinking about second mile acts along the lines of conventional morality. He notes that we would appropriately blame a soldier for the failure to discharge "institutional duties," such as falling asleep while on guard duties, and hesitate to blame a soldier for the failure to sacrifice his life. There is undoubtedly something harsh in judging that a soldier has violated his duty in failing to sacrifice his life for his comrades. Nevertheless, the standpoint of covenant love takes an uncompromising stand. Second-mile acts are required of moral agents; it is never optional whether or not to perform them. One must always go the second mile in showing love to one's neighbor. It is, Allen goes on to say, "a strict and demanding ethic."

Allen also points out that his position does not give one license to criticize or castigate a person who has failed to perform second-mile acts:

> It is quite another matter whether anyone ought to *verbalize* that blame to a soldier who did not sacrifice himself. We have no call to be self-righteous, and what we say by way of blame in such a situation, even if properly thought out, may well be misunderstood. Nor do we mean by "blame" anything like self-rejection. Blame refers here to moral disapproval. . . . it does not entail rejection of the person.[13]

A person who has failed to perform a second-mile act has thereby failed to fulfil a moral obligation. Such a person deserves moral disapproval for this failure, but it surely does not follow that another person has the right to verbalize or express this moral disapproval. Surely it is true that such verbal expression can be misunderstood, and Allen's position should by no means be taken as offering encouragement to those wishing to pass judgments upon the shortcomings of others.

In addition, Allen points out that there are often difficulties in knowing when and how one ought to be sacrificial. In particular circumstances it is often difficult to know what a person's obligation is, and it is difficult to know this when the person is someone else. For example, if another person has great financial or emotional needs, it is frequently far from clear how one might go about assisting the person through the performance of second-mile acts. In this connection Allen writes:

> The distinction between commands and counsels is still useful, not in regard to the accumulation of merit, nor in distinguishing second-mile actions from basic institutional requirements, but in judgments about particular cases where it is not altogether clear what one's obligation is, and especially where the judgment is about someone else's action.[14]

Thus, one's obligation to perform second-mile acts from the standpoint of covenant love is contingent upon one's being clear what one's obligation is. In circumstances where one is simply unsure what the appropriate course of action might be, Allen suggests that the distinction between commands and counsels is still useful.

It is not, however, entirely apparent what Allen has in mind in his suggestion that the distinction between commands and counsels is still useful. After a lengthy discussion of the strict and demanding nature of the ethics of covenant love, it may come as a bit of a surprise to the reader to find Allen admitting that this distinction still has a place in the moral life. But perhaps his idea can be explained in the following example. I meet two strangers who appear hungry. When I ask whether they would like something to eat, the first nods affirmatively but the second shakes his head as if to respond negatively. The first stranger I take to my house and feed, and with respect to this stranger I fulfil my obligation to perform a second-mile act. The second stranger, however, speaks a different language and is unaware of what I am asking him. Had he known that I was offering him something to eat, he too would have responded affirmatively.

Surely I cannot be expected to know under these circumstances that the second stranger really desires the same treatment as the first stranger, and hence my failure to prepare a meal for the second stranger is excusable. Under these circumstances, it is obligatory for me to feed the first stranger but not obligatory for me to feed the second stranger. Hence, just as it is not permissible to fail to do what is commanded to me and permissible to fail to do what is a counsel for me, so a failure to feed the first stranger is not permissible, while a failure to feed the second stranger is permissible. Therefore, I interpret Allen's reference to the distinction between commands and counsels as a statement to the effect that the strict demands of the ethics of covenant love are contingent upon being clear as to what these demands are in one's particular circumstances. One is under an obligation to perform second-mile acts, but an exception is made when one is not in a position to know what second-mile acts are appropriate in one's particular circumstances.

In spite of these qualifications, it is evident that Allen's ethics of covenant love bear a close similarity to Rahner's ethics of perfection. Rahner proposes that one has a moral obligation to be perfect, and Allen's scheme makes it obligatory for one to perform second-mile acts, even to the point of sacrificing one's life for one's comrades. Thus, it is hard to see how either system leaves room for supererogation (unless, in the case of Allen's scheme, one is in a position of confusion and nevertheless happens to perform the appropriate second-mile act). No matter how meritorious a person's behavior might be, it becomes swallowed up by duty. For Rahner it becomes swallowed up by the duty to be perfect, and for Allen it becomes swallowed up by the duty to go the second mile.[15] No matter how hard one tries to exceed the demands of duty, it is a futile endeavor.

Moreover, it is evident that the views of both Rahner and Allen bear a similarity to the position of the Protestant Reformers examined earlier. Motivated by the principle that human moral agents are incapable of building a treasury of merit through the performance of good works, the Reformers hold that there are no good works apart from what God has commanded. God's laws are not to be divided into the categories of obligatory commandments and optional counsels; all of God's ordinances are commandments (with the exception, for Melanchthon, of the counsel of chastity). Thus, all good works performed by human beings are swallowed up by the duties which emanate from God's law. Superabundant works are an impossibility, even for the holiest of the saints. No matter how hard one tries to perform superabundant works, one is doomed to failure.

What is common to the Reformers, on the one hand, and the anti-supererogationist theists of the twentieth century typified by Rahner and Allen, on the other hand, is a conception of moral obligation which involves radically enlarging the domain assigned to it by conventional morality. If God exists and has set down certain laws governing the lives of those whom he has created, it seems natural to regard these laws as binding upon his creatures. Or, from a slightly different perspective, if something is truly good and praiseworthy in the eyes of God, is it not something which ought to be done? Ought one not always pursue that which in the eyes of God is the best possible course of action? For one who is a theist, there seems to be a natural attraction to respond affirmatively.

A commitment to theism, then, has often led people to a conception of moral obligation which leaves little or no room for supererogation. On such an understanding it is possible for human beings to perform acts which are good or praiseworthy (although for the Reformers even this is possible only by virtue of Christ's atonement), but all such acts turn out to fall within the realm of the obligatory. The boundaries of the obligatory are extended to the point that, for all practical purposes, no good works can fall outside these boundaries. For Luther this includes all of the acts of martyrdom which the saints have performed. For Calvin this includes everything one does out of love for one's neighbor. For Rahner this includes whatever is required to attain perfection. And for Allen this includes going the second mile, even to the point of sacrificing one's life for one's comrades.

3. Objections to Theistic Anti-Supererogationism

It is tempting to dismiss the anti-supererogationism of Rahner, Allen, and the Reformers as implausible and unrealistic. For example, it might seem totally unreasonable to hold that the attainment of moral perfection is obligatory and that the slightest failure to achieve perfection is morally forbidden. And the idea that the saints were only fulfilling their obligation through their acts of martyrdom might seem wildly out of line with one's moral intuitions.

Such initial reactions, however, can be dangerously simplistic. It is common for the views of the anti-supererogationist theists to be dismissed out of hand as totally unacceptable without a careful account of how they are unacceptable. In the remainder of this chapter I will attempt to provide a somewhat careful account of the manner in which these accounts provide an exaggerated characterization of moral obligation. In this way I will express agreement with those who find these views implausible. However, I believe it is likewise important to emphasize that a careful examination of these views reveals a legitimate desire to avoid certain errors, and in subsequent chapters I hope to make clear that there are important lessons to be learned about the avoidance of these errors from the views of Rahner, Allen, and the Reformers. In so doing I hope to make clear that there are important ways in which philosophical ethicists can benefit from the insights of those who have reflected upon the religious dimensions of moral obligation. Thus, it will be my suggestion that these views have perhaps been dismissed out of hand too quickly in discussions of moral obligation, and for this reason the lessons to be learned from them have generally gone unnoticed. My position, then, is that the views of the theistic anti-supererogationists are problematic on philosophical grounds and yet deeply insightful in a way which sheds some important light on the issue of supererogation.

It is sometimes pointed out that the ideas under consideration in this chapter are objectionable on the grounds that they violate the principle that 'ought implies can'. That is, it is charged that they violate the principle that an agent ought to perform an act only if the agent can perform the act. If it is not in the agent's power to perform the act, then the agent cannot be under any moral obligation or duty to perform it. According to this principle, moral obligation is operative in one's life only in those areas in which one has the capacity of acting. Thus, I might have a moral obligation to feed the starving man at my doorstep, but I do not have a moral obligation to feed all of the world's starving people. And I might have a moral obligation to rescue a small child in the path of an approaching automobile, but I would not have such an obligation if I had myself just been struck by an automobile and were unable to walk.

While there might be some disagreement concerning the grounds or justification of this principle, it is a principle which enjoys almost universal acceptance among moralists. Clearly, it is a principle with a great deal of intuitive appeal. If a course of action is physically impossible for a particular person, there seems to be something unfair in judging that the person is nevertheless morally obliged to do it. It would seem unfair to judge that my failure to feed the entirety of the world's starving people is thereby a failure to fulfil my duty. And if I were seriously injured by a hit and run driver, it would seem almost cruel to judge that I had subsequently failed in my duty to rescue the child playing in the road nearby. One cannot reasonably be under an obligation to do that which is not in one's power to do. And this is the case even if the agent is at fault for having arrived at the state of affairs of being unable to act. In such instances the agent may have failed a different obligation, such as an obligation to stay alert, sober, or whatever, and the agent can surely be morally responsible for the outcome produced by this inability to act. But according to the principle that ought implies can, the agent nevertheless has no obligation to perform the specific act if it is not possible to do so.

The principle that ought implies can is not directly incompatible with the position that there are no acts of supererogation in human life. But it appears to be incompatible with the version of anti-supererogationism implicit in the words of Rahner quoted earlier, given the auxiliary assumption that living a life of moral perfection is not within the power of human beings. If one agrees that living a life of moral perfection is not within the power of at least most people, it follows on Rahner's view that such people have an obligation to do what they are unable to do. Hence the principle is violated. Of course, it is possible to challenge the assumption that human beings are unable to be morally perfect. According to Louis Berkhof, a wide variety of religious traditions have in one way or another embraced the view that perfection is attainable for each of us in this present life (including the Pelagians, some mystical sects such as the Labadists, Quietists, and Quakers, and a few "Oberlin theologians").[16] But given the assumption that we are unable to be morally perfect, Rahner's position clearly conflicts with the principle that ought implies can.

It is less clear that the principle is violated by an endorsement of Allen's ethics of covenant love. But a careful examination of Allen's remarks suggests that the principle is indeed violated. For regarding the soldiers who are saved by the sacrificial act of their comrade, Allen states in the passage quoted earlier that there is something that ought to have been done on the part of the soldiers who fail to sacrifice their lives to save their comrades. Each has an opportunity to sacrifice his life, and each fails to do so. Consequently, according to the strict requirements of covenant love, each has failed to fulfil an obligation.

The underlying principle appears to be that if an agent has an opportunity to perform a second-mile act (and on Allen's view it is crucial that the agent recognizes the opportunity), then the agent has an obligation to perform it. Assuming, then, that each soldier recognizes the opportunity to save the lives of the other soldiers by falling upon the live grenade, each has the obligation to do so. However, it is not possible for each soldier to fulfil this obligation because it is not possible for each soldier to fall upon the live grenade and thereby save the lives of the other soldiers. Either all of the soldiers will die in a simultaneous attempt to sacrifice their lives, in which case none has succeeded in saving the lives of any comrades, or some of the soldiers will survive. But if some of the soldiers survive, it follows that these soldiers have failed to sacrifice their lives for the sake of their comrades (although they might have attempted to do so). In either case it appears impossible for each of the soldiers to sacrifice his life and thereby save the lives of the others. Inevitably, some of the soldiers will turn out to have obligations which cannot be fulfilled.

Moreover, the principle that an agent has an obligation to perform second-mile acts whenever the agent recognizes the opportunity to do so seems to create situations in which individual agents have more obligations than is humanly possible to fulfil. There are myriad ways in which one has opportunities to perform second-mile acts for the sake of others, and from this principle it follows that one has obligations corresponding to each of these myriad opportunities. Allen introduces the distinction between commands and counsels in situations where such opportunities are not clear to one, but the strict requirements of covenant love make no provision for optional good works in situations where one's joint obligations exceed one's ability to fulfil all of them. One is simply in a position of being unable to fulfil all of one's obligations.

In two different respects, then, Allen's ethics of covenant love leads to situations in which the principle that ought implies can is violated. It is possible for several individuals in a group to have obligations to bring about a state of affairs where it is impossible for them to fulfil their individual obligations. And it is possible for an individual to have a multiplicity of moral obligations, where it is impossible to fulfil all of them. Perhaps it is possible for one to escape being in these situations by living in a remote area where one has little or no contact with other human beings. But as long as one is able to observe the opportunities to be of service to other people, there is the potential of an enormous number of obligations attaching to one.

I conclude that the principle that ought implies can is violated in both Rahner's ethics of perfection and in Allen's ethics of covenant love. If God desires of us to be perfect, then that is what we ought to do. And if God desires of us to go the second mile to be of service to another, then that is what we ought to do. Whether it is in our power to do these things is beside the point. What we ought to do is independent of what it is in our power to do.

On the basis of these observations, it is clear that one who is committed to the principle that ought implies can will find Rahner's ethics of perfection and Allen's ethics of covenant love unacceptable. Given that one can never be reasonably expected to do that which it is not in one's power to do, it is unreasonable to expect one to live one's entire life in a state of moral perfection. And it is unreasonable to expect that one will perform second-mile acts on all of the myriad occasions during every day that the opportunities present themselves.

It is important to realize, of course, that theism itself does not commit one to a rejection of the ought implies can principle. Many contemporary theists acknowledge that God's law places requirements upon his creatures but deny that God ever requires his creatures to do what they are genuinely unable to do. According to this way of thinking, God is sensitive to the needs and abilities of his creatures and never requires them to act beyond the limits of their capabilities. Thus, Christ's injunction in the sermon on the mount to be perfect is not to be taken as an ironclad commandment; it is to be taken as an exhortation to strive after perfection. Perhaps God's creatures can be expected to strive after perfection, but God does not expect any of his creatures to attain perfection.

Many theists, in fact, subscribe to a view according to which the ability to transcend the requirements of obligation is a special gift from God. By the grace of God, on this view, we have been given the capacity to go the extra mile and show love to our neighbor in special ways that are not strictly required. Accordingly, God has created his creatures with the capacity of a free and spontaneous outpouring of love which goes beyond strict obedience to what is required of them. Such outpouring of love need not be viewed as building a treasury of merit. Nevertheless, these acts fall outside the boundaries of obligation, and on this view it is a part of God's plan that his creatures are provided with opportunities to perform them.

Theists who subscribe to this position clearly view God's law differently than the anti-supererogationist theists. Reinhold Niebuhr argues that the law of God is less fixed and absolute than people have traditionally been led to believe. Based upon "a Stoic-Aristotelian rationalism which assumes fixed historical structures," Niebuhr believes that a mistaken conception about the law of God has evolved in both Catholic and Protestant thought:

> All law, whether historical, positive, scriptural, or rational, is more tentative and less independent in its authority than orthodox Christianity, whether Catholic or Protestant, supposes. . . . The final dike against relativism is to be found not in these alleged fixities, but in the law of love itself. This is the only final law, and every other law is an expression of the law of love . . . [17]

The law of God is not to be conceived as a fixed, absolute body of requirements or demands. It is the law of love which is central. All other laws are expressions of the law of love, formulated in terms appropriate to a person's historical circumstances.

Once love is made the central focal point, Niebuhr believes that much of the tension between Thomas and the Reformers is relieved. For "love means a perfect accord between duty and inclination in such a way that duty is not felt as duty."[18] Sacrificial love involves the readiness to sacrifice the self for the other; and when a person has a duty to make sacrifices for another, sacrificial love makes possible a perfect accord between duty and inclination. When sacrificial love manifests itself, a person is beyond the point of weighing the costs or benefits involved in making sacrifices.

> The final form of love is bereft of such calculation and meets the needs of the other without calculating comparative rights. Sacrificial love is therefore a form of love which transcends the limits of law. . . . it is a point which stands beyond all law, because the necessity of sacrificing one's life for another cannot be formulated as an obligation.[19]

Thus, sacrificial love has the capability of making possible a perfect accord between duty and inclination because it itself transcends the limit of law. It cannot be captured or embodied in terms of moral requirements. It does not make sense to ask whether one has an obligation to demonstrate sacrificial love, for it is not meaningful to speak of sacrificial love in terms peculiar to what is contained in the realm of law.

It is a consequence of Niebuhr's views that second-mile acts cannot neatly be classified within the realm of the obligatory. It is a mistake to conceive of God's law as placing strict requirements upon moral agents to perform second-mile acts whenever the opportunity arises. In particular, sacrificing one's very life for the sake of another cannot be regarded as an obligation. It is an ultimate expression of sacrificial love, and hence it exceeds the boundaries of obligation. Luther may have been correct in believing that the martyrdom of the saints does not succeed in building a treasury of merit, but it is a mistake to judge that the martyrdom of the saints is simply the fulfillment of God's commandments.

4. CONCLUSION

The principle that ought implies can appears to be rejected by theological moralists committed to views along the lines of Rahner's ethics of perfection and Allen's ethics of covenant love. From their perspective God's commandments make no allowances for human weaknesses and inabilities. Whether one disobeys God's commands out of perversity or out of inability, the fact remains that one has failed to fulfil one's obligations. On the other hand, there are theological moralists who accept the principle that ought implies can. On their view, God takes account of the needs and abilities of his creatures, never requiring a person to do what that person is unable to do.

It is difficult to offer a decisive proof in favor of the principle that ought implies can. And it is unlikely that those who endorse views of the sort described by Rahner and Allen will be inclined to alter their views regarding the nature of God's laws upon being confronted with arguments in favor of accepting this principle. Nevertheless, the principle has a strong intuitive appeal, and perhaps it is here that one will find views incompatible with it correspondingly less appealing or plausible than views which are compatible with it. Other things being equal, views which do not conflict with the principle that ought implies can are perhaps preferable to views which entail its denial.

More specifically, if one is committed to the view that God exists and has instituted moral requirements which are binding upon his creatures, one is still free to choose whether to accept or reject the principle that ought implies can. Since the principle has a strong intuitive appeal, there is perhaps a slight presumption in favor of rejecting views entailing its denial. Other things being equal, therefore, it seems preferable to interpret God's requirements in such a way that the principle is not violated. Of course, some theists will not grant that other things are equal, and hence one can grant that there is a presumption in favor of accepting the principle without granting that it is compatible with the requirements which God in fact places upon his creatures. Nevertheless, unless one can make a strong case that these moral requirements conflict with the principle (by way of showing, for example, that the relevant scriptural passages cannot plausibly be interpreted except as laying down ironclad requirements), it seems reasonable to opt for an understanding of God's law according to which moral agents are not required to perform acts which they are unable to perform.

Chapter 4

OTHER CONTEMPORARY ANTI-SUPEREROGATIONISTS

Although theism has led many thinkers to an anti-supererogationist position, there are a variety of other ways by which people have been motivated to repudiate the possibility of supererogation. It is frequently noted, for example, that act utilitarianism is inhospitable to the possibility of performing acts of supererogation. For if an agent ought always act in such a way as to bring about the greatest benefits to the greatest number, to take one version of act utilitarianism, then it would appear that the agent has a duty to bring about the maximally optimal outcome (in terms of maximizing benefits) in every situation. But if this is the agent's duty, it is difficult to see how the agent can perform an act which is both praiseworthy and fulfils no duty; no matter how hard one tries to bring about the greatest benefits to the greatest number, one is simply doing one's duty. It is not possible to maximize utility to the point where one rises above the call of duty within the framework of this type of theory.

Likewise, for considerably different reasons, Kantian ethics has frequently been judged to be anti-supererogationist. Roughly speaking, an act can be a moral act for Kant only if it is performed in obedience to duty.[1] Within the domain of morality there is no such thing for Kant as an act which is optional to perform or not to perform. If so, there seems to be no possibility that an act which is morally praiseworthy to perform can at the same time fall outside the confines of duty. Every such act is by its very nature performed in obedience to a law or command.

A great deal of scholarly debate has centered around the extent to which utilitarianism and Kantian ethics rule out the possibility of supererogation. While these two approaches to ethics are generally inhospitable to supererogation, recent scholarship suggests that in the case of each there are certain loopholes by virtue of which supererogation is not entirely ruled out. Various writers have argued that it is possible to interpret the writings of Kant in such a way that they are not entirely committed to an anti-supererogationist position. Similarly, there are versions of utilitarianism which can be demonstrated to be compatible with the possibility of performing acts of supererogation.

A third approach which is potentially inhospitable to the possibility of supererogation is 'ethical prescriptivism'. Very roughly, the idea is that when one expresses statements to the effect the something is good or right, one is exhorting others to regard it favorably. And this, according to at least one type of ethical prescriptivist, is a judgment with implicit prescriptions for action. Thus, to say that a certain course of action is good or worthy of praise is to imply that, given certain qualifications, one ought to perform it or at least be the kind of person that would perform it.

In this chapter I will discuss twentieth-century representatives of all three approaches and assess the extent to which each is committed to an anti-supererogationist point of view. Ross and Findlay I take to be representatives of the Kantian approach; Feldman, New, and Moore to be representatives of a broadly utilitarian approach; and Pybus to be a representative of the prescriptivist approach. (The figures will not be treated in precisely this order, for it will be useful to comment upon certain aspects of New's views against the backdrop of having discussed some of the points emphasized by Pybus).

1. C.D. ROSS AND J.N. FINDLAY

In a well known passage in his book *The Right and the Good*, C.D. Ross writes:

> In the first place it seems self-evident that if there are things that are intrinsically good, it is *prima facie* a duty to bring them into

existence rather than not to do so, and to bring as much of them into existence as possible.[2]

A person has a prima facie duty to bring into existence that which is intrinsically good. In the fifth chapter of his book Ross goes on to argue that there are three main things in human life which are intrinsically good: virtue, knowledge, and (with certain limitations) pleasure. And not only does one have a duty to bring these into existence, but one has a duty to bring as much of them into existence as possible.

Paul Eisenberg believes that in this passage Ross is committing the same error as that committed by Kant: treating as duties certain acts which are in fact acts of supererogation. After conducting a lengthy examination of Kant's moral writings and finding Kant guilty of this error, Eisenberg judges that Ross, in spite of trying to "discern common moral opinion," likewise errs by assigning acts of supererogation to the realm of duty. In doing so, he charges, both Kant and Ross have allowed their moral theories to be built upon a notion of duty which is unfaithful to the ordinary understanding of the term 'duty'. Consequently, both leave little or no room in their moral theories for acts of supererogation.[3]

Eisenberg fails to explain exactly how Ross commits the error of treating as duty what is in fact supererogation in the passage quoted above, and hence a brief examination of this passage is in order. Complicating the issue is the reference to prima facie duties in Ross's initial claim that one has a duty to bring into existence that which is intrinsically good. A prima facie duty can be contrasted with an all-things-considered duty in that only the former can be overridden by a conflicting duty. Thus, one's prima facie duty to refrain from deceiving others can be overridden by a conflicting duty not to jeopardize the lives of persons by divulging their whereabouts to the enemy. After the overriding process has been settled, the duty which survives is one's all-things-considered duty.

Curiously, after having stated that a moral agent has a prima facie duty to bring into existence that which is intrinsically good, Ross speaks later in the same passage of an agent's having a duty to bring into existence virtuous dispositions. The latter remark makes no reference to the duty's being of the prima facie variety, and hence it is not clear whether he is referring here to a prima facie duty or an all-things-considered duty. Nevertheless, it is the earlier statement which is crucial in determining to what extent Ross is professing an anti-supererogationist point of view, and in this statement the reference to prima facie duties is unambiguous. One has a prima facie duty to bring into existence that which is intrinsically good and to bring as much of these things (virtue, knowledge, and, with certain limitations, pleasure) into existence as possible.

Taking virtue as an example of an intrinsic good, it follows that a moral agent has a prima facie duty to bring as much virtue into existence as possible. This means that a moral agent has a duty to bring as much virtue into existence as possible, unless this duty is overridden by another duty. Suppose a moral agent, taking seriously such a duty, expends a great deal of time and energy promoting the virtue of justice in the world. There is much one can do to promote a greater measure of justice in human life, and, according to what Ross says, one has a duty to do precisely this. One has a duty to bring as much of it into existence as possible, and consequently (again assuming that no overriding duties interfere) one can never rest content with bringing into existence less than one is capable. With respect to promoting a virtue such as justice, duty requires promoting as much of it as one possibly can.

Within the realm of promoting the intrinsic goods of human life, Ross's view appears to leave little or no room for supererogation. It is meritorious to promote intrinsic goods, generally speaking, but for Ross it is also one's duty to promote intrinsic goods. And no matter how much of an intrinsic good one brings into existence, one is merely fulfilling a duty. Of course, it is a prima facie duty one is fulfilling, but this feature of Ross's theory does not seem to have any significant bearing upon whether there is any possibility of performing acts of supererogation in promoting intrinsic goods. Suppose I tirelessly labor to promote a greater measure of justice in human life. However, an overriding duty interrupts my work for several days or weeks. During this period of time I can rest assured that my failure to promote justice does not constitute a failure to fulfil duty, for my duty to promote intrinsic goods has been temporarily overridden. But it is hardly the case that I have now been afforded the opportunity to promote justice in a manner which is supererogatory, for my efforts must now be turned in the direction of satisfying the demands of the overriding duty. Thus, in the event that my duty to promote justice has been overridden by a greater duty, I am scarcely in a position to continue promoting justice and claim that my doing so is supererogatory. My doing so is no longer the fulfillment of a duty (at least not an all-things-considered duty), but since it involves violating an overriding duty I am no longer acting in a praiseworthy manner; hence, there is no possibility that I am performing an act of supererogation. Accordingly, the fact that Ross identifies one's duty to bring into existence that which is intrinsically good as a prima facie duty does not appear to have any effect upon whether bringing intrinsic goods into existence can qualify as an act of supererogation.

Eisenberg charges that Ross classifies as duties certain acts which ought properly to be classified as supererogatory, and I believe Eisenberg is correct. A person who labors tirelessly to promote the cause of justice is merely fulfilling a duty on Ross's view, assuming that this duty is not overridden. No matter how much of one's time and effort is directed toward promoting justice, one is merely doing one's duty. Arguably, this view makes unreasonably weighty demands upon moral agents. Such a person cannot plausibly be judged to have a duty to promote justice in such a manner as this, and those of us who fail to do all we can to promote virtue in human life (thus failing to be fantastically virtuous, as Kant puts it) cannot plausibly be judged to have failed in our duty.

At the same time it is important to realize that Ross does not rule out the possibility of performing acts of supererogation in areas of human life where intrinsic goods are not being promoted or brought into existence. Intrinsic goods, according to Ross, fall into the categories of virtue, knowledge, and, with certain limitations, pleasure. To the degree that a person can act in a praiseworthy manner without promoting these goods, the possibility of supererogation remains. Therefore, although Ross takes up an anti-supererogationist position with respect to that which is intrinsically good, it is inaccurate to classify him as an anti-supererogationist with respect to the entire range of human action. Hence it seems misleading for Eisenberg to accuse him of espousing a theory which leaves little or no room for supererogation. (Perhaps, though, Eisenberg's idea is that the duties to promote intrinsic goods make such incredible demands upon agents that at every moment of one's life one has an all-things-considered duty to promote them. However, it is not clear that this idea accurately reflects Ross's view. Perhaps Ross believes that agents have prima facie duties at every moment to promote them, but nothing in what he says suggests that these duties are all-things-considered).

Eisenberg goes on to accuse J.N. Findlay of making the same error as Kant and Ross, treating as duties certain acts which are in fact supererogatory. Understanding Findlay's view, however, requires understanding an important distinction between two different 'oughts', the 'hortatory' and the 'minatory'. According to Findlay, hortatory is used to urge a person to do something without necessarily urging the person not to omit doing it, while minatory consists in urging a person away from doing something (which might itself be an omission) without necessarily urging the person toward something.[4] An example of the latter, according to Findlay, is seen in an utterance such as "Never tell lies." When one ought never to tell lies, it is the minatory ought which is operative; one is urged away from telling lies with no explicit directive to tell the truth. On the other hand, the utterance 'You really ought to cultivate your mind' has a hortatory import. One is encouraged to move in the direction of cultivating one's mind, but there is no element of warning one not to remain uncultivated. One is not urged away from remaining uncultivated in the manner one is urged away from telling lies.

The relevance of this distinction to the issue of supererogation can be seen in a subsequent passage:

> It is therefore plain that what in a wide sense a man ought to do falls into two quite different segments: a fairly restricted focus consisting of what he is warned off from omitting and therefore ought, in a minatory sense, to do, and a much wider penumbra consisting of the things from whose omission he is not thus warned off, but which he ought, in a hortatory sense, to do. We shall find it convenient to use the word 'duty' to cover both segments of what we ought to do, since both are noble and serious. If we do so, however, not all duty will be 'stern', nor demanding punishment if violated. There will be duties that wear a purely winning aspect, and which will smile, perhaps wistfully, over a case of omission.[5]

A duty which reflects a minatory ought is understood to carry with it a strong urge to comply; one is "warned off" from omitting to do what one ought to do in a minatory sense. If one ought not to tell lies in the minatory sense, then one may be said to have a stern warning to comply. On the other hand, a duty which reflects what one ought to do in a hortatory sense does not carry with it a stern warning to comply; nor is punishment appropriate for one who declines to fulfil a hortatory duty. Someone who has a hortatory duty is positively urged to comply; a hortatory duty points out to one a desideratum to be realized. But a failure to fulfil such a duty warrants a wistful smile, not a stern reproach.

Findlay believes that the range of what one ought to do in a minatory sense is quite limited in relation to what one ought to do in a hortatory sense. There are certain things in life which we ought to do in a minatory sense, duties which carry with them a stern warning to comply. But there is a much wider class of duties binding upon us which are hortatory in nature. These are also things which we ought to do, and we are positively urged to comply with them. But the consequences of failing to comply with them are not the same as the consequences of failing to comply with minatory duties, for there is no sense in which one has a stern warning to comply. Findlay goes on to state that their nonfulfillment is morally indifferent.

It might be tempting to imagine that what one ought to do in a hortatory sense is not truly a duty. If the failure to comply with a hortatory duty is morally indifferent and appropriately causes one to do no more than "smile, perhaps a trifle wistfully," then it might be dubious that one is really describing a bona fide duty. Nevertheless, Findlay is insistent that hortatory duties are actual duties. They are, he says, both noble and serious. In spite of their omission being morally indifferent, hortatory duties state a "noble task" and are to be taken seriously by those on whom they are binding.[6] If a man has a hortatory duty to cultivate his mind, his failure to do so might elicit nothing more than a wistful smile. However, at the same time his failure to undertake this noble task is a serious matter. The failure to take one's hortatory duties seriously is not deserving of punishment, but he states that there is something almost tragic in this failure.

Eisenberg emphasizes the degree to which Findlay believes these duties are serious by quoting the following remark by Findlay concerning hortatory duties: "For every degree of positive value, there is a degree of effort which it would be . . . *shameful* not to make, should we know such effort to be probably effective."[7] If one knows that it is one's hortatory duty to undertake a noble task, then it is truly shameful to make no effort to undertake it. And for every degree of positive value which achieving the noble task realizes, there is a minimum threshold of effort below which it is shameful not to exert. Thus, one is not morally reprehensible for failing to exert the minimum effort appropriate for attempting to fulfil a particular hortatory duty, but it is shameful if one does not do so.

As with Ross, Eisenberg believes that Findlay assigns too wide a scope to the category of duty. And by failing to keep to the ordinary understanding of the term 'duty', he accuses Findlay of falling into the error of leaving little or no room for supererogation. Surely there is something initially plausible about Eisenberg's claim that Findlay leaves little or no room for supererogation, given Findlay's insistence that minatory and hortatory duties are both genuine duties. If the exhortation to cultivate one's mind is a hortatory duty, then one ought to do it. And while the failure to do it is morally indifferent, it can apparently never qualify as an act of supererogation. No act which truly fulfils a duty, no matter what the duty is, can qualify as an act of supererogation. And since Findlay believes that hortatory duties comprise a far wider class of potential human acts than minatory duties, it seems to follow on his view that that much of what is ordinarily considered supererogation falls under the category of duty. Whenever there is a desideratum which one ought to move toward, one has a hortatory duty to comply. Therefore, much of what moralists describe as supererogation can be characterized in terms of a desideratum which one ought in some sense of 'ought' to undertake.

Thus, the manner in which Findlay wishes to characterize hortatory duties appears to lead to the consequence that the theory leaves little room for supererogation or, at the very least, significantly narrows the range of what has traditionally been characterized as supererogation. However, there remains something peculiar about Eisenberg's criticism of Findlay. For while Findlay insists that hortatory duties are genuine duties, his accompanying description of hortatory duties does not seem compatible with the way duty is ordinarily characterized. Moralists ordinarily characterize duty in such a way that its omission is forbidden. It is morally forbidden to omit what one has a moral duty to do, and it is morally forbidden to do what one has a moral duty to omit. But hortatory duties are described by Findlay as morally indifferent to omit. Hence one might argue that, despite Findlay's insistence to the contrary, hortatory duties are not genuine duties and that Eisenberg's criticisms of Findlay's theory miss the mark.

Additional light can be shed upon the matter by attending to what Findlay says several pages later about the concept of 'obligation'.[8] Some duties, he says, are obligations and some are not. Hortatory duties are good to fulfil and morally indifferent not to fulfil. Some minatory duties are morally indifferent to fulfil and bad not to fulfil, and other minatory duties are obligatory to fulfil. Clearly, there are no hortatory duties which are obligatory; and even among minatory duties only some attain the status of obligation. It appears that no duty can qualify as an obligation as long as it is morally indifferent either to fulfil or to omit. The class of obligations, therefore, is not only considerably smaller that the class of duties, but it is also even smaller than the class of minatory duties. Indeed, Findlay complains that certain theists have attempted to extend obligation into the domain of all minatory and hortatory oughts by conceiving of God as legislating on every possible topic. Such theists allow obligations to spread their web over all of human conduct, and the end result is that men in relation to God have no sphere of rights. From such complaints as these it is tempting to suppose that Findlay wishes to distance himself from the views of the theistic anti-supererogationists discussed in the previous chapter. He is firmly opposed to the idea of extending the scope of obligation so that it covers virtually the whole of human conduct.

Further light is shed on the matter by Findlay's lecture to the British Academy, "The Structure of the Kingdom of Ends." Here he is critical of those who continually recast hortatory imperatives in the form of minatory imperatives, with the result of "forcing them into the mould of strict obligations."[9] In Findlay's opinion this practice has given rise to some disastrous developments, chiefly a variety of proposed systems of act utilitarianism. Within such systems it is made obligatory for each of us to "go as far as we can in the direction of infinity in the sheer multiplication of welfare."[10] In Findlay's opinion it is an absurdity to embrace a notion of obligations along these lines; it is a serious mistake to force all hortatory imperatives into the mold of strict obligation. Again, Findlay speaks as though he is critical of, rather than sympathetic toward, those who are inclined toward anti-supererogationism.

On the basis of Findlay's remarks concerning obligation, I believe Eisenberg's verdict is questionable. Eisenberg charges that Findlay, like Kant and Ross, subscribes to a theory which leaves little or no room for supererogation on the grounds that Findlay fails to keep to the ordinary understanding of the term 'duty'. Perhaps one can agree with Eisenberg that Findlay's views concerning duties are unorthodox. If everything covered by minatory oughts and hortatory oughts qualifies as a genuine duty, then the scope of duty for Findlay is considerably wider than what Eisenberg understands as the ordinary conception of duty. Findlay, in fact, assigns it a scope as wide as that typically assigned it by anti-supererogationists.

Nevertheless, even if it is true that Findlay's concept of duty is comparable in scope to that of the anti-supererogationists, it does not follow that Findlay can rightly be considered as leaving little or no room for supererogation. For Findlay understands duty in such a way that the failure to fulfil it is not necessarily morally forbidden. Hortatory duties, in particular, are morally indifferent to omit. It is a good thing to act in accord with one's hortatory duties, and one is encouraged to realize the desiderata which are made possible by fulfilling them. But the failure to fulfil hortatory duties is morally indifferent; there is no sense in which one who fails to fulfil them has done what is forbidden. Moreover, hortatory duties are never obligatory. One never has a moral obligation to do what one ought to do in a hortatory sense (and even certain minatory duties fail to qualify as obligatory).

It is plausible to interpret Findlay's view in such a way that his use of the term 'obligation' corresponds to what many moralists mean by the term 'duty'. The concept of duty is standardly understood in such a way that the failure to fulfil it is forbidden. Findlay seems willing to agree that this is true of obligations, but he is unwilling to agree that duties are automatically forbidden to omit. On this interpretation it is far from clear that Findlay's position is anti-supererogationist. Some of the things one ought to do in a hortatory sense, in fact, might qualify as acts of supererogation. Although Findlay insists that one has a duty to fulfil them, one has no obligation to fulfil them and their omission is morally indifferent. They are neither forbidden nor blameworthy to omit, and hence, if they are meritorious or praiseworthy to perform, they are arguably supererogatory.

To summarize, Eisenberg charges that Ross and Findlay, following the errors of Kant, assign too wide a domain to the category of duty. Consequently, they are charged with embracing views which leave little or no room for supererogation. In the case of Ross I have argued that Eisenberg's charges appear correct when applied to areas of human life where intrinsic goods are brought into existence (and this is true in spite of the relevant duties being designated as prima facie duties). A person has a duty to bring them into existence and to bring as much of them into existence as possible. However, in other areas of human life there is nothing Ross says which rules out the possibility of performing acts of supererogation, and this is a crucial point which Eisenberg apparently fails to take into consideration.

Regarding Findlay's views, Eisenberg's charges initially appear plausible. Findlay distinguishes between hortatory and minatory duties, treats them both as genuine duties, and describes them as having a very pervasive presence in human affairs. However, Eisenberg's conclusions rest upon a highly questionable interpretation of Findlay's discussion. Findlay's distinction between duties and obligations and his designation of failures to fulfil hortatory duties as morally indifferent (not to mention his criticisms of theists and act utilitarians eager to extend the boundaries of obligation into all areas of human life) suggest that it is his notion of obligation, not duty, which ought to determine whether his views are truly anti-supererogationist. And the role which he assigns to the notion of obligation seems perfectly compatible with the view that acts of supererogation are possible to perform.

2. Feldman: A Possible Worlds Approach

In his 1983 essay, "Obligations—Absolute, Conditioned, and Conditional," Fred Feldman begins with the observation: "In my view, the most fundamental principle about absolute moral obligation is that we ought to do the best we can."[11] In order to explain the precise meaning of this observation Feldman constructs a model of possible worlds. I will begin by describing the model he presents in this article; subsequently I will consider some additional details about this model and its interpretation which emerge from Feldman's 1986 book, *Doing the Best We Can*.

At the basis of this model is the concept of each person's having possible worlds in his or her power. This concept can be explained by imagining that when I came into existence, I was accompanied by an enormous set of possible worlds. These worlds were alike in respect to the facts of past history, necessary truths, and all aspects of the present and future over which I would never have any control. But they differed with respect to my behavior and its consequences. Each of them represented a possible way for me to live my life and everything that would happen to me if I were to so live my life. The set of these worlds can be described as the set of all the worlds accessible to me at the outset of my life.

As time goes by, I can act in such a way as to make huge blocks of these worlds no longer accessible. Suppose now that I am eating some peanuts, and it is now in my power to stop eating these peanuts. Of the worlds accessible to me right now, there are a multitude of worlds in which I continue eating peanuts during the next few minutes and also a multitude of worlds in which I do not. If I can stop eating these peanuts, then there are ever so many possible worlds in which I do stop eating these peanuts, and which are among my current accessibles. Two or three minutes from now, if all of the peanuts have been eaten, all such worlds will have been bypassed. None of them will ever again be accessible to me. Every world then accessible to me will be one in which I did eat those peanuts then.

A possible world that is in an agent's power at a given time is a world that was among the agent's original set of accessibles and which has not yet been bypassed. There is a way of living the rest of my life that is still open to me, and such that, if I do live my life that way, that world would be actual. In addition, all of the possible worlds are assumed to be ranked in terms of their intrinsic value. Feldman admits that such a ranking may not be of great interest in the absence of a specific account of what intrinsic value consists of, but it is nevertheless possible for the purposes of his project to presuppose that such a ranking exists. It is a ranking in which ties are possible, it imposes no boundaries as to how good or evil worlds can be, and it is a dense ordering in that it allows for degrees of value between any two degrees of value. Finally, it is a ranking which is "absolute." According to Feldman, the worlds are evaluated according to a measure that remains the same no matter what our point of view.

Moral obligation is introduced into the system by defining what a person ought to do at a particular time. Suppose that there is a p-world accessible to agent S at time t just in case there is a possible world where p is true and which is accessible to S at time t. Then one can say that S ought, as of t, to bring about p if and only if there is a p-world accessible to S at t, and there is no accessible not-p world as good as it. An agent ought to bring about a state of affairs p just in case, out of all the possible worlds accessible to the agent at the time in question, p is true in the world or worlds having the highest ranking.

Feldman employs the following illustration to explain this definition:

> So if I say that Smith ought to bake cookies tomorrow, what I mean is that there is a world now accessible to Smith in which he does bake cookies tomorrow, and there is no world now accessible to Smith that is as good as that one, and in which he does not bake cookies tomorrow.[12]

If this world contains the state of affairs of his baking cookies tomorrow, he ought to bake cookies tomorrow. On the other hand, if this world contains the state of affairs of his not baking cookies tomorrow, he ought not to bake cookies tomorrow (and this he can do by simply refraining from baking cookies).

It is in this sense, Feldman believes, that we ought to do the best we can when we ought to bring about a state of affairs. To say that someone S ought now to do something (bring about a certain state of affairs) at a certain time t is to say that if S acted in the very best way still available, S would have to bring about that state of affairs at t. And to say that S ought to do the best S can to bring about this state of affairs at t is to say that this state of affairs obtains in the highest ranked world or worlds at t of those accessible to S. The best S can do at t, relative to this state of affairs, is presumably to actualize the highest ranked world accessible to S at t in which this state of affairs obtains.

Up to this point Feldman's discussion pertains only to what he calls "absolute" moral obligation. In addition, he clearly distinguishes several types of conditional moral oughts, the most important of which is "conditional moral obligation." Here too the underlying idea is that we ought to do the best we can. Consider the judgment that, given that p occurs, I ought to bring about q. This means roughly that q does occur if I do the best I can consistent with the occurrence of p. Accordingly, if this judgment is correct, the following situation will hold. Among the worlds now accessible to me, there are worlds in which p and q both occur. The highest ranked such world (or worlds, in case of ties) will then be ranked higher than any other p world. In other words, there will be no p-world in which q fails to occur which will be ranked higher than this world.

Surely it is true that not all moral obligation is absolute in the relevant sense. I may not have an absolute moral obligation to pick up the litter which covers my neighbor's lawn. But I may nevertheless have a conditional obligation to pick up this litter if it is my dog which caused it to scatter by ripping open bags of garbage. And if I have this conditional obligation, then if I do the best I can consistent with the mess caused by my dog, the state of affairs of my picking up the litter occurs. If I have such a conditional obligation, then, of the worlds accessible to me now, there is a world in which my dog creates a mess and I pick up the litter such that no world in which my dog creates a mess and I do not pick it up is better than this world.

Both absolute and conditional obligation, then, are explicated in terms of doing the best that one can do. And the best that one can do at a given time is explicated in terms of identifying the best relevant world or worlds accessible to one at that time. It is a view of obligation which has much in common with act utilitarianism, for when one has an obligation with respect to a state of affairs there is a sense in which one ought to maximize the good in the process of actualizing it. Thus, Feldman judges his work to be a contribution to a utilitarian understanding of obligation.

Given its affinities with act utilitarianism, one might anticipate that Feldman's theory of obligation will leave little or no room for acts of supererogation. More specifically, it might appear that the theory will not allow for a moral agent to perform an act which transcends the bounds of duty or obligation. If one ought to do the best one can whenever one ought to do something, then it is hard to see how one can go beyond the requirements of what one ought to do. Suppose I ought to come to the assistance of a motorist with a disabled vehicle pulled off the edge of the freeway. When I pull over to ask whether I can be of any assistance, the motorist requests that I call for a mechanic. I make the call on my cellular phone, and thirty seconds later I am on my way again.

In this scenario I ought to come to the assistance of the motorist, and so I do. As I leave, I believe that I have fulfilled my moral obligation. However, it appears that I have failed to do my best. For it is in my power to bring about a better state of affairs. It is in my power to wait at the scene in case the mechanic fails to arrive; to offer the stranded motorist part of my sack lunch; or even to pay the bill for the repair work. If I do the best that I can in assisting the motorist, then it is plausible to suppose (assuming that these are states of affairs which would genuinely benefit the motorist if they were to be actualized) that I do some or all of these things. There is a world accessible to me right now in which I do these things, and, if there is no better world accessible to me in which I fail to do these things, the above criterion yields the result that I ought to do them. (This judgment will be qualified later in the light of the position developed in Feldman's book.)

There are typically a variety of ways in which one can fulfil one's moral obligations. Sometimes agents perform acts which barely succeed in satisfying the requirements of a particular obligation, and at other times agents perform acts which appear to go well beyond satisfying the requirements of an obligation. Feldman's theory is based on the idea that one ought to do the best one can all of the time. From this it seems to follow that one has failed to fulfil a moral obligation if one fails to do the best one can in satisfying its requirements. I fail to do the best that I can when assisting the motorist;

presumably, then, I have failed to fulfil my duty. There is a possible world accessible to me in which I do a great deal more than simply place a call on my cellular phone, and it is this great deal more that I really ought to be doing.

Going beyond the call of duty seems to be an impossibility if having an obligation really means doing the best one can. If one ought to bring about a state of affairs, then, no matter how much better one does in bringing it about, that is what one ought to do. And that is precisely what one does in an accessible world which is better than any world in which one fails to do so. Just as an act utilitarian who has a duty to bring about the optimal outcome in every situation cannot maximize utility to the point of rising above the call of duty, so one who ought to do the best one can is denied the opportunity of doing better than one ought.

I conclude that the theory so far described does not seem to allow for the possibility of transcending or going beyond the call of duty. In this manner one might say that the theory appears to be anti-supererogationist in at least one important way. However, in his book, *Doing the Best We Can*, Feldman presents a theory very much similar to that described in "Obligations—Absolute, Conditioned, and Conditional," but suggests an interpretation of the theory subtly different from that which I have taken the article to suggest. This interpretation is revealed in a section of the book in which Feldman responds to several objections, and I shall approach the interpretation by way of examining the objection which provides the context for it. The objection is that Feldman's concept of obligation is far too demanding. It requires that we do the very best that we can, perhaps to the point of devoting the rest of our lives to charity and becoming servants to humanity. Thus, a man who spends a quiet evening at home with his family has thereby violated a moral duty. But surely this is too demanding an account of moral obligation. Feldman calls this an objection based on 'moral rigor'. It charges that an account of moral obligation is overly demanding or rigorous if it requires moral agents constantly to do the best they can. A proper account of moral obligation should allow for agents to have periods of relaxation, even though there is much good they could instead be doing for the sake of humanity.

In response to this objection, Feldman first points out that the objection might be overestimating our capacity for good. Kurt Baier describes an ordinary man who, after a tiring day, puts on his slippers and listens to the radio. Is it really fair, Baier wonders, to judge that the man is failing in his duties on the grounds that he could instead be producing more good in the world? Feldman's first response to Baier is contained in the following words:

> Most decent people can't do very much better than they are already doing. There may be possible worlds in which Baier's tired worker becomes saintly, or works devotedly among the needy. But given the sort of character that man probably has, and his talents and opportunities, such worlds are probably not accessible to him. . . . His greatest possible contribution to human welfare is probably not very much greater than the contribution, meager as it is, that he is already making. He goes to work each day, earns some money to keep his family clothed, fed, and housed, and perhaps gives a bit of the excess to charity.[13]

Thus, while the objector might have visions of Baier's man spending his evenings laboring among the needy, enabling them to lead richer and more fulfilling lives, it is highly dubious that he is capable of acting out this vision. Given his character, his talents, and his opportunities, not to mention fatigue after a hard day's work, it seems almost ludicrous to imagine that worlds in which he emerges as a hero of the needy and oppressed during his evening hours are realistically within his power to actualize.

Surely Feldman's reply to Baier is plausible. One's absolute obligations are always restricted to worlds which are accessible to one on Feldman's approach, and hence these duties to engage in saintly or heroic behavior apply to those with extraordinary talen s or special training and in unusually opportune circumstances. Most of us can rest assured that we have no moral obligation to be spending our evenings driving to areas of town where needy and oppressed people live to be able to make an effort to improve their lives. Most of us, realistically speaking, are not capable of benefiting humanity all that much more than we are already doing.

Still, of course, we are not doing all that we are capable of doing. While there are many saintly or heroic deeds we cannot perform, there are certain courses of action open to us which can in some small way make the world a better place to live. We can do more for stranded motorists than place a telephone call, and we can do more for our lonely neighbors than give them a quick nod of greeting. And if this is true, then, according to the theory under consideration, this is what we really ought to do. It is easy to embrace a view of obligation which is too lax, but Feldman is convinced that morality really requires us to do the best that we can. If we really can do better than we are doing, then that is what we ought to be doing.

Feldman further replies to Baier's objection by noting that Baier seems to be attacking a view which requires a moral agent to identify the best of his alternatives and act accordingly. But the view defended in Feldman's book, the 'neo-utilitarian view', is subtly different, and the difference is revealed in the following passage:

> Old-fashioned act utilitarianism is apparently a view of this sort. My own neo-utilitarian view is different. It requires a person to do what he does in the best accessible worlds. Instead of focussing on some set of current alternatives, and insisting that the best of them be performed, it focuses on whole lives open to the agent. It requires him to live out the best of them. Thus, it may permit the tired worker to relax by the fireside each night so as to have the energy to return to modest saintliness on the following day.[14]

Baier's objection raises problems for views requiring agents to act in conformity with the best alternative currently open to them, but it would be a mistake to conclude that the objection thereby raises problems for the approach Feldman takes in his book. The 'neo-utilitarian' interpretation of the theory proposed by Feldman requires agents to act in conformity with the best life open to them, not the best short-term course of action open to them from one moment to the next.

The neo-utilitarian interpretation of the theory suggested in this passage differs from the interpretation discussed in connection with Feldman's article. The former interpretation was based on the idea that one ought at time t to bring about a state of affairs p just in case there is a p-world accessible to one at t and no not-p world as good as it. From this principle it follows that if p is the state of affairs of my remaining with the stranded motorist, offering part of my lunch to the motorist, and paying the repair bill, and if there is a p-world accessible to me and no not-p world accessible to me as good as it, then I ought now to bring about p. Under the former interpretation this was taken to mean that I am now required to bring about p. Under the neo-utilitarian interpretation, I am required to live out the best life available to me; perhaps this involves bringing about p, but there is no guarantee that the best life available to me is one I lead in a p-world. The best life available to me will be determined by an enormous number of factors involving the choices I make over periods of many years. The amount of good generated by actualizing p may turn out to be utterly trivial in the overall determination of the life I am required to live. Perhaps, then, there is no reason to think that the likelihood that such a world includes p is greater than the likelihood that it includes not-p.

Feldman points out that on this way of viewing things a moral agent can be justified in foregoing certain opportunities to do good. It may be consistent to living the best life open to one that certain opportunities to promote good can be bypassed. Such goods, in fact, ought not be pursued if one does not pursue them in the best life which is open to one. Again, the emphasis is not placed upon the short-term course of action upon which an agent is in a position to embark; the emphasis is to be placed upon the long-term life which an agent is in a position to live.

From these considerations it might appear that going beyond the call of duty is possible after all in the system proposed by Feldman. For if one can be justified in foregoing certain opportunities to do good, it might seem that an agent who seizes these opportunities to pursue good is in a position to do more than duty requires. Nevertheless, it is important to realize that in such cases one is *not* justified in pursuing the good. From the fact that one is justified in foregoing opportunities to do good, it does not follow that one is justified in seizing these opportunities. The reason is that in the best possible life open to one the opportunity is either seized or it is not. If it is seized, then seizing it is part of what one ought to do. If it is not seized, then foregoing it is part of what one ought to do.

The neo-utilitarian interpretation makes it evident that Baier's objection does not raise problems for Feldman's theory, but the prospects for accommodating the possibility of going beyond the call of duty remain substantially the same as before. With respect to any potential act, I either perform it or I do not perform it in the best life available to me. If I perform the act in the best life available to me, then I ought to perform it. If I do not perform the act in the best life available to me, then I ought not perform it. (If it is not in my power to perform it, of course, then by hypothesis performing it is not in the best life available to me; the same holds true of refraining from performing it.) In either case I am in no position to do more than duty requires. By performing an act I am either doing what I ought to be doing or what I ought not to be doing. The situation is slightly more complicated if there are several worlds tied for the honor of realizing the best life available to me; in this type of situation I might perform a given act in some but not all of these worlds. Feldman says nothing which commits him to the position that I ought to perform acts of this type; presumably, they are permissible both to perform and not to perform. However, it is Feldman's opinion that such acts will nevertheless fail to qualify as acts of supererogation or acts which go beyond the call of duty.[15]

When attention is directed at the best life which is open to a moral agent, it becomes clear that the agent is not constrained to take advantage of every opportunity to promote good. And this is the case even when these opportunities to promote good are within the agent's power. Thus, it is perfectly possible that Baier's tired worker is justified in relaxing by the fireside each night. Nevertheless, directing attention to the best life open to a moral agent makes it clear that neither the worker nor anyone else has the opportunity to go beyond the call of duty. If the worker is truly justified in relaxing, then relaxing is what he ought to do. Attempting to transcend the bounds of duty may well land him in the realm of the forbidden.

More generally, directing attention to the best life open to a moral agent raises serious questions as to whether it is ever possible to perform acts of supererogation. Again, if it is in my power to perform an act or not to perform an act, then either I ought to perform it or I ought to refrain from it (with the exception noted above regarding ties). I ought to perform it if I perform it in the best life available to me, and I ought to refrain from performing it if I refrain in the best life available to me. But if I either ought to perform it or ought not to perform it, there seems to be no possibility of performing it in a way which is both praiseworthy and fulfils no duty. Either I fulfil a duty by performing it or I do not. And if I do not fulfil a duty by performing it, then I ought not to perform it and my performance of it is forbidden. Thus, either I fulfil a duty by performing it or my performance of it is forbidden. And given the reasonable assumption that it is never praiseworthy to do that which is forbidden, it follows that for any act in my power to perform, my performance of the act either fulfils a duty or is not praiseworthy. I conclude, therefore, that Feldman's neo-utilitarian approach appears to leave no room for the possibility of performing acts of supererogation.

3. Pybus: A Prescriptivist Approach

Elizabeth Pybus sets out in her article "Saints and Heroes" to argue against the view that there is a realm of moral aspiration beyond duty or obligation. Urmson's classic paper of the same title has been widely influential in establishing the legitimacy of supererogation as a category of action which moral agents are capable of performing, but Pybus believes that Urmson's argument rests upon certain errors. Moreover, those who follow Urmson in acknowledging the legitimacy of supererogation unwittingly fall into these same errors.

Urmson's basic error consists of drawing a distinction between a morality of duty and a morality of aspiration. By separating duty from aspiration, Pybus charges, Urmson is effectively removing aspirations and ideals from the realm of morality altogether.[16] For, given Urmson's distinction, it is possible to commend others for performing certain types of acts without at the same time committing ourselves to the view that they are the sort of people we ought to be. In this fashion one can maintain that the commendation of another's behavior can have absolutely no implications regarding duties on the part of those who commend. But Pybus charges that this point of view removes such commendations from the sphere of morality altogether. One cannot express a moral point of view without there being such implications. If I say that something is truly a moral ideal, I cannot but feel that I have some sort of obligation to pursue it.

Suppose we observe a person who behaves in a heroic or saintly manner, and we commend the person for pursuing a moral ideal through this behavior. By commending this person we can either take ourselves to be committed to the view that we ought to be like that person, or we can take ourselves not to be committed to this view. Pybus believes that on the former alternative we are expressing a moral point of view, and on the latter alternative we are not expressing a moral point of view. Since Urmson believes that we can commend such people without being committed to the view that those are the sort of people we ought to be like, his view leads to the consequence that we are not expressing a moral point of view. He has removed such commendations from the realm of morality.

Urmson's basic error, then, consists in assuming that we are expressing a moral point of view when we commend saints and heroes in the absence of any commitment to the idea that these are the sorts of people we ought to be. Commendation in the absence of such commitment is possible, but one who expresses this commendation is not expressing a moral point of view. A second error Pybus accuses Urmson of committing, one which is closely related to the first error, is that he fails to realize that morality consists in the intertwining of evaluation and action. Urmson seems to operate on the assumption that one can morally evaluate the acts of moral agents in a detached manner, a manner which demands no action on one's own part. On Urmson's view one can remain aloof when passing moral judgments, detaching oneself from the situation to which one is directing these judgments.

Pybus conceives of morality as an enterprise in which evaluation and action cannot remain separate. Moral evaluations for Pybus inevitably commit one to action. One who expresses moral condemnation regarding the evil acts of another inevitably expresses the view that we all ought avoid acting like such people. And one who expresses moral approval regarding the good or saintly acts of another inevitably expresses the view that these are the sorts of people we ought to be. And this is the case even when we express approval of those who sacrifice their own life for others: "If I think that sacrificing one's life for others is the supreme moral ideal, but fail to connect this with any belief that I, and others, should pursue that ideal, I am confused."[17] Moral evaluation can never be made in the absence of some type of commitment to action.

This type of moral evaluation, Pybus hastens to add, does not mean that one is committing oneself actually to perform each and every type of act one praises others for performing. I do not commit myself to the actual sacrifice of my own life for others when I praise people for the sacrifice of their lives for others. According to Pybus, I commit myself only to the view that these are the sorts of persons I ought to be like. For when we praise others for what they have done, we are really praising the virtues which lie behind these actions. Thus, by praising the saints for what they have done I am not saying that I ought to perform these very same acts; I am saying that I ought to display the same sorts of virtues which have given rise to these acts.

Pybus's point is that moral praise or commendation implies a commitment to be virtuous in the manner that the one being praised is virtuous. And such a commitment clearly leaves open the possibility of performing acts of a different sort than those performed by the person being commended. One need not perform precisely the same sorts of acts that the saintly or heroic person performs, but one who makes a commitment to display a virtue is thereby making a commitment to act in a manner consistent with the possession of the virtue. Hence, if I praise a heroic man for his courageous behavior, I am implying that I ought to be courageous and to act in a courageous manner. According to Pybus, my praise is insincere if I praise the man without making such commitments regarding my own life.

To summarize, Pybus believes that moral commendation and moral condemnation essentially carry with them implications for action. When one commends a good person for what that person has done, one is committed to the view that this is the sort of person we ought to be. One who commends a person without implying that this is the sort of person one ought to be fails to express a moral point of view. Urmson's basic error consists in assuming otherwise. In addition, Urmson fails to appreciate the extent to which evaluation and action are intertwined. Pybus holds that moral evaluation always commits one to action; it does not allow one to remain aloof or detached from the situation being evaluated as Urmson assumes. One who commends is not committed to acting in the same manner as the person one is commending, but one is committed to acting in a manner consistent with the possession of the same virtues which motivate the acts of the person one is commending.

In the end Pybus believes that Urmson has failed to demonstrate that the traditional three-fold classification of human acts is inadequate. In addition to the categories of the obligatory, the (merely) permissible, and the forbidden, Urmson argues for the category of the supererogatory on the grounds that saintly or heroic acts cannot be subsumed under the category of the obligatory (in effect, though, Urmson is arguing that supererogation should be recognized as a special subcategory of the permissible). Pybus believes that Urmson's reasoning is faulty and that saintly and heroic acts are properly classified under the category of the obligatory. We should, she urges, resist the view that there is a realm of moral aspiration beyond duty or obligation. Aspiring to be the sorts of persons that saintly or heroic people are (assuming we find their behavior commendable) is what we ought to be doing. Consequently, Pybus holds that neither Urmson nor anyone else has demonstrated that a separate category of supererogatory acts needs to be acknowledged.

Patricia McGoldrick has commented on Pybus's views in her essay, "Saints and Heroes: A Plea for the Supererogatory." McGoldrick believes that Pybus has succeeded in dissolving part of the problem Urmson sets out to solve. Urmson asks whether we commit ourselves to the view that all persons ought to sacrifice their lives for others if we ascribe praise to the hero who sacrifices his life for his comrades. The answer Pybus defends, of course, is that we are not committed to this view. When we praise the saint or hero we do not commit ourselves to saying that we should all perform similar acts. Rather, we commit ourselves to saying that we ought to aim at inculcating within ourselves the dispositions and virtues from which acts of this type are produced. Again, moral praise is a matter of committing oneself to develop or display the virtue or virtues exhibited by the person one praises. This move, McGoldrick states, deals neatly with the apparent paradox Urmson introduces and upon which his own argumentation is constructed. McGoldrick's implication appears to be that it is a weakness in Urmson's argument that this point escaped his notice.

Nevertheless, McGoldrick is not convinced that Pybus has succeeded in establishing that we have a duty to develop the virtues from which the acts of the saint and hero spring and to act in accord with these virtues. McGoldrick quotes a passage in which Pybus argues that one cannot state that something is a moral ideal without feeling that one has an obligation to pursue it, and she charges that in this argument Pybus is guilty of circular reasoning:

> If we argue that any ideal to which we ascribe moral praise is one to which we all ought as a matter of duty aspire, then we beg the question in favor of the trichotomous taxonomy which Pybus purports to defend. That is to say, we may argue that moral commendation of an ideal logically entails that we ought *as a matter of duty* aspire to it if, and only if, we presuppose that all morally praiseworthy ideals are ideals of duty. But this is precisely the issue at stake, and thus just what cannot be presupposed. It may well be that all moral ideals are like this; but equally it may be that some moral ideals . . . are, as proponents of the supererogatory thesis would maintain, praiseworthy but not obligatory.[18]

McGoldrick sees Pybus as arguing for the trichotomous taxonomy on the grounds that moral commendation of an ideal entails that we ought as a matter of duty aspire to it. But these grounds derive their plausibility from the presupposition that praiseworthy ideals are ideals of duty, and this presupposition rests, in turn, on the assumption that the trichotomous taxonomy is legitimate. Thus, McGoldrick's construes the argument as circular.

It may not be evident from Pybus's discussion that she is guilty of such a blatant error of reasoning (although one other commentator, Russell Jacobs, finds McGoldrick's contention to be very persuasive).[19] Nevertheless, McGoldrick is correct in maintaining that Pybus's central premise, that moral commendation of an ideal entails that we ought as a matter of duty aspire to it, is not adequately substantiated. Pybus asserts that when commendation of an ideal is not taken to entail the existence of any such duty, then the commendation simply fails to qualify as a moral evaluation. But she does not appear concerned to argue in favor of this point; her assumption seems to be that if one reflects upon the nature of moral evaluation, then it will become evident that one cannot express a moral commendation without being committed to saying that one ought to aspire to the ideal which is being commended. McGoldrick sees Pybus as reasoning in a circular fashion, but I am inclined to diagnose the situation instead as one in which the central premise employed by Pybus is simply regarded by her as standing in no need of justification; it is regarded by her as evident to anyone who reflects on the situation. In any event, this premise is not adequately defended.

McGoldrick goes on to suggest that there is a core of truth in this premise. For, according to McGoldrick, " . . . logical consistency demands that any ideal which is thought of as morally praiseworthy must be thought of as worth aspiring to."[20] If I judge that a certain ideal is morally praiseworthy, I am committed to the belief that it is worth aspiring to. It would be logically inconsistent of me, on this view, to judge that a certain way of life is both morally praiseworthy and yet not worth aspiring to. If I believe that being charitable is not worth aspiring to because it damages an individual's chances of succeeding in business, then I am in no position to express moral commendation of a person's charitable behavior. I cannot consistently regard something as morally praiseworthy if I do not believe it is worth aspiring to.

McGoldrick accuses Pybus of turning this insight into something highly dubious by insisting that these ideals are worth aspiring to inevitably as a matter of *duty*. In other words, Pybus holds that any ideal which is thought of as morally praiseworthy must be thought of as worth aspiring to as a matter of duty. To judge an ideal as morally praiseworthy is to imply that one ought to aspire to it. On McGoldrick's view such ideals are felt to be worth aspiring to by one who judges them morally praiseworthy, but on Pybus's view the aspiration to such ideals must be regarded as a duty by one who judges them morally praiseworthy. Thus, what is dubious about Pybus's central premise is its reference to the concept of duty, not its claim that the moral commendation of an ideal commits one to a positive belief concerning one's aspiring to that ideal.

It is here that McGoldrick's views part ways with the views expressed by Pybus. An ideal judged to be morally praiseworthy must at the same time be considered worth aspiring to, but from this it does not follow that the ideal must be considered worth aspiring to as a matter of duty. One who judges something morally praiseworthy is committed to nothing in the form of a duty or obligation. When I praise the courage of a hero, I must regard such courage as worth aspiring to; but I am not committed to regarding such courage as worth aspiring to as a matter of duty. I need not regard the courage of a hero as something I ought to aspire to.

McGoldrick believes that the position she is advocating is consistent with the possibility of supererogation in human action. Returning to Urmson's example of the soldier who sacrifices his life on behalf of his comrades, consider a person who praises the soldier for his act of self-sacrifice. On McGoldrick's view such a person is then committed to regarding the virtue displayed by the soldier's act as worth aspiring to, but the person is not committed to regarding the virtue as something which ought to be cultivated or displayed. The person has no duty or obligation to cultivate or display this virtue. Nevertheless, such a person might in any event go on to cultivate this virtue. If so, then if the cultivation of this virtue is praiseworthy (and its omission is not blameworthy), it will qualify as an act of supererogation. On Pybus's view the cultivation is the mere fulfillment of duty, but on McGoldrick's view it can qualify as an act of supererogation.

To summarize, McGoldrick agrees with Pybus that the moral commendation of an ideal commits one to a positive belief concerning aspiring to that ideal, but she does not agree that it commits one to anything in the form of a duty or obligation. The central premise employed by Pybus, that moral commendation of an ideal entails that we ought as a matter of duty aspire to it, is used by Pybus to support the claim that the three-fold classification is adequate. McGoldrick charges that Pybus employs circular reasoning in the support for this claim. I am not convinced that Pybus is guilty of an error as blatant as this, but certainly the premise itself is not adequately supported by Pybus. In the end McGoldrick affirms a four-fold classification that includes the category of the supererogatory.

Pybus appears to sense that her central premise is not adequately supported in "Saints and Heroes," and, in a recent reply to McGoldrick, Pybus undertakes to provide additional support for it. The essence of her argument is that the distinction between spectator and agent points of view might be possible to maintain when discussing morality abstractly; however, as agents, making moral judgments, we cannot do this. Pybus imagines a situation in which one is watching an expert bridge player making a particularly skillful play. If one were a bridge player, she believes, it would be very odd to judge that this was a brilliantly played hand and yet to deny that this is how one ought to play one's own hand in such circumstances. Of course, if one resolves to be a mere spectator of the game, one might deny that this is what one ought to do. From a spectator point of view one need not worry about adopting the techniques of the good player.

But the distinction between a spectator and agent point of view cannot be maintained in one's capacity as a moral agent. As far as morality goes, according to Pybus, we are all players. With the possible exception of 'psychopaths', human beings cannot opt to be mere spectators.[21] And as players we need to adopt the techniques of the skilled players (namely, good people). We ought to live as they live, just as people who wish to participate in the game of bridge cannot deny that they ought to adopt the techniques of the skilled bridge players. Pybus describes this position as a 'modified prescriptivist' view; it emphasizes that there is an important connection between judgment and action.

Perhaps this argument will strike McGoldrick as removing the appearance of circularity from the structure of Pybus's reasoning. However, it remains to be seen whether McGoldrick will find this modified prescriptivist argument persuasive. Certainly, there are several points at which one might have questions concerning Pybus's new line of argument: Can morality appropriately be compared to a game?[22] Is it clear the bridge player ought to adopt the techniques of skilled players? If so, is the sense of 'ought' in which they ought to do so relevant to the ethical enterprise? Can it be concluded that moral agents ought to live as good people in a way that refutes Urmson's claims?

It might be noted, in conclusion, that if it is possible for the performance of an act to be praiseworthy without the agent's recognizing or realizing that it is praiseworthy, the position taken by Pybus may not be entirely anti-supererogationist after all (though, of course, her intent is to leave no room for a "fourth category"). Her entire argument is based upon situations in which moral judgments or evaluations are made; in all such situations duties are created, and the possibility of performing acts of supererogation is ruled out. However, it is consistent with her argument that an agent perform a praiseworthy act, having never stopped to think or consider that such behavior is praiseworthy, and hence having no attendant duty to perform it. In the absence of any realization that the act is praiseworthy the duty creating mechanism described by Pybus is absent, and supererogation seems possible after all. One who has never commended others for displaying an ideal or virtue by reason of having never realized that such behavior is praiseworthy leaves open the possibility of displaying the virtue oneself in a manner which fulfils no duty or obligation.

4. NEW AND MOORE

Like Elizabeth Pybus, Christopher New sets out to attack Urmson's contention that acts of saintliness and heroism are supererogatory. He too is convinced that these acts are properly characterized as acts which fall under the auspices of duty, and hence their omission is not to be regarded as permissible.

The heart of New's argument is stated in the following passage:

> We appear to have a duty not merely to make civilized life *possible*, but also to make it as *good* as we can. For in general we want to make civilized life *possible*, not for its own sake, but for the desirable results, the happiness, which are thereby achieved for human beings. But if the principle which justifies making civilized life *possible* is that it increases human happiness, then the same principle will justify making life as *good* as we can. If we have a duty to do x because it increases human happiness, it seems to follow that we have a duty to do y also if y increases human happiness.[23]

New believes that human beings clearly have a duty to make civilized life possible, and the basis of this duty lies in the desirable results which are brought about for human beings. But if one agrees that this is the basis of the duty to make civilized life possible, then one should likewise acknowledge that human beings have a duty to make life as good as possible. For making civilized life as good as possible likewise increases human happiness. Hence, if one accepts the claim that we have a duty to make civilized life possible on the grounds that it has desirable results, one should acknowledge that we have a duty to make life as good as possible, for this likewise generates desirable results.

Saints and heroes in particular go to unusual lengths in bringing about good in human life. But, contrary to what Urmson alleges, they are merely doing what is their duty; they are merely doing what they can to make life as good as possible. People are frequently encouraged to be saintly or heroic; why, New asks, do we encourage them in this manner if we do not think they ought to be saintly or heroic? He believes that it makes no sense to hold up saints and heroes as paradigms of human virtue if we are not intending to convey to our listeners that they ought to be like them. Just as Pybus holds that moral commendation of saintly or heroic people always implies that one ought to develop the virtues from which their acts originate, so New believes that if we hold up saints and heroes as paradigms of human virtue we are thereby saying that we are under an obligation to try to do likewise. We are not just encouraged to imitate them; we are required to imitate them.

Frequently saints and heroes respond to expressions of praise and admiration with the words, "I was only doing my duty." New states that these words express the literal truth of the matter. They express a modesty on the part of their speaker, but nevertheless it is perfectly true that saints and heroes are only doing their duty. Contrary to what Urmson believes, they are doing nothing which can be regarded as going beyond the call of duty. New concedes that people sometimes speak of agents as going beyond the call of duty. But these statements are made in the context of duties associated with special roles or special commitments. Someone might say that a lifeguard went beyond the call of duty by rescuing a swimmer while the lifeguard was not on duty, but this is just to say that the guard went beyond the duty of the specific role as a lifeguard. A person making such a statement knows perfectly well that as a human being the lifeguard has a moral duty to rescue the swimmer in distress. Permitting the swimmer to drown would be a tragic violation of a duty. Thus, the use of the phrase "going beyond the call of duty" in idiomatic language is perfectly compatible, New believes, with the position he is defending.

New is aware that most of us are unable to lead saintly or heroic lives, and he is willing to grant that saintliness and heroism are not duties for those who are unable to be saintly or heroic. In this way he shows a sensitivity for the principle that ought implies can. But from the fact that most of us have no obligation to be saintly or heroic, he argues, it surely does not follow that saints and heroes are under no obligation to be saintly or heroic. Otherwise we should conclude that honesty is not a duty for anyone on the grounds that some people are pathological liars and hence under no obligation to be honest. It might be argued that even pathological liars ought to try to be honest, and hence New is willing to agree that each of us has an obligation to try to be saintly or heroic. Those who can be saintly or heroic have an obligation to be saintly or heroic, while those who cannot still have an obligation to try to be saintly or heroic. And to the extent that trying to be saintly or heroic involves the cultivation of virtues which lead to saintly or heroic behavior, New appears to adopt a position similar to that defended by Pybus.

David Heyd grants that New's basic argument is correct if one presupposes that our moral obligations are determined entirely by an (act) utilitarian principle. If we are committed to make civilized life possible because we are committed to increasing human happiness, then we will be committed to making life as good as we can. If utilitarian grounds are the sole criterion for determining what we ought to do or ought not to do, then we will be committed to the view that we ought to make life as good as we can. In presenting this argument New is simply fleshing out the implications of his utilitarian presuppositions, as Heyd analyzes the situation.[24]

Heyd believes that New's conclusion runs counter to our common moral beliefs; it is not part of our common moral beliefs that we have a moral obligation to make life as good as possible. New, in effect, argues that when our moral beliefs conflict with utilitarian theory, our moral beliefs should be modified. Since our failure to believe that we ought to make life as good as possible conflicts with what utilitarian theory suggests we ought to believe, New's solution is to embrace such a belief. Heyd, on the other hand, believes it is the theory which ought to be modified. If utilitarianism demands the belief that we have an obligation to make life as good as possible, the most sensible course of action is to reject utilitarianism.

In addition, Heyd believes it is plainly false that encouraging someone to perform an act implies that the person has a duty to perform it. For one thing, the view "misleadingly makes use of the double role of 'ought'—the commendatory and the prescriptive."[25] If I encourage you to do something, there is a sense in which I am implying that you ought to do it. But this sense of 'ought' is the commendatory sense; it is in this sense, perhaps, that I imply that you ought to choose the cherry cheesecake upon hearing me encourage you to choose it. But from this it does not follow that when I encourage you to do something I am thereby implying that you ought to do it in the prescriptive sense of 'ought'. According to Heyd, it is not ordinarily my intent to convey the message that you ought to do it as a matter of duty.

In fact, at this point Heyd adopts the tactic of arguing that it is precisely when we *cannot* demand people to perform an act that we encourage them to perform it. Often we are aware that people have no obligation to perform a certain act, and this gives us reason to encourage them to perform it. We are in no position to demand that they act in this manner, for they have no obligation to do so; accordingly, we instead encourage them to do it. Of course, people sometimes need to be encouraged to do what they are under an obligation to do, and Heyd has no desire to dispute this point. For sometimes people are unaware of their obligations, and sometimes people who are aware of their obligations need to be encouraged by others to fulfil these obligations. Nevertheless, on many other occasions we encourage people to perform acts which neither we nor they believe to be their obligation to perform. No doubt Heyd has in mind certain saintly or heroic acts whose performance would be desirable but which we have right to demand of others. "Encouragement implies a pro-attitude to its objects," according to Heyd, "but not usually a belief that the object is obligatory."[26] Situations in which encouragement implies that the object is obligatory are in Heyd's opinion the exception, not the rule.

Perhaps New will be reluctant to admit that encouragement ever fails to imply that the object in question is obligatory. But Heyd notes that, even if he does not admit this possibility, he cannot possibly deny that on some occasions the reason we do not encourage people to perform certain acts is that we regard them as involving too great a sacrifice (even when they can be judged good on utilitarian grounds). Suppose that a number of people are waiting in line to be cleared by customs before boarding their overseas flight. A man at the head of the line presents documents which the officials regard as highly problematic, and it is evident that clearing him for customs will be an inordinately lengthy process. Those waiting behind him are concerned that they will miss their flights, and they are hopeful that he will step aside and allow them to be cleared ahead of him. However, they are aware that this course of action will greatly increase the likelihood that he will miss his flight. In the end they decline to encourage him to step aside, for they are aware that it is too much to ask of a man to give up his place in line under the circumstances (and this is true even if the most utility would be produced by his stepping aside).

Clearly Heyd is correct in stating that sometimes we are reluctant to encourage people to act in certain ways because we feel that their performing these acts would involve too great a sacrifice on their part. I am not convinced, however, that this observation refutes New's claim that encouraging one to perform an act invariably carries with it the implication that one ought to perform it. Perhaps New can respond that we refrain from encouraging people to act in these situations because we are aware that it is incorrect to express the idea that they ought to act in this manner. If we believe that someone has no obligation to perform an act, we will withhold expressing encouragement, since such encouragement carries with it the implication that we regard them as obliged to perform it. We do not encourage the man to step aside precisely because we do not feel that he has an obligation to make such a sacrifice. Thus, it is open for New to argue that our reluctance to encourage people to act when we feel that it is too much of a sacrifice for them is perfectly compatible with his view concerning encouragement. We do not wish to convey the message that we feel such action is obligatory on their part, for we do not consider it obligatory.

Nevertheless, the wider point Heyd argues for cannot be brushed aside so easily: New's conclusion that moral agents have an obligation to make life as good as possible conflicts with our common moral beliefs. To the extent that such conflicts arise, New assumes that our common moral beliefs require revision. Heyd, on the other hand, is inclined to reject the utilitarian assumptions which he believes to underlie New's argument and to retain our common moral beliefs. It is not part of our natural disposition to assign so considerable a proportion of human action to the realm of duty, and, if utilitarian principles dictate otherwise, so much the worse for these principles. Again, a commitment to act utilitarian presuppositions propels one strongly in the direction of anti-supererogationism, and Heyd feels that New's own moral theory is a case in point.

Heyd feels that another case in point is G.E. Moore. He is of the opinion that Moore too arrives at an anti-supererogationist position by means of "purely utilitarian considerations".[27] For Moore states that to say that a given act is obligatory is to say that performing it is the best thing to do. Heyd believes that Moore is led to this conclusion by way of observing that the uniqueness of any act that is our absolute obligation consists in the total goodness of its performance. In Moore's words, the act "will cause more good to exist in the Universe than any possible alternative."[28] At any given moment, on Moore's view, the agent has a duty to perform the optimific act, that which will cause more good than any alternative act open to the agent at that moment. Heyd notes that Moore makes exceptions to the principle that we ought to perform the optimific act in situations where two or more potential acts are perceived as having equally good consequences. Aside from these situations (which Heyd believes to be somewhat rare), Moore's position is close to that of New. Our moral duty consists in choosing the alternative open to us which will produce the most good and acting in accord with that choice.

Moore's position appears to be anti-supererogationist in two separate but closely related ways. First, if one has an obligation to do something, it is the best thing to do of that which is within one's powers. One never is permitted to settle for a course of action if a better alternative is available. To use Feldman's terminology, one ought to do the best one can.

Technically, a person can affirm this point and avoid a denial that supererogation is possible by denying that human beings ever have obligations. It would be possible to affirm that, if we had moral obligations, they would be to choose the best available course of action, while denying that we ever have moral obligations. However, Moore's second point rules out the possibility of denying that we have moral obligations. According to him, we have a definite moral obligation to choose the optimific course of action. At any moment our moral duty is determined by what will bring about the most good. And unless there are two or more courses of action which are perceived to produce equally good results (and I am inclined to challenge Heyd's claim that this occurs only in rare circumstances), there is a unique course of action upon which the moral agent has an obligation to embark.

In summary, New stands in agreement with Pybus on two key issues. Both believe Urmson is incorrect in classifying acts of saintliness and heroism as supererogatory, and both believe that to express moral commendation of saintly or heroic people is to express an obligation to be (or to try to be, in the case of New) like them, but New's theory is motivated by an underlying commitment to an act utilitarian perspective, according to which we have a duty to make life as good as possible. New does not push his anti-supererogationist ideas to the point of repudiating the ought implies can principle, as some of the others have done, for he insists that those who cannot lead saintly or heroic lives have the obligation to try to lead such lives, not the obligation actually to lead them. Nevertheless, New's position appears to be thoroughly anti-supererogationist. One can never perform an act in a manner which is praiseworthy and does not at the same time directly fulfil a moral obligation.

Moore's position appears to be an even more straightforward acceptance of the utilitarian claim that at any moment we ought to perform the act which causes more good in the universe than any other act which is open to us. We have a definite moral obligation to choose the optimific course of action in every situation. Like New, Moore seems to allow no room for acts of supererogation in human life. An agent who fails to perform the act which causes the most good in human life, of all the acts open to the agent, thereby fails to do that which is obligatory.

5. Conclusion

There are many twentieth-century moralists whose approaches are, in one way or another, anti-supererogationist. Those familiar with the literature will know that I have by no means conducted an exhaustive survey; it would be possible to lengthen this discussion considerably by discussing the views of philosophers such as Hastings Rashdall, L.A. Reid, and Yogendra Chopra. In this chapter I have selected only those whom I judge to be the most important contemporary representatives of three different ethical approaches.

In fact, of the writers who have been considered, there is one which, I have argued, does not actually deserve to be considered an anti-supererogationist. In the case of J.N. Findlay I have argued that it is little more than appearance which leads others to classify him as anti-supererogationist. Much of what Findlay writes about duty, for example, leaves the distinct impression that acts of supererogation are impossible to perform. However, it has been my suggestion that a careful reading of what he says leads to the opposite conclusion: Findlay not only acknowledges the possibility of supererogation but criticizes certain theists and utilitarians for permitting the spreading of obligations over the whole web of human conduct. Hence, I believe philosophers have been mistaken to regard Findlay as an opponent of supererogation.

Eisenberg likewise describes Ross as an opponent of supererogation. With regard to that which is intrinsically good in human life, Eisenberg's interpretation seems accurate. Ross clearly states that moral agents have a duty to bring intrinsic goods into existence and to bring as much of them into existence as possible. From this statement it is hard to see the possibility of performing acts of supererogation involving the promotion of intrinsic goods. Nevertheless, Eisenberg concludes on the basis of this statement that Ross is committed to a theory which leaves little or no room for supererogation, and I have argued that this conclusion is too strong. For Ross says nothing which commits him to a rejection of the possibility of supererogation beyond the promotion of intrinsic goods. Although supererogation is ruled out in the area of promoting intrinsic goods, it by no means follows that the possibility of supererogation is ruled out across the board.

Feldman describes his approach as a 'neo-utilitarian view'. Roughly speaking, it requires agents to live in accord with the best possible world accessible to them; each agent is required to live out the best life available. Feldman designs a possible worlds approach to moral obligation which is intended to capture the insight that obligation involves doing the best one can. Unlike act utilitarianism, which focuses upon individual acts which one ought to perform, the theory defended by Feldman focuses upon living the best life available to one. I have argued that this theory leaves no room for acts of supererogation on the grounds that in the world which embodies the best life available to me (at any given time) I either perform the act or I do not. If I perform the act in this world, then it is part of the best life available to me and I ought to perform it. If not, I ought not to perform it. As a result, there is no possibility of acting in a way whose performance is both praiseworthy and fulfils no duty.

Pybus sets out to show that the standard three-fold classification of human acts (the obligatory, permissible, and the forbidden) is adequate, and she believes Urmson has failed to show the legitimacy of supererogation as a fourth category. On her view there is no realm of moral aspiration beyond duty. If we find the behavior of saints and heroes commendable, we have a duty to aspire to be the sorts of people they are. One cannot express moral commendation of them without implying that this is the sort of person one ought to be.

New agrees with Pybus both that Urmson has failed to demonstrate the legitimacy of supererogation as a fourth category and that the expression of moral commendation with regard to saintly or heroic people implies obligations to try to be like them. But, unlike Pybus, New's theory is clearly rooted in a utilitarian point of view. According to him, moral agents have a duty to make life as good as possible. Saintly or heroic persons who go to great lengths to make life as good as possible are simply doing their duty, and those of us who fall short of making life as good as possible to the best of our ability are failing in our moral duties. G.E. Moore reflects a similar way of thinking in his view that each of us ought to do that which will bring about the most good of the alternatives open to us. Our obligation is to perform the optimific course of action.

Feldman, New, and Moore are led to their views by way of broadly utilitarian presuppositions, and I have argued that each is committed to a denial that acts of supererogation are possible. Pybus expresses a point of view which may not entirely succeed in ruling out the possibility of performing acts of supererogation, but she nevertheless professes to resist attempts to recognize supererogation as a legitimate category of human action. Hence it is at least her intent to embrace an anti-supererogationist stance.

It has not been my primary aim in this chapter to criticize or refute the writers treated in it. My primary aim has been to describe their views and determine the extent to which their views are anti-supererogationist. And, with the possible exception of Findlay, characterizing their views as anti-supererogationist will not in their estimation constitute a criticism. For the most part, these writers actively stand in opposition to theories which allow or accommodate acts of supererogation, and it is by no means their desire to accommodate acts of supererogation in their own theories.

In a previous chapter I argued that there are circumstances in which acts of supererogation are possible. While I am not prepared to admit into the ranks of the supererogatory all of the alleged examples which have been identified in the literature as acts of supererogation, I believe that Urmson is correct in identifying supererogation as a legitimate "fourth" category of human action. Moreover, I believe that Urmson is correct in identifying (most typical) acts of saintliness and heroism as supererogatory. Hence I believe that the writers treated in this chapter are mistaken to have ruled out the possibility of accommodating acts of supererogation. Even Ross, whose anti-supererogationist views are confined to promoting intrinsic goods, strikes me as mistaken. I believe that each of us has a duty to promote intrinsic goods such as justice. However, it is my view that it is possible to promote the cause of justice in a manner which is supererogatory.

It would be possible at this point to pursue a lengthy refutation of these writers, examining their arguments and attempting to identify false premises and faulty inferences. But a more fruitful exercise, I believe, is to ask why there has been so much opposition to the concept of supererogation throughout the history of modern philosophy. In the previous chapter part of the motivation for this opposition was identified as theological in character; many have construed God's commands in such a way that moral agents are obliged to do whatever good they are capable of doing (and in some cases they are obliged to do good which they are incapable of doing). However, the prevalence of anti-supererogationist views among writers for whom theism plays no essential role in their theorizing suggests that the anti-supererogationist impulse requires further explanation.

Much work has been done in examining the anti-supererogationist nature of Kantian moral philosophy and utilitarianism, as well as the impact each has had upon twentieth-century moral philosophy. I have no desire to call into question the accuracy of this work. Rather, it is my belief that more work needs to be done in the explanation of the anti-supererogationist impulse itself. For one frequently finds among non-philosophers the same reluctance to acknowledge acts of supererogation as one one finds among philosophers. In particular, one frequently finds among people having no acquaintance with Kantian or utilitarian philosophy a reluctance to concede that praiseworthy or meritorious behavior can escape being bound up with duty or obligation. This is a phenomenon which has scarcely been noted, let along addressed, in the literature on supererogation, and in the next two chapters I propose to introduce some concepts which will be useful in approaching some tentative explanations for this phenomenon.

Chapter 5

Quasi-Supererogation

In this chapter I propose to introduce a category of human acts which I shall call acts of 'quasi-supererogation'. Roughly speaking, an act of quasi-supererogation is similar to an act of supererogation, except that it is blameworthy to refrain from performing it. That is, the performance of an act of quasi-supererogation is praiseworthy and fulfils no obligations (directly) and its omission is blameworthy. As far as I am aware, there has been no prior mention of these acts in the literature,[1] and it is my hope that by calling attention to them it will be possible to shed some light upon the anti-supererogationist impulse which one commonly finds among both philosophers and non-philosophers.

Some might immediately object to the notion of quasi-supererogation on the grounds that it is hard to conceive of an act whose performance is praiseworthy and whose omission is blameworthy (given that its performance is non-obligatory). If someone's performance of an act is genuinely worthy of praise, how can the nonperformance of the act possibly qualify as worthy of blame? How can someone rightly be faulted for simply failing to do that which is genuinely worthy of praise? I do not deny that this is a reasonable concern, and I will make an attempt to address it in the course of explaining the nature of quasi-supererogation. In addition, I will present an argument for the conclusion that it is no less reasonable to acknowledge that acts of quasi-supererogation are possible than it is to acknowledge that acts of supererogation are possible. In other words, I will argue that it is reasonable to doubt that acts of quasi-supererogation are possible only if one doubts that acts of supererogation are possible.

In the first section of this chapter I employ two lines of argument to establish that acts of quasi-supererogation are possible. In addition, I introduce the concept of quasi-offence, and I argue that it is likewise reasonable to hold that there can be acts of quasi-offence in human life. The second section explores the implications which an acknowledgement of quasi-supererogation as a legitimate category of human action might have for understanding the extent to which people commonly gravitate toward a rejection of supererogation as a genuine category of human action. And in an appendix to this chapter I discuss some of the formal features of the categories of quasi-supererogation and quasi-offence, and I present a formal deontic scheme to show their relationship with other types of acts.

1. THE NATURE OF QUASI-SUPEREROGATION

In this section I shall advance some considerations to suggest that acts of quasi-supererogation are possible to perform. An act of quasi-supererogation I define as an act which (1) Fulfils no moral obligations directly; (2) Is morally praiseworthy to perform; and (3) Is morally blameworthy not to perform. Earlier I defined an act of offence as one which (1) Is not forbidden to perform, (2) Is nevertheless morally blameworthy to perform, and (3) Is not morally praiseworthy to omit. More will be said about these acts in chapter eight. For now my concern is to define an act of quasi-offence as an act which is just like an act of offence, except that it is praiseworthy to omit. And just as I allege that quasi-supererogation is a legitimate category of human action, I shall attempt to suggest that the same is true of acts of quasi-offence.

Those who subscribe to the idea that acts of supererogation and offence are legitimate categories of human action sometimes claim that all human acts can be classified into one of five categories: obligation, supererogation, neutral, offence, and forbidden (where an act is said to be neutral just in case its performance is neither obligatory, forbidden, praiseworthy, or blameworthy). However, I shall suggest that this scheme is incomplete as it stands, and that there are human acts which fit into none of the categories. More specifically, I shall argue that it is plausible to hold that acts whose performances are neither obligatory nor forbidden can be praiseworthy to perform and blameworthy not to perform. And that it is plausible to hold that acts whose performances are neither obligatory nor forbidden can be blameworthy to perform and praiseworthy not to perform.

My proposal, then, is that the five-fold system give way to a seven-fold scheme: obligation, supererogation, quasi-supererogation, neutral, quasi-offence, offence, and forbidden (with no claim that even this system is exhaustive). The ordering of these categories reflects the fact that there is a sense in which acts of quasi-supererogation can be viewed as having a subordinate status relative to acts of supererogation, for the latter are so meritorious that the failure to perform them is still above reproach; for similar reasons the category of quasi-offence precedes that of offence. However, I do not wish to attach too great a significance to this ordering. Here my main point is that the five-fold scheme needs to be expanded to a seven-fold scheme, and I am willing to concede that the ordering I have proposed is somewhat arbitrary.

It is customary to understand 'praiseworthy' as worthy or deserving of moral praise and 'blameworthy' as worthy or deserving of moral blame. So understood, it might seem impossible for an act which is truly praiseworthy for an agent to perform to be blameworthy for the agent not to perform. For example, if it is truly praiseworthy to perform an act of great sacrifice for another, it does not seem reasonable to judge that it is blameworthy to refrain from this act. And the same may be felt true for any paradigm example of a truly praiseworthy act.

For this reason I believe it is important to recognize that the concepts of 'praiseworthy' and 'blameworthy' are concepts which admit of degrees.[2] Although two acts are each praiseworthy for an agent to perform, one of the acts may be more deserving of praise than the other. If it is praiseworthy for me to take a disadvantaged child to my cabin for the weekend, perhaps it is more praiseworthy for me to take five disadvantaged children. And if it is blameworthy for me to insult one person, perhaps it is more blameworthy for me to insult five persons.

In this way it is important to acknowledge that the performance of some acts are praiseworthy (or blameworthy) to a high degree, and the performances of other acts are mildly praiseworthy (or blameworthy). In the present context this point is of considerable importance, for if the performance of an act is praiseworthy to a very high degree—such as a sacrifice of heroic proportions—it would strike many (who are not anti-supererogationists) as unreasonable to suggest that it is blameworthy to refrain from performing it. One who chooses not to perform such an act could not reasonably be blamed for the failure to perform it. On the other hand, the same does not hold true for an act which is praiseworthy to a modest degree for an agent to perform. With respect to an act whose performance by a particular individual is only modestly praiseworthy, it is not nearly so evident that the failure to perform it is not deserving of blame.

To develop this point in greater detail, consider situations in which agents resist temptation. In certain circumstances, I believe, it is plausible to regard the resisting of temptation as an act of quasi-supererogation. Begin by considering an act o whose performance by agent S is an offence. Perhaps S is in a restaurant and o consists in walking to the next table and emptying the contents of his plate upon a man whose behavior is particularly obnoxious. I believe it is plausible to consider the performance of such an act as blameworthy (but not forbidden) and the omission of such an act non-praiseworthy. It would be blameworthy of S to perform this act, and there does not seem to be anything praiseworthy in and of itself if S were to refrain from it. (The choice of example is not crucial. If this example is not clearly one of an offence, fill in for o an example which does clearly fit the conditions required to qualify as an offence.)

Assume next that the temptation for S to perform o is extremely strong. Suppose, for example, that the man at the next table is making loud jokes and mocking gestures about the physical disabilities of S's wife. For this reason S is livid with rage, and it requires great effort for S to resist the temptation to perform o. But suppose that S succeeds in resisting the temptation, and he proceeds to ignore the man's behavior.

Here it seems reasonable to judge that S's resisting the temptation to perform o is morally praiseworthy. Although it might not be praiseworthy to a heroic or saintly degree, it appears to be praiseworthy to at least a modest degree. S is strongly tempted to express his anger and outrage, and he succeeds in overcoming his strong urge to do so. It requires great effort to resist this temptation, and someone who is aware of this fact would be justified in praising S for the restraint he exercises. The mere omission of o is not praiseworthy in and of itself, but under the circumstances it is praiseworthy of S to resist the temptation to perform o. Simply refraining from an act is not the same as resisting the temptation to perform the act; the latter can be praiseworthy even if the former is not.

Consider, however, a world w which is as similar as possible to the actual world, except that S refrains in w from resisting the temptation to empty the contents of his plate on the man. In this world S deliberately chooses not to resist his strong desire to seek revenge, and he ends up causing great anguish to his wife and the restaurant's owner, as well as ruining the man's expensive three-piece suit. Here it seems reasonable to judge that his refraining from resisting temptation is deserving of blame. It is in his power to resist the temptation in w, and he deliberately chooses not to do so, knowing full well the consequences which will result. The other man's behavior, of course, is highly blameworthy, but S's (in w) is blameworthy as well. One would be justified in having expected better of him, for he could at least have made an effort to resist temptation, and he can justifiably be criticized for his failure to do so. The performance of o by S is blameworthy (since by hypothesis its performance is an offence), and it is plausible to judge that the same is true of S's refraining from resisting the temptation to perform o.

In this example, then, S's resisting the temptation is an act which is praiseworthy to perform and blameworthy to refrain from performing. I do not claim that resisting temptation is highly worthy of praise or that refraining from it is highly worthy of blame. I claim only that S's resisting temptation is not a neutral act, for it is at least somewhat worthy of praise, and his refraining from doing so is at least somewhat worthy of blame. It would be difficult to defend the view, I believe, that S's resisting temptation is not the least bit deserving of praise and S's refraining from resisting temptation is not the least bit deserving of blame.

In order for S's resisting the temptation to qualify as an act of quasi-supererogation it must also be the case that S's resisting the temptation directly fulfil no moral duties. Many cases in which one's resisting temptation is praiseworthy and one's refraining from doing so is blameworthy fail this condition. One might have a perfect opportunity to embezzle company funds with no possibility of getting caught, and I believe that resisting this temptation is obligatory in addition to its being praiseworthy. Employees have a moral obligation to refrain from embezzlement, and hence it is plausible to suppose that they have a moral obligation to resist the temptation to engage in it. (Some might be skeptical of this last claim; however, if it is false that employees have a moral obligation to resist the temptation to embezzle such resisting itself turns out to be an act of quasi-supererogation).

In the example under consideration, however, the situation is different. While employees have a moral obligation to refrain from embezzlement, S does not have a moral obligation to refrain from performing o. The performance of o by S is an offence, and hence it is not forbidden for S to perform it. Thus, it would be a mistake to draw a parallel between S's behavior in w and the behavior of the embezzler. Employees have a moral obligation to resist the temptation to embezzle, since they have an obligation to refrain from embezzlement. But S has no obligation to refrain from performing o, and hence it is hard to see on what basis S could have an obligation to resist the temptation to perform o.

One might argue, as some have, that it is never morally permissible to act in a blameworthy manner, and given this conclusion it follows that S's resisting the temptation in the restaurant is obligatory. On this line of reasoning it is always forbidden to do what is blameworthy, and hence S does in w that which is forbidden. Clearly, however, one can subscribe to this line of argument only at the cost of regarding acts of offence as impossible. If it is always forbidden to do that which is morally blameworthy, then there is no possibility of one's act qualifying as an offence.

This line of reasoning bears a close similarity to those who argue that an act can be praiseworthy to perform only if it is obligatory to perform. If one argues that it is always forbidden to do that which is blameworthy, one is presenting the mirror image of the anti-supererogationist argument that it is always obligatory to do that which is praiseworthy. The former is an argument that acts of offence are impossible to perform, and the latter is an argument that acts of supererogation are impossible to perform. Just as it is sometimes argued that there can be no praiseworthy acts outside the realm of obligation, so it can similarly be argued that there can be no blameworthy acts outside the realm of the forbidden.

Nevertheless, such arguments are not strictly relevant at this point in the discussion. In chapter eight I shall examine more fully the concept of offence and reasons for calling into question the very possibility of performing acts of offence. But here my purpose is to argue that if the standard system is legitimate in the sense that there can be acts falling under each of its five categories, then there is good reason for regarding the standard system as incomplete. If one agrees that acts of supererogation and offence are possible, then one ought to acknowledge the possibility of acts of quasi-supererogation and quasi-offence. Thus, it is not reasonable to deny the possibility of quasi-supererogation and quasi-offence as legitimate categories of human action while affirming that supererogation and offence are legitimate categories of human action.

In the example under consideration the assumption that it would be an offence for S to perform o leads to the conclusion that S's resisting the temptation to perform o is an act of quasi-supererogation and that S's refraining from resisting the temptation in w is an act of quasi-offence. I believe there are many other varieties of examples which can likewise be constructed, given the assumption that there are acts of supererogation and offence, and hence I believe that acts of quasi-supererogation and quasi-offence ought to be acknowledged as types of acts which moral agents not only can perform but also as acts which moral agents commonly do perform.

In the present example S's resisting temptation would qualify as an act of supererogation were it not for the fact that refraining from it is blameworthy. And S's failing to resist temptation in w would qualify as an act of offence were it not for the fact that refraining from it is praiseworthy. I have argued that refraining from resisting temptation need not be blameworthy to a significant degree and resisting temptation need not be praiseworthy to a significant degree to prevent them from being assimilated to the ranks of offence and supererogation, respectively. No doubt the failure to acknowledge acts of these types has been due in part to the assumption that permissible acts are neutral to perform or refrain from performing unless they are significantly praiseworthy or blameworthy to perform or refrain from performing.

Some writers have shown an inclination to suppose that acts of supererogation must involve behavior whose praiseworthy status is comparable to the deeds of saints and heroes. But Chisholm, Heyd, and others have pointed out that acts of supererogation can include small gestures of courtesy and kindness. Such acts are presumably praiseworthy to a considerably lesser degree than acts of heroic self-sacrifice; nevertheless, they qualify as acts of supererogation, for their performance is at least somewhat praiseworthy. And in like manner I wish to suggest that there can be permissible acts which are mildly praiseworthy to perform and mildly blameworthy not to perform. While it is perhaps dubious that there can be acts of quasi-supererogation which are highly praiseworthy to perform or highly blameworthy not to perform (or acts of quasi-offence which are highly blameworthy to perform or highly praiseworthy not to perform), I hope to have shown that the same is not true of acts whose performances or omissions are praiseworthy or blameworthy to a modest degree.

Up to this point my argument for the legitimacy of quasi-supererogation and quasi-offence has depended upon examples involving the resistance of temptation. Given an offence o, resisting the temptation to perform o is a candidate for quasi-supererogation, and refusing to resist the temptation is a candidate for quasi-offence. There is, however, another approach to arguing for the legitimacy of quasi-supererogation and quasi-offence. This approach involves imagining a moral agent who is faced with a sequence of opportunities to perform acts of supererogation. By definition, it is never blameworthy to refrain from performing an act of supererogation, and hence there is nothing blameworthy in refraining from each act one at a time. However, when a person repeatedly passes up opportunities to perform acts of supererogation, it is sometimes tempting to find fault with the person.

Suppose that each Saturday I have an opportunity to drive my elderly neighbor to the supermarket. She is no longer able to drive an automobile, and each Saturday she walks a considerable distance, in spite of varicose veins, to purchase her groceries. Each Saturday the thought crosses my mind that I could spare her the trouble of walking by offering to drive her, but I always dismiss the idea on the grounds that on weekends it is my custom to relax with my coin collection.

In this example it is reasonable to judge that on any given Saturday my offering to drive my neighbor to the supermarket would constitute an act of supererogation. Of course, the anti-supererogationist would disagree; but my aim in this section, once again, is to argue that if supererogation and offence are legitimate categories of human action, so too are quasi-supererogation and quasi-offence. Hence I assume that I have the opportunity to perform a sequence of acts, each of which would be supererogatory to perform. Each Saturday I have the opportunity to offer my neighbor a ride, and on any given Saturday my failure to do so is the failure to act in a supererogatory manner.

On any given Saturday one might be tempted to regard my failure to offer my neighbor a ride as blameworthy. It is not impossible to imagine someone expressing criticism or rebuke at my failure to act (such a person might, in fact, hold the view that offering her a ride on any given Saturday is an act of quasi-supererogation, not supererogation). But if my failure to act is in fact the failure to act in a supererogatory manner, there is nothing blameworthy in its omission. One cannot justly blame me for the failure to offer my neighbor a ride if my offering her a ride would have qualified as an act of supererogation. The failure to perform an act of supererogation is never blameworthy in and of itself.

Nevertheless, a person who has observed my failure to act for many weeks might level a different criticism: "Each week you have an opportunity to help that poor woman, and you never offer to help. I know that you are under no moral obligation to help her, and I know that you can't be blamed each time that you decide to remain with your coin collection. But the fact is that you never offer to help her, and for this I am disappointed in you. For your repeated failure to help, your behavior is definitely open to criticism." According to this appraisal of my behavior, my individual failures to act are not morally blameworthy; but my failure to act after many repeated opportunities is worthy of blame. It is never blameworthy to refrain from performing an act of supererogation, but it can be blameworthy persistently to pass up opportunities to perform acts of supererogation.

Some philosophers have introduced the concept of a 'disjunctive act' to describe situations in which an agent performs an act which itself consists of performing one or more acts in a group or series. Given a series of acts $x_1, x_2, \ldots, x_n$, one can describe the disjunctive act 'x_1 or x_2 or $\ldots$ or x_n' as the act one performs if and only if one performs at least one of the acts in the series. An agent who refrains from performing each of the acts in the series fails to perform the disjunctive act, but an agent who performs only one of the acts in the series succeeds in performing the disjunctive act.

Consider the disjunctive act of my offering to drive my neighbor at least once in the series of opportunities afforded to me. Since I repeatedly fail to take advantage of these opportunities, it follows that I fail to perform the disjunctive act. And the criticism directed to me is that my failure to perform this disjunctive act is worthy of blame. Having failed to perform a single act in the series, I am in a position which deserves moral criticism. No single omission of the acts in the series is blameworthy, but the omission of the disjunctive act itself is morally blameworthy.

If it is granted that I have the opportunity to perform an act of supererogation each time I have the choice to offer assistance to my neighbor, it is plausible to identify the disjunctive act of offering assistance at least once as an act of quasi-supererogation. Since each act in the series is praiseworthy to perform, the disjunctive act itself is praiseworthy to perform. Hence, if its performance directly fulfils no obligation and (as already suggested) its omission is blameworthy, it qualifies as an act of quasi-supererogation. It is not my intent to argue that every disjunctive act whose components are acts of supererogation qualifies as an act of quasi-supererogation. After missing only two opportunities to help my neighbor, it is no doubt premature for someone to criticize me for never helping her. In a situation of this nature there must be sufficiently many disjuncts for the disjunctive act to qualify as an act of quasi-supererogation. And in other situations the point may never be reached where the failure to act eventually becomes blameworthy, as when the individual acts of supererogation consist in making extraordinary sacrifices. It is possible that I cannot be blamed for the failure to perform such acts, no matter how many opportunities I fail to act upon. Nevertheless, I believe that many acts of quasi-supererogation are of this nature: an agent who performs at least one in a series of potential acts of supererogation performs the quasi-supererogatory act of having performed at least one of them.

It might be objected that there are no such entities as disjunctive acts. Perhaps a man can refrain from performing each of the acts in a series, but it is evident that he thereby refrains from their disjunction? I have no conclusive argument that there are such entities as disjunctive acts, and I shall simply assume that an appeal to the manner in which people commonly make moral judgments renders plausible the assumption that there are such acts. For it is common to find fault with someone for never having performed an act of a certain kind, even though each individual failure is not by itself enough to warrant criticism. It is hard to make sense of these moral judgments if one steadfastly refuses to acknowledge that one can refrain from disjunctions of acts in addition to refraining from their individual component acts.

It is likewise common to praise someone for never having lapsed into a certain kind of behavior after many repeated opportunities to do so. Perhaps each individual refusal to lapse does not merit praise, but after many such refusals the person's behavior attains the status of the praiseworthy. Here too there is a strong indication that it is the failure to perform a disjunctive act which is morally significant. Such acts, in fact, frequently qualify as acts of quasi-offence. When the individual components in a disjunctive act are potential acts of offence, it is possible for the disjunctive act to be praiseworthy to refrain from. It is never praiseworthy to refrain from an act of offence, but after having repeatedly refrained from potential acts of offence, moral commendation may be in order. If so, it is likely that it is by virtue of having refrained from an act of quasi-offence that one's omission is praiseworthy.

I have argued that performing a disjunctive act whose individual components are acts of supererogation frequently qualifies as an act of quasi-supererogation. It has often been noted, however, that one's performance of such acts can fulfil obligations, and hence they cannot qualify as acts of quasi-supererogation. John Stuart Mill raises this point in his discussion of imperfect duties.[3] Recall from chapter two that, according to Mill, particular acts of charity are not required of moral agents, but moral agents are required to perform acts of charity at some time or other. An agent who never performs acts of charity is for Mill guilty of having failed to fulfil a moral obligation.

The relevance of this point to quasi-supererogation is clear. Suppose a man has a great many opportunities to perform acts of charity over a significant period of time, and he refrains from acting each time. One can then say that he refrains from performing the disjunctive act of having performed an act of charity at least once during the period of time. (Mill does not not specify the period of time necessary to constitute the failure of an obligation, but this point is not crucial to the present discussion.) I have argued that the failure to perform a disjunctive act of this type is likely to qualify as the failure to perform an act of quasi-supererogation, for his failure to act is morally blameworthy. Mill would agree that the man's failure to perform the disjunctive act is blameworthy, but Mill is also committed to the view that the man's failure is the failure to fulfil a moral obligation. As such it is forbidden, and hence it cannot qualify as an act of quasi-supererogation.

It might seem paradoxical that a man who repeatedly passes up opportunities to perform acts of supererogation should eventually find himself in violation of duty. For the very essence of an act of supererogation is that it fulfils no duty (directly) and hence that its omission violates no duty. How, then, can one violate duty by refraining from a series of potential acts of supererogation? Once again, the puzzle is resolved by distinguishing between the omission of individual acts and the omission of the disjunctive act having these individual acts as components. An agent can never violate duty by refraining from an act of supererogation, but from this it does not follow that the agent can never violate duty by refraining from a disjunctive act whose components are potential acts of supererogation.

I believe Mill is correct in holding that a person can succeed in violating duty merely by a repeated failure to perform potential acts of supererogation. While it may be a matter of controversy whether this situation can arise with the failure to perform acts of charity (I believe it can), it is reasonable to accept Mill's general claim that imperfect duties can be constituted by potential acts of supererogation. If so, the picture which emerges is the following. Sometimes the disjunctive act which is constituted by potential acts of supererogation is neutral to refrain from, at other times it is blameworthy to refrain from, and at still other times it is forbidden to refrain from. A man who elects not to perform two or more acts of supererogation may be (and typically will be) immune from criticism. In some circumstances, however, his inaction may be serious enough to be worthy of blame. And in the most extreme circumstances (such as a lifetime of having never given to charity) his inaction may actually qualify as forbidden.

A similar observation might be made in the case of a person who refrains from a series of potential offences. It is never praiseworthy to refrain from performing an act of offence, but I have argued that after having repeatedly refrained from a series of potential offences a person's act may become praiseworthy. Such a person has refrained from a disjunctive act, and this act may qualify as an act of quasi-offence. However, just as refraining from a series of potential acts of supererogation can constitute the violation of a moral duty, so it might be supposed that a parallel phenomenon occurs in the realm of offence. Is it not possible that a person who refrains from a series of potential offences over a period of time eventually succeeds in fulfilling a duty? One can never fulfil a duty by the mere omission of an act of offence, but is it not possible to fulfil a duty by the omission of a disjunctive act whose components are potential acts of offence?

In chapter eight I shall argue that the apparent symmetry between supererogation and offence is less real than one might initially suspect. There are many respects in which this symmetry breaks down, and I am inclined to believe that the phenomenon under consideration is a case in point. It is true that refraining from a series of potential acts of supererogation can constitute the violation of duty, but from this it does not follow that refraining from a series of potential acts of offence can constitute the fulfillment of duty. It is very hard to imagine cases in which the disjunctive act whose components are potential acts of offence is initially neutral to refrain from, then praiseworthy to refrain from as the disjunction grows longer, and finally (as it continues to grow) the fulfillment of an obligation. In chapter eight I will have more to say about the respects in which the symmetry between supererogation and offence breaks down, but for the present I shall only note that the phenomenon under consideration appears to be an instance of this asymmetry.

To summarize, I have argued that quasi-supererogation and quasi-offence are legitimate categories of human action. They will almost certainly not be acknowledged by those who do not acknowledge the legitimacy of supererogation and offence, but I hope to have shown that an acknowledgement of supererogation and offence coupled with a refusal to acknowledge quasi-supererogation and quasi-offence is unreasonable. On the basis of the arguments presented in this section, one cannot reasonably admit that acts of supererogation and acts of offence are possible and simultaneously refuse to admit that acts of quasi-supererogation and quasi-offence are possible.

My case for the legitimacy of quasi-supererogation and quasi-offence consists of two lines of argument. According to the first, if it is an offence for a person to perform a certain act o, then resisting a strong temptation to perform o can qualify as an act of quasi-supererogation. Alternatively, succumbing to this strong temptation to perform o can qualify as an act of quasi-offence. According to the second, performing a disjunctive act whose components are potential acts of supererogation can qualify as an act of quasi-supererogation (although it can at times also qualify as the fulfillment of duty). And performing a disjunctive act whose constituents are potential acts of offence can qualify as an act of quasi-offence. It can be blameworthy to repeatedly pass up opportunities to perform acts of supererogation, and it can be praiseworthy to repeatedly pass up opportunities to perform acts of offence.

2. IMPLICATIONS

Suppose, then, that acts of quasi-supererogation and quasi-offence are possible. Are these categories of action of any significance for normative ethics? And if there are acts of quasi-supererogation and quasi-offence in human life, do these acts have any bearing upon the controversy between the proponents and opponents of supererogation?

There is a real sense in which a moral agent who passes up an opportunity to perform an act of supererogation is entirely above reproach. Such an agent can neither be accused of failing to fulfil a duty nor be found blameworthy for passing up this opportunity. But to the anti-supererogationist there is something deeply unsettling about judging that a person who willfully declines to do good is entirely above reproach. From the anti-supererogationist perspective an agent ought not willfully decline to do good; seizing opportunities to perform good deeds in life is what each of us ought to be doing. People who pass up these opportunities are, very simply, failing to fulfil their duty. From this perspective it is tempting to argue that acknowledging acts of supererogation is a grave error, for it involves showing too much tolerance for those who proceed through life treating these opportunities to perform good deeds with impunity.

On several prior occasions I have expressed disagreement with those who argue for the conclusion that there can be no acts of supererogation in human life. But is there not something plausible in the contention that a supererogationist is in danger of being too tolerant of those who regard these opportunities to perform good deeds with impunity? Perhaps this is one area in which philosophical ethicists can benefit from taking seriously the insistence of theological anti-supererogationists that in some sense moral agents ought to be doing what they can to be of service to others. If the supererogationist allows that a person who declines to take advantage of these opportunities is entirely above reproach, morally speaking, perhaps the supererogationist unwittingly endorses a moral point of view which is too lenient toward those who do not go out of their way to benefit others. People who regard their opportunities to perform good deeds with impunity deserve moral condemnation, and the supererogationist appears to be in the position of being forced to tolerate this behavior.

There are two respects in which one must be sympathetic to the view of the anti-supererogationist. First, there is something morally suspect about a person who adopts a disdainful attitude toward acts which are praiseworthy or meritorious to perform. A person who sneers at opportunities to perform good deeds seems deserving of moral criticism; it seems wrong to regard these opportunities with utter impunity. And to the extent that one adopts a moral point of view which tolerates this type of attitude, there seems to be something deficient in the moral point of view.

Fortunately, the supererogationist is not committed to this particular form of tolerance. There is a significant difference between declining to perform a potential act of supererogation and adopting a disdainful attitude toward performing potential acts of supererogation. The former is an act of omission, and there is nothing blameworthy in simply omitting an act of supererogation. But from this it cannot be concluded that there is nothing blameworthy in adopting a disdainful attitude toward performing potential acts of supererogation. In adopting this attitude one actively cultivates a disposition to avoid performing acts of supererogation, and the supererogationist is not committed to regarding this type of behavior as acceptable. It is perfectly consistent with a recognition that acts of supererogation are possible that one condemns this type of behavior. It is acceptable to refrain from performing an act of supererogation, but it is not acceptable to cultivate a disdainful attitude toward performing acts of supererogation. On this point the instincts of the anti-supererogationist appear to be well founded.

Second, one ought to be sympathetic to the anti-supererogationist's point of view concerning agents whose failure to take advantage of opportunities to do good has become habitual. There are some individuals who consistently decline to perform potential acts of supererogation simply because such behavior has become habitual. It is not that they sneer at the opportunities to perform these acts or that they regard these acts with disdain. They simply see no need to exert the effort which is necessary to perform them, and they gradually fall into the habit of consistently passing up these opportunities.

Some individuals who allow their failure to perform potential acts of supererogation to become habitual are nevertheless scrupulous in the fulfillment of their moral obligations. In their judgment the moral life makes requirements in the form of these obligations, and we are all constrained to know precisely what these requirements are and to live in accord with them. However, the moral life makes no further requirements upon moral agents in their view, and we are entitled to regard the performance of good works over and above our moral obligations as entirely optional. A person might have opportunities to perform good works which fall beyond the realm of moral obligation, but there is nothing shameful or disgraceful in refraining from performing them.

These sentiments can perhaps be dramatized by imagining a man who scrupulously attempts to fulfil all of his moral obligations but regards all other good works as supererogatory and having absolutely no claim on him. Over the course of time he faithfully does the former and consistently declines to do the latter. He faithfully performs acts which are explicitly required and refrains from acts which are explicitly forbidden. But it is also apparent that he never goes out of his way to help another when under no strict obligation to do so. Never one to attend to the small needs of those around him, he likewise never volunteers for church or community service. When approached by another with the request of a small favor, he politely declines without fail. And if he is rebuked for declining the favor, he retorts that the rebuke is out of place on the grounds that the omission of an act of supererogation is never blameworthy.

An individual of this type epitomizes the anti-supererogationist's worst fears concerning the acknowledgement of supererogation as a genuine category of human action. Above all else, the concern is that supererogation will be held up by people as an excuse to ignore the needs of others and to concentrate on maximizing their own comforts and pleasures. And certainly this is a legitimate concern. Very few, I believe, would be inclined to admire this man's behavior or attitude. There does seem to be something fundamentally wrong about his approach to living the moral life. He is clearly a legalist of sorts, perhaps the worst of sorts, and it would not be an exaggeration to think of him as a type of modern day Pharisee.

Indeed, it is reasonable to argue that his approach to morality is actually self-defeating in the long run. He is scrupulous in his observance of what is morally required of him, and yet, given Mill's insights concerning imperfect duties, it can easily turn out that his habitual refraining from potential supererogatory acts causes him to leave certain moral obligations unfulfilled. Good works which are optional on any specific occasion may well turn out to be obligatory to perform at some time or other. Thus, while it may be optional to do a favor for one's neighbor on a specific occasion, one who never goes out of one's way on behalf of another violates a duty of imperfect obligation. If Mill is correct, therefore, the man described above appears to violate some of his moral obligations after all.

Here there might be some disagreement concerning exactly what is objectionable about this man's behavior or attitude. But it is tempting to locate at least some of the blame for his disagreeable behavior in the assumption that acts of supererogation are possible. For he is able to justify his behavior on the grounds that it is never blameworthy to omit performing acts of supererogation. And it is precisely this type of justification which may convince some, following Luther, Calvin, and Melanchthon, that acts of supererogation are little more than the imaginary constructs of people who wish to escape from life's burdensome moral obligations. Those who are unwilling to affirm that we ought to go out of our way to help others when the opportunities arise seek refuge in the claim that doing so falls under the category of the supererogatory and is hence optional.

I believe that much of the anti-supererogationist impulse is built upon this perception of supererogation, and here the writings of the theistic anti-supererogationists are instructive in understanding this impulse. If supererogation makes possible the attitude that good works are entirely optional and superfluous in living the moral life, then it is easy to see how supererogation can be viewed as an undermining influence in cultivating the values and attitudes which are thought to be demanded of such a life. In short, supererogation becomes a natural scapegoat for the widespread failure of people to feel the importance of going beyond the bounds of duty for the sake of others. Of course, there are some people who show little interest even in the fulfillment of their moral duty, and their situation is more serious than that of the legalist. But the anti-supererogationist is concerned about those who attend to the fulfillment of their moral duties and regard all other good works as optional and superfluous. It is this phenomenon which can lead one to regard supererogation as the invention of those who are unwilling to tolerate moral requirements over and above the strict requirements of moral obligation.

The idea that one can consider all good works outside the bounds of duty as optional and superfluous is closely related to a concern of Kant's, that the performance of such works will be accompanied by a feeling of smugness and superiority. Marcia Baron describes this concern in her essay, "Kantian Ethics and Supererogation": "One can puff up with self-satisfaction at having done something 'extra' for someone; it is more difficult to feel smug and superior about doing what, one believes, anyone in those circumstances is morally required to do."[4] It is difficult to feel smug and superior about merely discharging one's moral duty, but these feelings can easily arise when one is doing what one believes to be supererogatory. Baron contends that Kant was worried about the possibility that people will regard the performance of good works in this manner, and she contends that Kant's fears are indeed confirmed in our own society. Once these good works are viewed as cut loose from duty, people tend to regard them as nice, inessential extras. In their minds there is no need to perform them, and consequently one seems justified in feeling smug and superior on those occasions on which one happens to perform them. As before, the anti-supererogationist is concerned about the enormous changes in the way people think about the performance of good works when they countenance the possibility of good works outside the realm of duty.

Obviously the refusal to acknowledge supererogation as a legitimate category of human action cannot reasonably be based solely on pointing out these problems. That supererogation is used by some as an excuse for being unwilling to do more than what is strictly required by moral obligation (or used by others as an excuse for smug self-satisfaction) is not by itself reasonable grounds for concluding that there can be no such thing as an act of supererogation. The point I wish to stress is that these concerns need to be taken seriously; the anti-supererogationist is justly concerned over the possibility that some will use supererogation as an excuse for being unwilling to do more than what is strictly required by moral obligation, and this concern can and does (as with the Reformers) serve as a strong motivator for going on to formulate arguments discrediting supererogation.

Nevertheless, it is here that quasi-supererogation is capable of addressing the concerns of the anti-supererogationist. For if it is correct that acts of quasi-supererogation are possible, then there are occasions in which one can be deserving of blame for failing to go beyond the call of duty. There are also times in which moral agents can reasonably be expected to go beyond the call of duty. One who fails to perform an act of supererogation is immune to criticism, but it does not follow that the failure to perform praiseworthy acts (which fulfil no moral obligation) automatically renders one immune from criticism. If acts of quasi-supererogation are possible, one is not in a position to plead that the failure to go beyond the call of duty is automatically above reproach.

Thus, there are times at which one can be expected to do that which is praiseworthy but non-obligatory. And I believe this point has far-reaching implications for one who is attempting to live the moral life. A person is always expected to do that which is morally obligatory, but this is not all that can be expected of us. We can likewise be expected—at times—to do more than that which is strictly obligatory.

From these observations it follows that going the second mile is not always supererogatory. It is never blameworthy as such to refrain from an act of supererogation, but one can frequently be blamed for failing to go the second mile. The legalist (described earlier) who defends his right to refrain from acts of supererogation is correct in assuming that such refraining is not blameworthy. But his mistake is to assume that each time he refrains from a praiseworthy act which fulfils no moral obligations, he thereby refrains from an act of supererogation. Hence, he wrongly concludes that each time he passes up an opportunity to go out of his way to help another, it automatically follows that he is immune from blame or criticism. Surely one can reasonably expect that he will not always decline opportunities to go out of his way for the sake of another, and the same holds true for all moral agents who are presented with such opportunities.

The anti-supererogationist's worst fear is that supererogation will be held up by people as an excuse to ignore the needs of others and to concentrate on their own well being, and the legalist described above does precisely this. But the point I am making is that the reasoning of the legalist fails to take into account the possibility that acting for the sake of others can frequently fall into the domain of quasi-supererogation. Hence the legalist's attempt to employ supererogation as an excuse and to ignore the needs of others appears to be based upon fallacious reasoning. And an awareness that this reasoning is fallacious ought to provide the anti-supererogationist with less reason to regard supererogation as an excuse for moral insensitivity. This is not to say that an awareness that the legalist's argument ignores the possibility of quasi-supererogation will remove all motivation for opposing the idea that acts of supererogation are possible. But it does serve to call into question what I suspect is one of the most significant motives operative in people's thinking.

In the end, therefore, the legalist I have described is mistaken in thinking that he is above moral criticism. If morally praiseworthy acts which fulfil no moral obligations can reasonably be expected of moral agents under certain circumstances, then one can justly criticize a person whose only moral objective is to refrain from behavior which is forbidden. If such a person entirely neglects performing praiseworthy non-obligatory acts while faithfully carrying out all other moral obligations, then that person can still be criticized for refraining from performing acts of quasi-supererogation. Certain acts which are morally praiseworthy but non-obligatory cannot be omitted without becoming blameworthy in the process. Under certain conditions, for example, a person can be expected to resist temptation even when under no moral obligation to do so. Thus, one can be expected to perform certain praiseworthy acts even when they fulfil no moral obligation.

A further corollary can be derived from these considerations. If there are acts of quasi-supererogation, one can be expected to live in such a way as to aim higher than the simple avoidance of what is forbidden. The presence of quasi-supererogation in human life implies that there are moral requirements over and above the requirements of strict obligation. It is not enough that an agent attends to the requirements of obligation; sooner or later one must take stock of one's opportunities to perform praiseworthy acts which go beyond these strict requirements. A failure to do so is an omission for which one deserves blame.

The anti-supererogationist is fond of pointing out that these praiseworthy acts are acts which agents ought to perform, and perhaps this way of stating the point has merit. On the basis of the foregoing discussion, perhaps it can be agreed that there is a sense in which we ought to perform these acts. But the anti-supererogationist typically equates doing what we ought to do with the fulfillment of duty; hence all such praiseworthy acts fall into the domain of duty. The point I have tried to make is that there is an important middle ground between what is neutral to omit and what is forbidden to omit. The anti-supererogationist is determined to remove morally praiseworthy acts from the realm of what is neutral to omit, and the end result is that they are transported wholesale into the realm of what is forbidden to omit. I have argued, on the other hand, that acts of quasi-supererogation are neither neutral nor forbidden to omit. They provide a basis for criticizing those who never go out of their way to perform good works (above and beyond duty) without resorting to the drastic expedient of regarding all praiseworthy acts as obligatory.

Similarly, acts of quasi-offence provide for an important middle ground between what is neutral to omit and what is obligatory to omit. Many would be inclined to relegate all blameworthy behavior to the category of the forbidden; according to this way of thinking, one always has a moral obligation to refrain from acts whose performance would be blameworthy. But if one acknowledges that there are acts of quasi-offence, one is in a position to acknowledge that certain acts which are blameworthy to perform are likewise praiseworthy to omit. Thus, just as quasi-supererogation provides a basis for criticizing those who never go out of their way to perform non-obligatory good works, the category of quasi-offence provides a basis for praising those who go out of their way to refrain from blameworthy behavior. And just as quasi-supererogation allows one to level criticism while avoiding the drastic expedient of regarding all praiseworthy acts as obligatory, quasi-offence allows one to bestow praise without resorting to the drastic expedient of relegating all blameworthy acts to the domain of the forbidden.

To summarize, an act of quasi-supererogation is similar to an act of supererogation, except that its omission is blameworthy, and an act of quasi-offence is similar to an act of offence, except that its omission is praiseworthy. I have presented two lines of argument for the conclusion that, if supererogation and offence are legitimate categories of human action, quasi-supererogation and quasi-offence are legitimate categories of human action. I have pointed out some implications this conclusion has for normative ethics, and I have endeavored to show that these implications address some of the concerns of the anti-supererogationist. Specifically, I have suggested that quasi-supererogation undercuts the argument that praiseworthy acts which fulfil no obligation are entirely superfluous. And to the extent that the possibility that some might appeal to this argument plays a role in the anti-supererogationist's rejection of supererogation, there is less reason for concern over the recognition that acts of supererogation are possible.

Of course, addressing this particular concern hardly exhausts the areas of concern which can potentially motivate one to repudiate the possibility of supererogation. In the next chapter I will suggest that a discussion of the concepts of virtue and vocation can shed additional light upon the debate between the proponents and opponents of supererogation. I believe that some of the points which emerge may help its proponents better understand some of the fears that give rise to the anti-supererogationist impulse and at the same time enable its opponents to reassess some of these fears.

Appendix

The following is a taxonomy of alleged types of human action in which "S" stands for a moral agent, "a" stands for an act, and it is assumed from the outset that S's performance of a is neither obligatory nor forbidden (from which it follows that S's refraining from a can be neither obligatory nor forbidden):

126   Beyond the Call of Duty

1. Action a is such that: (i) S's performing a is neutral, and (ii) It is blameworthy for S to refrain from performing a.
2. Action a is such that: (i) S's performing a is neutral, and (ii) It is praiseworthy for S to refrain from performing a.
3. Action a is such that: (i) It is praiseworthy for S to perform a, and (ii) It is blameworthy for S to refrain from performing a.
4. Action a is such that: (i) It is blameworthy for S to perform a, and (ii) It is praiseworthy for S to refrain from performing a.
5. Action a is such that: (i) It is praiseworthy for S to perform a, and (ii) S's refraining from performing a is neutral.
6. Action a is such that: (i) It is blameworthy for S to perform a, and (ii) S's refraining from performing a is neutral.
7. Action a is such that: (i) S's performing a is neutral, and (ii) S's refraining from performing a is neutral.

The list could be lengthened to include mention of acts which are praiseworthy for S both to perform and not to perform, as well as acts which are blameworthy for S both to perform and not to perform. However, it seems dubious that such acts are possible, at least for human moral agents. Hence I shall limit the taxonomy to the possibilities already listed.

The first point to be noted is that acts of type five qualify as acts of supererogation. By hypothesis the performance of each type of act is non-obligatory, from which it follows that the performance of acts of type five directly fulfil no obligation. Moreover, acts of type five are praiseworthy to perform and neutral not to perform. Hence they are praiseworthy to perform and not blameworthy not to perform. Therefore, acts of type five meet the three conditions required to qualify as acts of supererogation.

In addition, it can be noted that acts of type six correspond to the category of the offensive. Acts of type six are blameworthy to perform and neutral not to perform, from which it follows that their omission is not praiseworthy. And by hypothesis the performance of each type of act is neither obligatory nor forbidden; hence acts of type six are not forbidden to perform. I conclude that acts of type six qualify as acts of offence.

In addition, acts of type seven clearly qualify as neutral acts. Acts of type seven embrace acts whose performance and non-performance are both neutral. While it is not true that all acts which are neutral to perform are acts of type seven (some are acts of types one or two), it is obvious that all acts of type seven are neutral to perform.

For the purposes of this discussion I shall refer to the 'standard system' as the system which recognizes the legitimacy of the five categories of the obligatory, the supererogatory, the neutral, the offensive, and the forbidden, but no additional categories. According to the standard system, there can be human acts falling under any of these categories, but there are no additional categories. Already I have indicated that the standard system accommodates acts of types five, six, and seven. Acts of type five qualify as acts of supererogation, acts of type six qualify as acts of offence, and acts of type seven qualify as neutral acts. It is not clear, on the other hand, how acts of types one through four fare with respect to the standard system. If the standard system can claim to be exhaustive, it must presumably accommodate all possible types of human action. Thus, if the standard system fails to accommodate some of these types, one must either admit that the standard system is not an exhaustive classification or hold that the types of acts it fails to accommodate are not types of acts which are possible to perform.

Already I have argued that the standard system is incomplete in its failure to accommodate acts of quasi-supererogation and quasi-offence, and perhaps one can be assisted in appreciating the arguments already presented by noting that these acts are represented in the formal scheme by types three and four, respectively. Acts of type three are similar to acts of supererogation, except that it is blameworthy not to perform them, and acts of type four are similar to acts of offence, except that it is praiseworthy not to perform them. Hence acts of type three just are acts of quasi-supererogation, and acts of type four just are acts of quasi-offence. Given the structure of the scheme, there appears to be no reason to acknowledge acts of supererogation and offence while refusing to acknowledge acts of quasi-supererogation and quasi-offence, and this observation, of course, correlates with what I have argued in the preceding sections. There is no reason to think that acts of types three and four have any less legitimate a place than acts of types five and six, and in this way a formal scheme such as this can help guarantee that such acts will not be overlooked.

In conclusion, it is interesting to note that acts of types one and two cannot be accommodated by the five-fold classification as characterized above. However, with the aid of the following auxiliary principles a place for them can be found in the standard system:

p1. To refrain from performing an act is itself to perform an act;
p2. If one performs an act, then one refrains from refraining from performing it;
p3. It is praiseworthy (or blameworthy or neutral) to perform an act if and only if it is praiseworthy (or blameworthy or neutral) to refrain from refraining from performing it.

The following is a formal demonstration that, given principles (p1)-(p3), an agent performs an act of type one if and only if the agent refrains from an act of offence.

Consider a person who refrains from an act of offence. Such a person refrains from performing an act a whose performance by this person would be blameworthy. By principle (p1) this person thereby performs an act a*. But by definition it is neutral to refrain from performing an act of offence, and hence the performance of a* is neutral. Moreover, by principle (p3) it is blameworthy to refrain from performing act a*. For to refrain from a* is to refrain from refraining from a; but performing a is blameworthy. Hence by (p3) refraining from refraining from a is blameworthy, and so refraining from a* is blameworthy. Thus, act a* meets both of the conditions which are required to be an act of type one, and I conclude that one refrains from an offence only if one's act is an act of type one, given principles (p1)-(p3).

Suppose next that S's performance of a is an act of type one. Then S's performing a is neutral, and it is blameworthy for S to refrain from performing a. To show that S refrains from an act of offence, it must be shown that S refrains from an act which is blameworthy to perform and neutral to refrain from performing. By principle (p2) S refrains from refraining from performing a. And since it is blameworthy for S to refrain from performing a, S refrains from an act which is blameworthy to perform. Moreover, the same act (refraining from performing a) is neutral to refrain from performing. For S's performing a is neutral, and hence by (p3), S's refraining from refraining from performing a is likewise neutral. Thus, S's refraining from performing a meets the conditions which are required to be an act of offence, and hence S refrains from an act of offence. Given principles (p1)-(p3), therefore, one performs an act of type one if and only if one refrains from an act of offence.

A similar argument shows that one performs an act of type two if and only if one refrains from an act of supererogation, given principles (p1)- (p3). Together with these three principles it can be shown that the standard system accommodates acts of types one and two. More specifically, given these principles it follows that one performs an act of type one if and only if one refrains from an act of offence, and one performs an act of type two if and only if one refrains from an act of supererogation.

Thus, acceptance of (p1)-(p3) makes it possible for the standard system to accommodate acts of types one and two. Of course, I do not presume to maintain that these principles will elicit universal agreement. It would be possible to examine at great length various objections which can conceivably be raised concerning these principles. However, the main focus of this chapter has been upon acts of quasi-supererogation, and hence I shall conclude this section with the observation that the standard system's prospects of accommodating acts of types one and two are by no means hopeless. There are auxiliary principles which allow the standard system to handle acts of these types. In the event that these principles should turn out to be problematic, it can be concluded either that the standard system is even less exhaustive than what has already been alleged (that it fails to accommodate acts of types three and four) or that there are other auxiliary principles less objectionable than (p1)-(p3) which establish that acts of types one and two are accommodated by the standard system. In any case, the fate of the standard system in this regard is of only secondary concern.

Chapter 6

SUPEREROGATION, VIRTUE, AND VOCATION

Since the time of Aristotle, it has been commonly assumed that a complete ethical theory must include both a theory of right and wrong and a theory of virtue. While theories of right and wrong have for centuries received a disproportionate share of attention by philosophers, recent work by Alasdair MacIntyre and others has led to a resurgence of interest in the virtues and their role in the moral life. Predictably, philosophical discussions of supererogation have largely ignored the relationship between supererogation and theories of virtue. David Heyd has treated individual virtues such as gratitude in their relation to supererogation, and his discussion of these virtues has in certain ways promoted a greater understanding of supererogation. But the relation between supererogation and theories of virtue has until recently received almost no attention.

In 1986 Gregory Trianosky published his paper, "Supererogation, Wrongdoing, and Vice: On the Autonomy of the Ethics of Virtue," the first substantive attempt to discuss supererogation specifically in the context of virtue ethics. Actually, Trianosky attempts an even more grandiose objective—analyzing the connection between theories of right conduct and theories of virtue—and the concept of supererogation is employed as a device to help explain points of contact (or the lack thereof) between the two. In the course of the discussion he introduces some important and innovative ideas regarding supererogation and its place in regard to theories of virtue, and I shall use his discussion as a point of departure in a continuing effort to probe more deeply into the concerns of the anti-supererogationist. I shall suggest that his ideas have significant implications for understanding the debate between the proponents and opponents of supererogation and possibly for resolving some of the issues dividing them.

Another concept with significant potential for understanding this debate is that of vocation, and subsequent sections of this chapter deal with an explanation of how vocation sheds light upon the issues surrounding it. I will argue that an understanding of vocation as it has evolved in Protestant thought enables one to think about supererogation as it relates to certain restricted portions or segments of one's life and that consequently the Protestant concept of vocation has great potential for addressing some of the key concerns of the theistic anti-supererogationist. In the final section I show that these consequences can be generalized to fit an understanding of vocation which is not specifically connected with the Protestant conception of vocation.

1. TRIANOSKY ON SUPEREROGATION

Trianosky's general aim in "Supererogation, Wrongdoing, and Vice" is to show that the "fit" between a theory of right conduct and a theory of virtue is fairly loose; one's views about what motives are vicious and one's views about what conduct is wrong need not be correlated in any clear or systematic manner. He announces at the outset that he proposes to approach the issues indirectly by way of a discussion of supererogation and its connections with virtue and vice. A supererogatory act is defined by Trianosky as an act whose performance is recommended but not required and whose omission is permitted rather than forbidden.[1] Trianosky does not explain precisely what is meant by saying that an act's performance is recommended. But his accompanying discussion seems to suggest that it is because it possesses certain meritorious qualities that a certain act comes to be morally recommended, and hence it does not seem inaccurate to describe these as acts which are praiseworthy or meritorious to perform. He also makes no explicit requirement that their omission cannot be blameworthy. However, he remarks that, given his characterization of supererogation, "it is plausible to think that blame for failure to perform is appropriate only when the act in question is obligatory and not when it is merely supererogatory."[2] One might be puzzled as to how he thinks one might be led to this conclusion solely on the strength of his definition if one believes there are more ways to merit blame than to do that which is forbidden. But the important point is that he in fact regards the failure to perform an act of supererogation as neutral, not blameworthy, and hence it can be concluded that what he has in mind by supererogation is for all practical purposes what I have referred to as the standard characterization.

Trianosky believes that there is an intimate connection between the concepts of 'blame' and 'excuses'. Roughly speaking, when a person deserves blame for the failure to perform an act, excuses function to deflect the blame. Thus, it is appropriate to make excuses for the failure to perform an act when such a failure is blameworthy. And, Trianosky notes, it is never appropriate to make excuses for the failure to perform an act when the failure is not blameworthy. From this it follows that it is never appropriate to make excuses for omitting an act of supererogation. Given this intimate connection between blame and excuse making, no excuse is ever necessary for failing to perform an act of supererogation, for it is never blameworthy to omit such an act.

No sooner does Trianosky derive this principle than he notes a phenomenon which seems puzzling. Sometimes, he observes, we are challenged to perform acts that are good to do but not required, acts which are commonly regarded as acts of supererogation, by people who are already committed to performing them. Examples might include such challenges as, "Would you help us with the telethon this year?" or challenges which involve a lengthy commitment, such as, "Why don't you join the Peace Corps with me?" What is puzzling about these situations is the reaction which is frequently elicited by these challenges. Although the acts which people are challenged to perform are acts of supererogation, according to Trianosky, people often react by offering excuses. Challenged to perform acts of supererogation by people who are already so committed, our instinctive response often seems to be the offering of excuses. Therefore, while it is never appropriate to offer excuses for the failure to perform an act of supererogation, according to the reasoning offered earlier, people in fact frequently feel the need to offer excuses when they plan to refrain from performing acts of supererogation.

Trianosky believes that the reason people feel the need to make excuses in these situations is that they feel uncomfortable or even ashamed to refrain from these challenges. When they are unwilling to go the extra mile, people often feel uncomfortable or ashamed; accordingly, they feel the need to make excuses. Often this feeling is strong enough to impel them to make excuses which they know to be false.

But, again, it is puzzling that people should have these feelings at all, given that the acts they are challenged to perform are acts of supererogation:

> But if what we are challenged to do is supererogatory, it would suffice to say, politely, "No thanks, I'm not in the mood" or "No thanks, I'm interested in saving up for a new tennis racket" or "No thanks, I like my current job too much." Yet these replies seem somehow infelicitous.[3]

The logic of the situation seems to demand nothing more than a polite statement of intent to decline the challenge. Even the explanation that one is saving for a tennis racket or that one likes one's current job too much arguably constitutes more explanation than the situation demands. The explanation, "No thanks, I'm not in the mood" perhaps best captures the type of response which satisfies the minimum demands of the situation. Nothing more seems to be required by the logic of the situation. Yet this type of response seems infelicitous, and herein lies the puzzle. The logic of the situation demands considerably less than what seems to be demanded by the situation in real life.

Trianosky notes that there are a variety of ways in which one might attempt to argue that there is really nothing puzzling about this situation. In particular, he considers the argument that the acts we are challenged to perform in these situations are acts which fulfil imperfect duties. Thus, while we may have no duty to perform such an act, we might have a duty to perform any one of a range of acts which includes this act. And if this is the case, an excuse may be perfectly appropriate. If I have a duty to perform an act of charity at some time or another, then perhaps it is appropriate to explain why I am not performing the act of charity you are now challenging me to perform.

He counters this suggestion by noting that, even if it is true that excuse making is appropriate in these instances, the puzzle still arises in situations where the agent has obviously fulfilled the requirements of the imperfect duty which is supposedly operative. Suppose I have an imperfect duty to perform an act of a certain kind and I perform an act which fulfils this duty. Suppose in addition that a short time later someone challenges me to perform another act of this kind, and I make an excuse for not doing it. Trianosky's point seems to be that in this scenario my feeling the need to make an excuse is a puzzling phenomenon which cannot be explained by the principle (even if it is true) that it is appropriate to make excuses for failing to perform an act which fulfils an imperfect duty. There are many situations in which people make excuses for failing to perform acts which do not fulfil imperfect duties, and this is a puzzle which remains to be explained.

Trianosky concludes that offering excuses for the failure to perform acts of supererogation is a phenomenon which is indeed puzzling. And while one might fault him for failing to consider some additional ways in which one might seek to explain this puzzling phenomenon (such as the suggestion that we sometimes make excuses because we know that the other person believes, even though we do not, that our performance of the act is obligatory), I am inclined to think that he is correct that the puzzle cannot be satisfactorily explained by appealing to traditional moral concepts. As might be evident by now, his suggestion is that the explanation requires one to venture into the area of virtue ethics.

He begins his own explanation by distinguishing between two types of negative moral judgments. Negative deontic judgments directed to an agent are judgments about the wrongness of an agent's performing or failing to perform some particular act. Included in the category of negative deontic judgments are judgments of blameworthiness, judgments of culpability, fault, or negligence, and judgments of responsibility for reparations. In contrast, negative aretaic judgments are described as follows:

> Negative aretaic judgments of the person presuppose a judgment about the viciousness of some conative or affective state of the agent's. They are of two kinds: those which presuppose judgments about the viciousness of standing traits or dispositions, and those which presuppose judgments about the viciousness of occurrent motives or states. Judgments about what a bad person someone is, or about how cowardly or dishonest a person he is, are aretaic judgments of the first sort. Judgments about how inconsiderate someone was on a certain

occasion or about how insensitive, dishonest, or cowardly it was *of him* to do what he did are aretaic judgments of the person of the second sort.[4]

If I judge that someone is a bad person, my judgment is a negative aretaic judgment of the first sort. And if I judge that on a given occasion someone exhibits a particular vice, then my judgment is a negative aretaic judgment of the second sort. Neither is a negative deontic judgment, however, for neither logically presupposes that the agent performs or omits a particular act by virtue of which the negative judgment is appropriate. I can judge that you are insensitive, dishonest, or cowardly on a given occasion, even though it is not possible to isolate a particular act you perform which justifies me in judging you are demonstrating one of these vices.

Given this distinction, according to Trianosky, it is easy to resolve the puzzle described above. When an agent fails to perform an act of supererogation, one cannot appropriately make a negative deontic judgment about this failure. On strictly deontic grounds, the failure to perform an act of supererogation can never warrant the ascription of moral blame; it is never morally blameworthy to omit an act of supererogation.

However, from the fact that a negative deontic judgment is never appropriate with respect to the failure to perform an act of supererogation, it does not follow that a negative aretaic judgment cannot appropriately be made when an agent fails to perform an act of supererogation. Indeed, it frequently happens that a negative aretaic judgment is warranted by an agent's failure to perform an act of supererogation. According to Trianosky, this situation can arise when a person's failure to act arises from a less than virtuous motive. Often people are presented with an opportunity to perform an act of service for another and react with total indifference. It is one thing to refrain from an act of supererogation with accompanying feelings of regret and concern for those that one elects not to help, but it is another thing to demonstrate a total indifference to their needs. In the latter case one's failure to act arguably arises out of a less than virtuous state of mind, and there is a very real possibility that a negative aretaic judgment is in order.

In more extreme cases an agent's failure to perform an act of supererogation may arise from a decidedly vicious motive. Perhaps I have an opportunity to perform an act of great service for another person, and I refrain from doing so strictly out of spite. It gives me a perverse pleasure to withhold benefits, and for this reason I refrain from doing so (such malicious interest in another's misfortune Kant describes as a "fiendish joy").[5] Certainly the motives out of which I fail to perform an act of supererogation in this example are open to moral criticism, and the type of moral criticism appropriate to this situation is a negative aretaic judgment. More specifically, it is a negative aretaic judgment of the second type which Trianosky distinguishes. On a particular occasion my behavior is motivated by a vicious state of mind, and my occurrent motives warrant a negative aretaic judgment.

It must be emphasized that negative deontic judgments are not appropriate in these situations, given that the acts the agent refrains from are acts of supererogation. Again, it is never blameworthy in and of itself to refrain from an act of supererogation. But the point of the present discussion is that the motive or state of mind accompanying the failure to act warrants moral criticism, and Trianosky maintains that it warrants moral criticism in the form of a negative aretaic judgment.

The possibility that the failure to perform an act of supererogation arises out of motives which warrant a negative aretaic judgment provides an explanation why people commonly make excuses when it is their intent to omit acts of supererogation. People are aware that others may perceive their failure to act as arising from motives which are less than virtuous or even vicious, and they do not want to appear driven by such motives. Hence they make excuses for their failure to act. These excuses, according to Trianosky, serve to deflect negative judgments about their motives, and there is good reason for offering these excuses. Because others are likely to suspect that the underlying motives are less than virtuous, it is frequently important to reassure them that such is not the case. And this objective is accomplished through offering excuses. Of course, the objective is not automatically accomplished through offering excuses, since others may not believe that the excuses are sincere. But this does not alter the fact that people have good reason to make excuses in these circumstances.

People do not offer these excuses, then, to deflect negative judgments of a deontic nature. They are not making excuses for failing to perform acts of supererogation. As has already been shown, there is no rational reason to do so. They offer excuses to deflect negative aretaic judgments, for there is often a real possibility that others will suspect their failure is grounded in a less than virtuous state of mind. Often people do in fact refrain from acts of supererogation as the result of these states of mind, and hence the suspicions of others are no less understandable than feeling the need to make excuses on the part of the person who refrains from acting.

Philosophical discussions of supererogation almost invariably characterize acts of supererogation in entirely deontic terms. But to characterize them in purely deontic terms, according to Trianosky, is both misleading and incomplete. It is misleading because it invites the inference that the omission of a supererogatory act can never warrant a negative moral judgment; on the basis of the preceding discussion it is abundantly clear that negative moral judgments are sometimes appropriate when a person refrains from a potential act of supererogation. And characterizing supererogation in purely deontic terms is incomplete because it is incapable of providing an explanation of why the failure to perform an act of supererogation may provide grounds for some critical judgment. In this respect the concept of supererogation differs from the concept of obligation. When a person omits an obligatory act, the grounds for criticizing the person are clear; and these grounds are specifiable in purely deontic terms. But to explain why negative judgments are sometimes appropriate when a person omits an act of supererogation requires one to appeal to moral concepts which lie beyond the realm of the deontic. And this is the reason why people's propensity to offer excuses for omitting acts of supererogation remains genuinely puzzling as long as one operates strictly within the realm of the deontic.

A complete characterization of supererogation must appeal to moral concepts from theories of virtue as well as theories of right conduct. Discussions of supererogation almost invariably disregard the role of virtue and vice in the moral evaluation of agents who either do or do not perform acts of supererogation, and it is Trianosky's aim to emphasize the importance of their respective roles.

Up to this point Trianosky's discussion has concentrated upon the less than virtuous motives which sometimes accompany occasions in which people refrain from acts of supererogation. However, people who perform acts of supererogation frequently display great virtue. Saints and heroes are often praised for their acts of great self-sacrifice, but here too it is important to go beyond the typically deontic characterization of their behavior. For it is virtue which underlies the heroic and saintly acts which they perform. Not only do they perform these acts when the opportunities arise, but they display an ongoing willingness to help those in need even at great risk or inconvenience to themselves.

Trianosky describes a "fully virtuous person" as one who is willing to do both what morality requires and what morality recommends and who has the personal qualities sufficient to maintain this commitment. To be a fully virtuous person it is not enough to do in fact both what morality requires and recommends when the opportunities arise; one must in addition possess an ongoing willingness to act in this manner. The fully virtuous person is always willing to do more than what is required, and this shows that there is a straightforward connection between virtue and supererogation. The fully virtuous person is naturally disposed to perform acts of supererogation. This is a point which would seem so obvious as to be hardly worthy stating were it not for the degree to which virtue ethics has been disregarded in the literature on supererogation.

Of course, people who are highly virtuous sometimes perform wrong acts. Thus, it is sometimes appropriate to make a negative deontic judgment about an act which a saintly or highly virtuous person performs. Conversely, people who are egregiously lacking in virtue sometimes act in a morally praiseworthy manner. When this happens it may be appropriate to make a positive deontic judgment about an act (perhaps even an act of supererogation) which proceeds from a character which deserves a negative aretaic judgment. There is no perfect correlation between positive deontic and aretaic judgments or between negative deontic and aretaic judgments.

To summarize, Trianosky's important paper calls attention to situations in which a person's failure to perform an act of supererogation proceeds from a less than virtuous motive. Hence while no negative deontic judgment can justly be made about the person's omission, it may nevertheless be appropriate to make a negative aretaic judgment about the motives or underlying character leading to the omission. The failure to perform an act of supererogation cannot by its very nature be judged blameworthy in and of itself, but this failure may well proceed from a less than virtuous disposition or underlying character which can be criticized on aretaic grounds.

This phenomenon, Trianosky argues, explains why people frequently feel a need to make excuses for the failure to perform acts of supererogation. When asked to donate time or money for charitable causes, people tend to feel that a simple "no" is inadequate. From a deontic point of view, of course, no further response is necessary. From a deontic point of view there is no need to apologize for the omission of a supererogatory act. Nevertheless, people sense that others will make a negative judgment if it is not made clear that the omission is occasioned by circumstance, not a lack of virtue. Thus, people are aware that the omission of a supererogatory act invites the possibility of negative judgments regarding the dispositions or underlying character of the agent which gives rise to the omission.

2. Virtue and Supererogation

In the previous chapter it was my suggestion that the failure to recognize that acts of quasi-supererogation and quasi-offence are possible can have a considerable impact upon the degree to which one is attracted to an anti-supererogationist point of view. For if one is of the opinion that a praiseworthy, non-obligatory act is never blameworthy to omit, then it appears that moral agents can with impunity make a practice of omitting these acts. They can make a practice of performing only those praiseworthy acts which fulfil moral obligations and regard the rest as merely optional. This scenario embodies the worst fears of the anti-supererogationist: that one is essentially using supererogation as an excuse for being morally insensitive to the needs of others. It is understandable that this fear will make one more likely to be attracted to the arguments of the anti-supererogationist. Nevertheless, I have attempted to argue that these fears are based upon misunderstanding. It is simply not the case that the omission of praiseworthy, non-obligatory acts are never blameworthy, and hence a person who makes a practice of performing only those praiseworthy acts which fulfil moral obligations is frequently subject to moral criticism.

On the basis of Trianosky's discussion of supererogation in "Supererogation, Wrongdoing, and Vice," it becomes apparent that people who regard the performance of praiseworthy, non-obligatory acts with impunity are subject to moral criticism on additional grounds. For if a person makes a practice of refraining from praiseworthy, non-obligatory acts, that person almost certainly acts on the basis of a motive or an underlying character which is less than virtuous. Hence, a person who habitually refrains from acts of supererogation (or, for that matter, acts of quasi-supererogation) is subject to negative aretaic judgments. While the person's individual failures to perform these acts may not be subject to negative deontic judgments (they will be in the case of quasi-supererogation), they are subject to negative aretaic judgments.

If Trianosky is correct in believing that such people are subject to negative aretaic judgments, there are significant implications regarding the debate between the proponents and opponents of supererogation. For to the extent that the anti-supererogationist impulse is rooted in the fear that such people are taking advantage of a system which provides no penalties for moral insensitivity, it is rooted in a misunderstanding. Moral insensitivity arises from defects of character, and hence it bears a close connection with the absence of virtue in one's character. Where moral insensitivity is present, virtues of various sorts are lacking, and I believe this is true even when one's moral insensitivity is entirely unintentional (in fact, it is trivially true if moral sensitivity is itself recognized as a virtue). Accordingly, where moral insensitivity is present there is a very real possibility that negative aretaic judgments are in order. There is, therefore, a very real possibility that people who refrain from performing acts of supererogation are deserving of moral criticism. There is no such thing as taking advantage of a system which provides no penalties for moral insensitivity; as the work of Trianosky shows, the system cannot be taken advantage of in this manner. And those who think otherwise fail to reckon with virtue ethics and its connection with supererogation.

Earlier I made reference to situations in which an agent, out of spite for another, takes great delight in refraining from a potential act of supererogation which would benefit the other person. Here the motive giving rise to the agent's omission is blatantly wrong, and one could accurately judge that the agent's occurrent state of mind is characterized by vice. Clearly, such situations fall under the model Trianosky has constructed; they are, in fact, extreme examples of cases in which negative aretaic judgments are appropriate. When it is out of spite for another that an agent refrains from an act of supererogation, judgments about the viciousness of the occurrent motives are certainly in order.

Nevertheless, I believe it is important to recognize that in these situations it may also be appropriate to make negative deontic judgments about these spiteful agents. Suppose that I make a conscious decision to withhold certain goods from a man. It is in my power to give these goods to him; they are of little use to me, and I know they would be of great use to him. But I also know that I have no moral duty to give these goods away, and I resolve that I will not give them away. Because I dislike the man, I find pleasure in my ability to withhold these goods from him.

Assuming that my giving these goods to the man would count as an act of supererogation, I am not blameworthy in my failure to perform this act. A negative deontic judgment cannot appropriately be made with respect to this omission. Nevertheless, it is important to see in this example that my failure to act is precipitated by a prior act. I make a conscious resolve to withhold certain goods from the man, and this act leads me to refrain from the act of supererogation. This conscious resolve is not itself the omission of an act of supererogation; it is a decision to omit an act of supererogation. I believe it is an act which is deserving of moral blame, unlike the subsequent omission which it precipitates, and hence it is an act for whose performance a negative deontic judgment is appropriate.

Trianosky rightly points out that negative aretaic judgments are often appropriate when people fail to perform acts of supererogation, but his discussion may leave the impression that negative deontic judgments are never appropriate when people fail to perform acts of supererogation. Thus, I believe that it is important to augment his discussion with the observation that people often make conscious decisions to omit acts of supererogation, and these decisions frequently qualify as acts which can be criticized on deontic grounds. No doubt these decisions themselves frequently arise from a set of dispositions or underlying character which can be criticized on aretaic grounds, and it is likely that this is true of the example I have offered. But often there is an intermediary decision between the underlying disposition or character and the eventual failure to perform an act of supererogation, and often this decision can be criticized on deontic grounds.

Because Trianosky makes no mention of this point, what he says about excuse making may seem somewhat incomplete. People commonly make excuses for their failure to perform acts of supererogation, and he attributes this behavior to the realization that others are likely to suspect that the underlying motives are less than virtuous. These excuses serve to deflect negative judgments about their underlying character or occurrent motives. People do not offer these excuses to deflect judgments of a deontic nature. There is no reason to make excuses for the failure to perform acts of supererogation, and Trianosky concludes that the excuses are made to deflect negative aretaic judgments, not to deflect negative deontic judgments.

In the example of the agent who makes a conscious decision to withhold certain goods from a man, it is apparent that a negative deontic judgment can appropriately be made about the agent's behavior. The agent can appropriately be blamed for resolving to withhold these goods, given the circumstances described above, even though the agent cannot appropriately be blamed for omitting the act of supererogation. It is possible, then, that an agent's decision to refrain from an act of supererogation is itself blameworthy. The decision can constitute a moral wrongdoing, and it is appropriate to criticize the agent for acting in this fashion.[6] To the extent that the decision reflects a less than virtuous character or set of occurrent motives, it might in addition be appropriate to make a negative aretaic judgment. But certainly the appropriateness of a negative aretaic judgment does not rule out the possibility that a negative deontic judgment is likewise appropriate.

I believe it is common for people to exhibit this type of behavior, making a conscious decision to refrain from a potential act of supererogation in a way which deserves moral blame. And I believe it is common for people to make excuses in situations where they intend to refrain from acts of supererogation precisely because they wish to deflect negative judgments about their decision to refrain. My decision to refrain from an act of supererogation might be perfectly justifiable, but others may suspect otherwise. Hence my expression of remorse for failing to perform the act of supererogation can function to reassure others that my decision to refrain is indeed justifiable. As Trianosky points out, people sometimes offer excuses in order to deflect negative aretaic judgments about their underlying character or occurrent motives. But there are also occasions in which people offer excuses in order to deflect negative deontic judgments regarding their decision to refrain from an act of supererogation.

The excuses people offer might even serve to deflect both negative aretaic and deontic judgments simultaneously. Suppose that during the night there is a significant snowfall. Although I am under doctor's orders to limit my physical activity, I proceed to clear the snow from my own driveway. My elderly next door neighbor, unable to shovel snow, is forced to remain indoors until her grandson comes after school late in the day to clear her driveway. It is in my power to clear her driveway, and I must make a decision whether to do so. Eventually I conclude that it would be unwise for me to engage in additional strenuous activity, and with regret I decide not to offer my services to my neighbor.

Imagine that others are present on the occasion of my arriving at this decision. If they are aware that I am entertaining the possibility of offering my services to my neighbor, I might simply announce that I have decided against doing so. But it would be perfectly natural for me to explain that I am under doctor's orders to limit my physical activity and that I have already cleared my own driveway. The excuse

I offer explains my decision not to clear my neighbor's driveway, and by offering this excuse I deflect negative judgments that others might form about my decision. It is not my intent to apologize for my failure to clear my neighbor's driveway; there is no need to make excuses for omitting to perform this act (which, for the purposes of this example, I am assuming to be an act of supererogation). But I do feel a need to explain my decision to refrain, for people frequently decide to refrain from acts of supererogation in a blameworthy manner. In this scenario my decision is not blameworthy, and by offering an excuse I can make this point clear to the people I am with. Because it is an excuse for the performance of an act rather than an excuse for occurrent dispositions or an underlying motive, it serves to deflect a negative deontic judgment.

It might be objected that my real intent is to convince my listeners that I am a virtuous person in spite of deciding not to come to the aid of my neighbor. My explanation concerning the doctor's orders to limit my physical activity might simply be a way of restoring their confidence in me as a virtuous person, and if this is true then my excuse serves to deflect a negative aretaic judgment. On this line of reasoning my excuse does not in reality serve to deflect a negative deontic judgment, for it is not simply an excuse for the particular decision I make.

Here I am willing to grant that the intent of my excuse is both to explain the decision I make and to portray myself as virtuous. My immediate intent is to explain the decision, but perhaps it is also part of my design to remove any suspicions on the part of my listeners that I am a less than virtuous person. After all, one's decisions are closely connected with the state of one's underlying motives and character. If so, my excuse can conceivably be characterized as serving to deflect negative judgments of both a deontic and aretaic nature.

However, I am not willing to concede that people never make excuses for their decisions to refrain from acts of supererogation. Such decisions are often difficult or painful, and people are understandably concerned that others come to see them in a favorable light. Often those who witness these momentous decisions already have a deep familiarity with the agent's underlying character or motivational structure, and there is no need for the agent to deflect negative aretaic judgments. Saintly people might arrive at a painful decision to refrain from a particular act of supererogation, feel a need to explain the decision, but feel no need to defend their underlying character or dispositions. Such people are concerned to deflect negative deontic judgments, not to deflect negative aretaic judgments, and the same is true of many non-saintly persons who feel no need to enlighten their listeners about their character.

I conclude that Trianosky is correct in pointing out that those who offer excuses for failing to perform acts of supererogation are frequently concerned to deflect negative aretaic judgments. They are concerned that others will suspect that their underlying character or motives are less than virtuous, and this is the reason for offering their excuses. I have attempted to show that Trianosky's account needs to be augmented, for there are times when the focus of an agent's concern is the decision to refrain from an act of supererogation. These decisions are themselves blameworthy, and there is good reason for people to defend their decisions when others are likely to suspect that these decisions are indeed blameworthy. When this happens people are making excuses to deflect negative deontic judgments, not negative aretaic judgments (though there are situations in which their excuses serve to deflect both).

It might be observed that Trianosky's model does not apply to situations in which the person refraining from an act of supererogation mistakenly believes that it is not an act of supererogation. A person might offer an excuse for refraining from the act on the false assumption that its performance fulfils a moral obligation. It is forbidden to refrain from an obligatory act, and people who refrain or intend to refrain from an act presumed to be obligatory might offer an excuse to deflect negative judgments about their character or motives. After all, some motives for omitting one's duty are better than others, and people wish to put the failure to do their duty in the best light possible. Consequently, when people mistakenly believe that they are failing to fulfil a moral duty, they may be similarly inclined to offer excuses.

Trianosky's model also does not apply to situations in which people refraining from an act of supererogation are convinced that other people will regard the omission as a failure to fulfil their duty. Suppose I am in a position to perform an act of heroic self-sacrifice, and I decline to perform it. My failure to perform this act does not warrant an apology or excuse. However, I am painfully aware that those who witness my obvious failure to act are anti-supererogationists. They will surely regard my failure to act as a failure to discharge my duty in this situation, and hence I may feel the need to offer excuses.

There is admittedly something feeble about the excuses offered in situations of this type. An excuse such as, "I really cannot do this—I have too many good years of life ahead of me," when accompanying a refusal to perform an act of heroic self-sacrifice, will likely make a favorable impression on few of my anti-supererogationist companions. Nevertheless, as feeble as these excuses might be, the truth is that people may feel the need to offer them. Concerned that others will jump to the worst possible conclusions about my reasons for (what they see as) shirking my duty, I may offer excuses with the intent of deflecting negative judgments about my character or motives. Thus, while they will definitely make negative deontic judgments about my failure to act, it may be possible to abort their arriving at negative aretaic judgments about me by my explanation.

There is one additional respect in which Trianosky's analysis may be open to further refinement. Trianosky emphasizes that people do not need to offer excuses for the failure to perform acts of supererogation as such, because there is no need to offer excuses for the omission of these acts. Hence the explanation for their offering excuses must lie elsewhere, and he eventually locates the explanation in the realm of virtue ethics. Already I have indicated that the explanation he offers is accurate. Often the excuses people offer for their motives are aimed at reassuring others that those motives are virtuous, and this explanation squares with the fact that excuses are unnecessary with respect to omitting to perform potential acts of supererogation.

However, this analysis presupposes that people offer excuses only when it is necessary to offer them. Since there is no point in offering excuses for the failure to perform acts of supererogation, Trianosky concludes that people must offer them for other reasons. But surely it is conceivable that on at least some occasions people will behave in a less than rational fashion by offering excuses which are not necessary to offer. In particular, it is possible that people will, for whatever reason, feel the need to offer excuses for the very failure to perform an act of supererogation. Sometimes excuses of this type seem to be offered in situations where there is not a great deal at stake. If there is only one cupcake left on the plate by the time it reaches me, it would arguably be an act of supererogation for me to leave it for the woman seated on the other side of me. However, I decline this opportunity to perform an act of supererogation, and I take the cupcake. While there is no need for me to do so, I may nevertheless offer an excuse such as, "Sorry, I cannot easily resist these."

It might be argued that my excuse functions to deflect a negative aretaic judgment, but it seems possible to imagine that I have no concern whatever as to how virtuous the woman's estimate of me might actually be. For all I care, she might conclude that my underlying character is thoroughly vicious. It might strike me as more important that I get the cupcake. Thus, although Trianosky is surely correct that people frequently offer excuses in order to deflect negative aretaic judgments when omitting acts of supererogation, it seems possible that at least occasionally people offer unnecessary excuses. And in particular it appears that they offer excuses for the failure to perform acts of supererogation.

In this section I have discussed some ways in which Trianosky's analysis can be expanded to take into account situations where people make excuses for their decisions to omit acts of supererogation or can be further refined to recognize that people do sometimes make excuses for omitting acts of supererogation even when there is no logical need to do so. But the overall point to be stressed is that, in having shown that the need people feel to make excuses for omitting acts of supererogation requires (at least partially) for its explanation an excursion into virtue ethics, his discussion breaks new ground. The feelings people have about the moral status of supererogation in human life cannot adequately be analyzed in terms of the ethics of right conduct, and Trianosky's discussion provides much insight into the role virtue ethics can play in understanding these feelings. Therefore, one can expect future discussions of supererogation to pay greater attention to virtue ethics.

It has also been my aim in this section to point out that Trianosky's analysis addresses certain key concerns of the anti-supererogationist. There is a close connection in many people's minds between supererogation and moral insensitivity: a person who has no desire to go out of the way to help others can conveniently escape moral criticism by arguing that it is never blameworthy to refrain from acts of supererogation. In this way supererogation is sometimes viewed as a device to vindicate those who wish to do no more than simply discharge their moral duties. Baron uses the term "yuppie ethics" to describe this treatment of duty as totally separate from the good which one can choose as one pleases: "I have done 'my duty' . . . now my time, my choices are all mine . . . . Any other attention to morality is, for me, strictly optional."[7] Such a separation encourages the idea that one need only be concerned about discharging one's duty. However, I have argued that Trianosky's discussion shows that those who seek to escape moral criticism are subject to moral criticism of a different sort. Although they cannot be criticized on deontic grounds, their behavior and underlying attitude certainly warrants negative aretaic judgments. There is, therefore, a real possibility that those who refrain from acts of supererogation deserve moral criticism after all. Much of the stigma attached to the concept of supererogation is the result of misunderstanding, and the recognition that such people deserve moral criticism has the potential for removing much of this misunderstanding.

3. Supererogation and the Protestant Concept of Vocation

Another area with the potential for removing some of the misunderstanding—and some of the stigma attached to the concept of supererogation—is that of vocation. Just as an examination of the relationship between virtue and supererogation can lead to a reexamination of the feelings which lead people to embrace anti-supererogationism, the same is true of an examination of the relationship between vocation and supererogation. I shall begin by introducing the Protestant concept of vocation, and I will suggest that an examination of its relationship with supererogation serves primarily to address the concerns of the theistic anti-supererogationist. Those who have rejected the possibility of supererogation on theological grounds are those whose concerns are most likely to be affected by the issues raised in this section. In the next section I shall suggest that an understanding of vocation in non-theological terms has the capability of addressing the concerns of anti-supererogationists in general.

Recall from chapter three the general line of reasoning by which people have typically rejected supererogation on theological grounds. God is pictured as the supreme creator of the universe and all of the creatures which inhabit it. As the creator of all humans, God has instituted certain moral requirements governing their lives. In particular, since God loves good and hates evil, God requires humans to do good and to turn away from evil; we are morally obligated to pursue good and refrain from evil. When presented with the opportunity to do that which is morally good or praiseworthy, we ought to seize the opportunity. And when presented with the opportunity to do evil, we ought not seize the opportunity. As creatures of a good God, therefore, we are obliged to do whatever is good or praiseworthy and we ought to avoid whatever is evil or blameworthy. (A milder version of this view would incorporate the ought implies can principle.)

The picture presented here is one which would probably strike a good many theists as acceptable. A person who is convinced that we are all creatures of a God who loves good and hates evil might readily agree that it is our obligation as creatures of God to do whatever is good or praiseworthy and to refrain from whatever is evil or blameworthy. Clearly, the picture presented here leaves no room for supererogation. If we are obliged to do whatever is praiseworthy, there is no possibility of performing an act which is both praiseworthy and fulfils no obligation (from which it also follows that acts of quasi-supererogation are impossible). In addition, the picture presented here leaves no room for acts of offence (or quasi-offence), for whatever is blameworthy also turns out to be forbidden; refraining from blameworthy acts inevitably fulfils a moral obligation.

Although some theists may wish to reconsider their acceptance of this view upon discovering that it rules out the possibility of supererogation, others have been willing to accept these anti-supererogationist implications. To their way of thinking there is something powerfully wrong-headed about the idea that a supremely good God could make it morally permissible for his creatures to pass up opportunities to do that which is morally good. If it is God's intent that his creatures pursue the path of good and turn away from evil, for what possible reason would God not require of us that we take advantage of these opportunities? And, although theological ethicists have seldom discussed acts of offence, it is easy to imagine a similar puzzlement about God's regarding as permissible certain acts which are morally blameworthy to perform. If it is God's intent that his creatures turn away from evil, for what possible reason would he not declare as morally impermissible whatever is evil or blameworthy?

It is in considering these questions that the concept of vocation may be capable of shedding some light. The basic idea, as it has evolved primarily in Protestant thought, is that God calls his creatures into various areas of work or service. It is part of God's plan that his purposes on earth be brought about or realized through the efforts of his creatures, and each of his creatures is called to a particular area of service. Of course, it is within God's power to bring about these states of affairs apart form the work or cooperation of his creatures; but it is a part of God's plan to utilize the talents and abilities of his creatures in such a way that they play an essential role in the realization of his overall designs.

Naturally, since it is God who endows us with our talents and abilities in the first place, it is misleading to describe God as first endowing us with abilities and later choosing an appropriate vocation for us. More accurately, perhaps, God endows us with talents and abilities in the light of the vocation to which we are called. And since the carrying out of his designs requires a multiplicity of persons in differing areas of service, God endows people with differing talents and abilities. Having decided upon the purposes to be realized through the collective efforts of his creatures on earth, God calls his creatures to a variety of vocations and equips each with the appropriate abilities to engage in the assigned vocation with adequate success.

Many questions are raised by the notion of vocation as described here. For example, there is much unclarity as to the relation between one's vocation and one's occupation. When a person is called by God into a particular vocation, to what extent should the person regard this call as a directive to enter a particular occupation or seek an occupation in a particular area? Moreover, how exactly does a person ascertain the vocation to which each is called? An examination of one's abilities and opportunities presumably serves as a potential indicator, but many questions may remain. It is far easier to know which areas of vocation one is ill equipped to enter than it is to pinpoint the vocation God has in mind for one. Hence on a practical level a person who desires to fulfil God's purposes may encounter considerable difficulty.

Here my aim is to describe the significance of the concept of vocation for the debate between the theistic proponents and opponents of supererogation, and it is not necessary to settle the practical questions of ascertaining the vocation to which one is called or, having learned this, what occupation one ought to enter. The important points are that God calls his creatures to vocations for which they are suited according to their talents and abilities, that each person is called to a unique area of vocation and service, and that God has special expectations of his creatures according to their particular vocations. Of course, God expects his creatures to serve him in all areas of their lives, but the notion of vocation, as described in the Protestant tradition, carries with it the implication that God's expectations are not the same for persons within the area of their vocation as they are for persons outside the area of their vocations.

It is at this point that the issue of supererogation becomes vitally relevant. The theistic anti-supererogationist typically operates with a picture of God's expectations as uniformly distributed over the areas of his creatures' lives. God's expectations of his creatures are uniformly high in the sense that his creatures are expected to take advantage of all opportunities to perform praiseworthy acts. No discriminations are made between those areas of one's life in which one possesses considerable talents and abilities and those areas of one's life in which one possesses little or no ability. No matter how well equipped one is to be of particular service to others, one has a moral obligation to attempt to be of service (and, again, whether this encompasses acts which are not in the agent's power to perform depends upon the version of theistic anti-supererogationism one embraces).

The situation changes dramatically when the concept of vocation is introduced. If God calls me into a particular area of service or vocation and equips me with the appropriate talents and abilities, then God's expectation concerning my behavior within this area of my life will be particularly high. It will be particularly important for me to take advantage of opportunities to be of service within this area of my life, more so than others who have been called into other areas of service or vocation. For God has specifically designated me as an instrument to contribute to the realization of his purposes in this area of life.

Conversely, in an area of life beyond the scope of my vocation God's expectations of me will presumably be less than his expectations of others who have specifically been called to be of service in that area. The vocation to which I have been called is suited to the talents and abilities with which I have been endowed, and the areas of life to which others have specifically been called are suited to their talents and abilities. Hence I will often find myself far less capable of being of service in some area of human life than others who have specifically been called to that area of service. This is not to say that I am excused from serving others in areas which lie beyond the bounds of my own vocation. When no physician is present at the scene of a horrible accident, perhaps I ought to do what I can to help relieve the suffering of the accident victims. However, the expectations regarding my service are less than those accruing to individuals specifically called to that area of service.

What emerges from this way of viewing expectations is that the performance of acts of supererogation within the area of one's vocation will be more difficult than outside the area of one's vocation.

Each person is called to be of special service within a particular area of life, and within this area of life there will be considerable expectations that one will take advantage of opportunities to be of service beyond what might otherwise be the call of duty. In other words, a person becomes morally obligated to perform praiseworthy acts, acts whose performance would qualify as supererogatory were they outside the scope of the person's vocation. Within the scope of one's vocation the possibility of performing acts of supererogation is significantly diminished, for one is expected to be of special service.

Naturally, the anti-supererogationist will emphasize that the possibility of performing acts of supererogation within the area of one's vocation is zero. And on this point the theistic supererogationist may be sympathetic. Perhaps there is an area of life for each of us in which there is effectively no possibility of performing acts of supererogation. Perhaps God's demands on us are sufficiently high within this area of life that it is not possible to transcend the bounds of duty. According to this line of reasoning, to have a vocation is to have an area of life in which one must always go to the limit to be of service.[8]

In this way the concept of vocation may enable one to comprehend the attraction of the theistic anti-supererogationist perspective when examining the special area of service to which each person is called. If it is God's intent that a man pursue a particular vocation, having been endowed with the necessary abilities to pursue it, for what possible reason would God not require of him that he take advantage of all possible opportunities to promote the cause of good in the exercise of these special abilities? If a person is endowed with special gifts to be of special service in one area of life, what would be the point of allowing the use of these gifts to be morally optional? The conclusion that there simply is no room for supererogation in the exercise of these special abilities may strike many supererogationists as quite plausible.

Of course, the supererogationist views the situation differently when considering those areas of life in which one is not equipped for special service. In these areas of life one still has obligations to fulfil, and the failure to fulfil these is a serious matter. Moreover, in these areas of life there may be acts of quasi-supererogation, and the failure to perform these is morally blameworthy. But beyond these the supererogationist envisions acts which fulfil no moral obligation, acts whose performance is praiseworthy and whose omission is not blameworthy. I have many opportunities to be of service both inside and outside the area of my vocation, but with respect to the latter my taking advantage of these opportunities is sometimes morally optional. Outside the bounds of my vocation I am not required to go the extra mile on every occasion, and when I elect to go the extra mile there is a genuine possibility of performing an act of supererogation.

The theistic anti-supererogationist refuses to recognize that there is anything different about promoting good whether it is inside or outside the scope of a person's vocation. In all areas of life God requires us to do that which is good or praiseworthy, and there is nothing optional in fulfilling these requirements. Curiously, it was Martin Luther who contributed significantly to articulating the Protestant concept of vocation,[9] but there is nothing in Luther's writings which suggests that his anti-supererogationist ideas are thought to be operative only within the area of a person's calling or vocation. For him the possibility of performing acts of supererogation simply does not exist, and what he says about vocation appears to make no difference on this score.

The acceptance of the Protestant notion of vocation does not force one to recognize that acts of supererogation are possible. It is not inconsistent to operate with this notion of vocation and maintain a solidly anti-supererogationist position. Rather, it is my suggestion that this notion makes possible an alternative point of view which takes seriously many of the theistic anti-supererogationist's concerns about a supremely good God with high expectations of his creatures and yet recognizes that in certain areas of their lives these creatures are capable of performing acts of supererogation. The debate between the theistic supererogationist and anti-supererogationist need not be pictured in terms of a total rejection of supererogation as opposed to a wholesale, across-the-board affirmation of supererogation. An important middle alternative consists in rejecting the possibility of supererogation within the area of one's special vocation or calling in life and affirming its possibility within other areas of life.

Like the notion of virtue, an examination of vocation addresses the concerns of the theistic anti-supererogationist and points the way to a more moderate alternative. One is not forced to give up the idea that God has high expectations for his creatures when one allows that in some areas of life they can perform good works which go beyond the bounds of God's requirements. One simply draws a distinction between the requirements associated with one's special calling in life and the requirements associated with other areas of one's life which God has placed upon them. Because they are endowed with special gifts to live out their vocations, much is expected of them. But the same is not true when they have not been endowed with special gifts.

An interesting connection between the concepts of virtue and vocation, as they bear on the issue of supererogation, emerges in the writings of Kierkegaard. In a recent article entitled "Vocation," Robert M. Adams's comments on Kierkegaard's conception of vocation points to an important respect in which the relevance of vocation to duty is connected with the relevance of virtue to duty:

> Kierkegaard's conception of vocation is intimately related to his ideas about selfhood. It is significant that the crucial statement in the verdict on Quidam is not, "This is not what he ought to *do*," but, "This is not what he ought to *be*." Kierkegaard sees the vocation first and foremost as a vocation to be a certain kind of person.[10]

If Adams has correctly interpreted Kierkegaard's conception of vocation, Kierkegaard is insisting that vocation be understood in terms of the mandate to be a certain kind of person. And if this is what he is insisting, the suggestion seems to be that the obligations arising out of one's vocation often require one to possess virtues of various sorts. To be a certain kind of person presumably requires, among other things, the possession of certain virtues or the absence of various vices. Accordingly, if being a certain kind of person implies that one has come to possess such virtues, the requirements of vocation as understood by Kierkegaard go well beyond the requirements to perform certain kinds of action.

Clearly, Kierkegaard's insight ties in neatly with the conclusions of the previous sections. The manner in which one approaches one's moral obligations can be judged on both deontic and aretaic grounds. There is an intimate connection between virtue and vocation if one follows Kierkegaard in thinking of vocation in terms of a mandate to be a certain kind of person. Pursuing one's vocation is more than seizing the right opportunities to be of service; it also involves the cultivation of the virtues appropriate to one's particular vocation. Perhaps one is summoned to go beyond the call of duty within the scope of one's vocation, but the additional point which emerges from Kierkegaard's insight is that the manner in which one actually responds to this summons can be judged on both deontic and aretaic grounds. Again, it is not enough in responding to this summons that one perform certain types of action; one must also cultivate and display certain types of virtue. Thus, Kierkegaard's emphasis reaffirms the conclusions arrived at earlier in this chapter: the requirements of the moral life go beyond the realm of the deontic.

In this section I have suggested that the Protestant notion of vocation has significant relevance for the debate between the theistic proponents and opponents of supererogation. The basic idea is that God has called his creatures into areas of service or vocation according to the special gifts with which they are endowed. As a result, the manner in which one conducts one's life outside these areas differs from the manner in which one can be expected to conduct one's life within these areas. For in the process of pursuing one's vocation one has a calling frequently to go beyond the strict fulfillment of duty, being of service to others in ways which are not strictly required. Within these areas of life one can be expected to transcend the fulfillment of duty to the point of excelling in service to others.

This way of viewing vocation might initially appear to support or confirm the views of the anti-supererogationist, since it makes dubious the idea that one can perform acts of supererogation while pursuing one's vocation. But upon close inspection it becomes evident that one can understand the concept of vocation in such a way that areas in one's life beyond the scope of one's vocation qualify as areas in which supererogation can be operative. The supererogationist would argue that a person cannot be expected to excel in service to others in every conceivable area of life, and hence the possibility of performing acts of supererogation in other areas of life is preserved. Thus, while the possibility of supererogation tends to fade or diminish in areas where one has a special calling, the same does not happen outside these areas.

4. SUPEREROGATION AND VOCATION

The Protestant concept of vocation has been tremendously influential in shaping the way that concept has come to be understood in Western culture. However, there are those who reject this understanding of vocation, and in this section I will briefly attempt to generalize some of the issues raised in the preceding section as they might pertain to other ways of viewing vocation. In particular, for those who view the concept of vocation in non-theological terms, I shall suggest that the basic conclusions of the preceding section are essentially the same. Within certain areas of one's life there may be few if any opportunities to perform acts of supererogation, and in other areas of one's life there may be frequent opportunities to perform such acts.

The idea that God calls persons into areas of special service is at the heart of the Protestant concept of vocation. However, it is possible to believe that one is called into an area of special service without believing that this results from any action on God's part. A person who is unsure about the existence of God might nevertheless subscribe to the notion that some, or even all, human beings have a special calling in life. Others who are convinced of God's existence may decline to make a connection between anything God has specifically ordained and the special calling that some have; on such a view there are people called to areas of special service, but God is not viewed as the agent initiating the call. For that matter, it is possible to hold that there is no agent initiating the call in question. It is possible to hold that one is simply called to be of special service in some area of life without specifically being called *by* anyone or anything.

Suppose that a woman very nearly loses her life as the result of a drug overdose. After a period of recovery she feels a strong sense of calling to be of special service to drug addicts. She does not believe that her calling is from God or anyone else, but she nevertheless feels called to help drug addicts and to help them to the limit of her abilities. Administering this help sometimes requires great sacrifices of time and effort on her part, but she is convinced that she ought to help drug addicts in whatever ways she can. There may be room to go beyond the call of duty in other areas of her life, but in these pursuits she has a special sense of vocation to go the extra mile whenever a need arises.

In many diverse respects people may feel a special calling to be of service or assistance without believing that the calling is from God or any other particular source. In some instances people may feel called to take up residence is areas of the world where they can be of direct assistance to the poor or oppressed. But in a less dramatic fashion people might simply regard their special calling in terms of providing a wholesome home environment in which to raise their children. They might form the conviction that there is no going beyond the call of duty in guaranteeing that their children receive the best upbringing the parents are capable of providing. They are determined to do everything in their power to maximize the quality of their children's upbringing.

Other examples of this sense of calling may involve one's work. Some people regard their work as demanding an ultimate commitment of effort. They feel called to do the best job they are capable of performing, and to their way of thinking no degree of effort or energy can qualify as more than enough. Their work requires the best that they can do, and there is no respect in which they feel they can rise above the level of this requirement by pouring more effort into their work than it demands.

In each of these examples people feel a calling to be of special service in a particular vocation or area of their lives, and without this calling as having actually been issued by God or anyone else. They simply feel called to be of service. Naturally, it is open for others to argue that their efforts are misguided or based upon faulty assumptions. I might challenge my spouse's belief that she is called to an ultimate commitment of effort in discharging the requirements of her job. She is convinced that there is no possibility of going beyond the call of duty in discharging the duties of her work, but I might believe she is mistaken. In my view she is constantly going beyond the call of duty by working eighty to ninety hours per week. Nevertheless, such differences of opinion are by no means unique to situations in which one's concept of vocation is of a non-theistic nature. For it commonly happens that people engage in disputes as to whether God has called one to some specific area of service. The point is that if one does have a calling to be of special service in a particular area of life, it is reasonable to regard this as an area in which the possibility of supererogation is significantly restricted.

In his book *Moral Thinking* R.M. Hare offers an account of morality in which vocation is assigned a role very much along the same lines as suggested in the foregoing. His account is based upon two levels of moral thinking, the intuitive and the critical. The intuitive level is the level of prima facie principles, and the critical level is the level at which these principles are evaluated when they conflict, are incomplete, or should be discarded altogether. Within the intuitive level are various 'sublevels' of prima facie principles:

> First there will be those principles which nearly everyone has to accept if they are to be workable and fulfil their purpose: principles requiring honesty and truthfulness, for example . . . and principles forbidding cruelty. . . . Then at another sublevel there will be principles which each person takes as binding upon himself and on those like him, but which he does not expect to be obeyed by everybody . . . For example, if I were

very saintly like Albert Schweitzer or Mother Teresa, I might have much more exacting principles than in fact I have.[11]

At the first sublevel are principles of morality that are binding upon all moral agents, and it is demanded of everyone that they conform to these principles. At the other sublevel are principles of morality that are binding upon certain persons and not others; they are demanded of those individuals who take them to be binding upon themselves.

Hare believes that there is at least one more sublevel intermediate between these two. There is a sublevel consisting of prima facie principles which are common to "particular roles" in life. In this connection Hare introduces the concept of vocation and distinguishes between two of its senses. There are some principles which are appropriate to those which occupy certain roles or vocations in a professional sense. Thus, there are certain courses of conduct which can be expected or even demanded of one in one's capacity as a physician or as a lawyer. In addition, this sublevel includes principles proper to one's vocation in a more "personal" sense. One can have a vocation in life over and above one's vocation in a professional sense, and here too there are certain demands which come to be placed upon one.

In this passage Hare appears to be making a point closely related to what has been emphasized above. One's vocation has a definite effect upon what can be morally demanded or expected of one. Some of the obligations which are binding upon one do not depend upon one's special roles or vocations in life, but there are other obligations which definitely do. One takes on special obligations as a result of having chosen a certain vocation, either professionally or in some other manner. Consequently, the possibility of performing acts of supererogation is restricted by virtue of the special obligations which are generated within the area of one's vocation, but the possibility of supererogatory conduct in other areas of one's life is unaffected. (In parallel fashion at the sublevel where individuals choose to be subject to more demanding principles of morality the possibility of performing acts of supererogation is restricted, but the possibility of supererogatory conduct by moral agents in general is unaffected.)

In the previous section it was my suggestion that an understanding of the Protestant concept of vocation has the potential for addressing some of the theistic anti-supererogationist's chief concerns. Similarly, it is now apparent that an understanding of a nontheological notion of vocation has the potential for addressing some of the concerns of anti-supererogationists in general. For if one is indeed called to be of special service in some particular area of life, one recognizes that one is subject to the highest expectations within this area of life. Surely it can be reassuring to the anti-supererogationist that people who are committed to acknowledging supererogation are willing to take their duties seriously within this area of their lives. It is important to recognize that those who acknowledge supererogation do not automatically seek to take the easy way out with regard to what life demands. A person who is inclined to perceive supererogation as providing the easy way out for those with no desire to take these demands seriously may well be attracted to an anti-supererogationist point of view, and it is such a person for whom an understanding of vocation is particularly instructive. For that person it is crucial to see that there is an important middle ground between regarding praiseworthy acts as entirely optional in all areas of life and regarding them as entirely obligatory.

5. Summary: Virtue, Vocation, and the Anti-Supererogationist

In differing respects an analysis of the concepts of virtue and vocation shed a great deal of light upon the debate between the proponents and opponents of supererogation. More specifically, an analysis of each concept addresses concerns of the anti-supererogationist in such a way as to remove certain misconceptions about supererogation. In the case of virtue, it has been seen that people who appeal to supererogation as an excuse for being morally insensitive to the needs of others (practicing what Baron calls "yuppie ethics") are definitely open to moral criticism. By distinguishing between negative deontic judgments and negative aretaic judgments, it becomes apparent that the widespread view that people who refrain from acts of supererogation are immune from moral criticism is a misconception. In the case of vocation, it has been seen that one can acknowledge that acts of supererogation are possible while at the same time acknowledging that in a particular area of one's life going beyond duty (or, more accurately, going beyond what would otherwise be a duty) is what is required and expected of one. Thus, it is a misconception to assume that a recognition of supererogation in human life rules out the possibility of taking seriously the idea that one can be expected to excel in service to others or that one simply has a special calling to excel in service to others.

The previous chapter likewise attempts to expose a misconception about supererogation. It is easy to fall into the trap of assuming that it is never blameworthy to refrain from a praiseworthy, non-obligatory act, and hence of assuming that one can make a regular practice of refraining from them without becoming worthy of blame. By arguing that acts of quasi-supererogation are possible, I hope to have dispelled this misconception. Accordingly, I hope to have shown that certain potential fears of the anti-supererogationist regarding an acknowledgement that acts of supererogation are possible have no real basis in fact.

The net effect of this and the preceding chapter is hopefully twofold. First, there is a great deal of misunderstanding regarding supererogation and its place in human life. Through a discussion of the concepts of quasi-supererogation, virtue, and vocation I have attempted to create the possibility of correcting some of these misconceptions (with no pretence of having addressed all possible misconceptions about supererogation.) Second, the misconceptions I hope to have created the possibility of correcting bear a close connection with what I have called the anti-supererogationist impulse. Each of these misconceptions has the potential of portraying supererogation unfavorably and driving one in the direction of denying its possibility. To the extent that the anti-supererogationist impulse feeds off these misconceptions, therefore, this discussion will hopefully undercut some of the reasons people are attracted to the position that there can be no acts of supererogation in human life.

Chapter 7

A Cost-Benefit Analysis

It is frequently pointed out that there are both costs and benefits involved in performing acts of supererogation. There are costs on the part of the agent performing the acts, costs which can range from the very sacrifice of the agent's life to inconveniences so minor as to be scarcely noticeable. The benefits which accrue from acts of supererogation are generally directed to the needs of others or the improvement of life in general, and they can range from highly significant to trivial. In addition, these benefits often accrue to the agents themselves either directly or indirectly (an example of an indirect benefit would be the improvement of one's character through the practice of making sacrifices on behalf of others).

A recent article by Barry Curtis entitled, "The Supererogatory, the Foolish, and the Morally Required" makes the intriguing claim that weighing the costs and benefits actually determines whether an act qualifies as an act of supererogation. In this chapter I shall examine the highlights of Curtis's discussion and shall attempt to come to a clear understanding of his central claim. Since this claim embodies some beliefs about supererogation which are actually fairly common, it is my concern to assess it carefully. I will argue that the general outlook suggested by his approach (and that of others) is quite plausible in some respects, but in other respects it is problematic. I will conclude that this model portrays supererogation in too simplistic a fashion.

1. CURTIS ON MORAL REASONS AND REASONS OF SELF-INTEREST

When agents contemplate performing acts, they are often aware of moral reasons in favor of performing them. On the other hand, agents are often aware that there are reasons of self-interest in favor of not performing certain acts. And it frequently happens that agents are aware that, with respect to the same act, there are both moral reasons in favor of performing it and reasons of self-interest in favor of not performing it (or reasons of self-interest in favor of performing it and moral reasons in favor of not performing it). When this situation occurs the agent is called upon to make a judgment whether to perform the act or not perform it. These judgments are made from what Curtis calls the "the perspective of wisdom" because the skill with which they are made is a factor which determines whether we consider the agent to be wise. The perspective of wisdom is required to decide whether to act in accord with the moral reasons which favor performing the act or to act in accord with reasons of self-interest which favor not performing the act.

Two questions might immediately arise at this point of the narrative. First, will not the perspective of wisdom always decide in favor of performing an act when there are moral reasons in favor of performing it? Will a wise person not invariably give these moral reasons priority over reasons of self-interest? Curtis answers in the negative. There are times when it is foolish to give these moral reasons priority over reasons of self-interest, and several examples he offers will be examined shortly. A wise person will not automatically act contrary to self-interest. Hence skill is required of a wise person to decide whether to perform these acts in each situation.

The second question which might arise concerns the comparison of moral reasons with reasons of self-interest. How, it might be asked, can the two be compared without the intermediary of a common denominator in terms of which their relative significance can be compared? Curtis notes that utilitarians employ net utility as their common denominator and that others, like W.D. Ross, cash out everything of significance in terms of prima facie duty. However, Curtis does not believe that the perspective of wisdom requires a precise method of comparison which makes use of a formal common denominator. A wise person can take the relevant circumstances into account and arrive at a wise judgment without the benefit of such calculations. Wisdom gives one the ability to make these judgments without formal calculations, and hence Curtis rests the full weight of making comparisons between moral reasons and reasons of self-interest upon the proper function of the perspective of wisdom.

When the comparison is made between moral reasons and reasons of self-interest, there are three possible outcomes. First, the perspective of moral wisdom will generate the conclusion that the moral reasons for action override the reasons of self-interest to refrain from acting. When this occurs, one ought, all things considered, to perform the act. Curtis states that since the reasons in favor of performing the act are moral reasons it follows that one morally ought to perform it. When the moral reasons for performing the act outweigh the reasons of self-interest in favor of omitting the act, therefore, the act is a 'moral duty' or 'morally required' of the agent (compare with Sidgwick's characterization of the duty of beneficence: "a positive duty to render, when occasion offers, such services as require either no sacrifice on our part or at least very much less in importance than the service rendered").[1] Curtis does not commit himself to the view that all moral duty is of this nature, but he does hold that one always has a moral duty to perform an act when the moral reasons for action outweigh the reasons of self-interest for inaction. And here it is important to bear in mind that the action for which one has moral reasons might itself consist in refraining from a particular course of action.

Second, the perspective of wisdom may discover that the reasons of self-interest for refraining from an act override the moral reasons in favor of performing it. This situation is precisely the opposite of the first possible outcome, and here Curtis states that the agent ought not, all things considered, perform the act. Despite the moral value of performing the act, the agent ought not perform it. Here the 'ought' in question is not a moral ought as is the case with the first outcome. Hence the agent does not have a moral duty to refrain from acting when the reasons of self-interest for refraining override the moral reasons for not refraining. Curtis's view is simply that refraining is what one ought to do, all things considered.

Curtis concedes that his view might initially seem "morally outrageous," but he is convinced that it is correct. Moreover, he believes that his view actually conforms to our ordinary beliefs:

> It corresponds to our ordinary and quite sensible belief that it is possible to go so far in self-sacrifice, even for the sake of a morally good end, as to be foolish. Aristotle taught us that foolish acts of morally inspired self-sacrifice are not morally good, however noble the motives of the agent.[2]

It is possible to press self-sacrifice to the point of being foolish, and when this occurs the agent can no longer be said to do that which is good or right.

Examples of this phenomenon are offered by Curtis in the following passage:

> For a wide variety of cases, Aristotle seems to have been right. All other things being equal, if I risk my life to keep a trivial promise, if I go deeply into debt to buy my girlfriend a new Mercedes (for moral reasons, of course), if I quit my excellent job to protest a minor social injustice on the part of my employer, no one would praise me for the "moral goodness" of my actions. On the contrary, everyone would rightly say that I had been a damned fool to do these things.[3]

It is one thing to risk my life for the sake of protecting the lives of others, but risking my life for the sake of keeping a trivial promise is foolhardy. However good or noble my intentions, it is not good to risk my life for something so insignificant. According to Curtis, it is not only something I need not do, it is something I ought not do. Likewise, I ought not go deeply into debt to buy my girlfriend a new Mercedes or quit my job to protest a minor injustice. In each case it is foolish to give precedence to moral reasons for acting over reasons of self-interest for not acting.

While there may be some disagreement over Curtis's choice of examples, I believe his basic point is correct. It is foolish automatically to give precendence to the moral reasons for acting over against the reasons of self-interest for refraining from action. Where the moral reasons for acting are clearly seen to be trivial in comparison with the reasons of self-interest for refraining, it may be foolish to take action. Curtis describes this situation as one which appears morally outrageous at first glance, but upon closer examination his position is quite reasonable. There are times when the perspective of wisdom will identify situations in which the reasons of self-interest in favor of refraining from action will clearly override the moral reasons in favor of action. And when this happens, taking action does not seem to be the wisest alternative. As Knut Tranoy puts it, "If you give a million dollars to a home for deprived orphans you are a benefactor; if you give the same sum of money to a home for red-haired, ageing unmarried daughters of federal employees you are likely to be called an eccentric."[4]

Third, the perspective of wisdom may discover that neither the moral reasons for action override the reasons of self-interest for inaction nor do the latter override the former. In this situation there is no clear reason for action over against inaction, nor any clear reason for inaction over action. Therefore, the principles established by Curtis do not apply: the agent neither ought to act nor ought not to act. There is no "best thing to do, all things considered"; whether the agent acts or fails to act, the agent is not acting contrary to what Curtis calls the "all-things-considered 'ought'."[5]

At this point Curtis introduces the concept of supererogation. For he believes that the perspective of wisdom allows a place for supererogation precisely in situations where neither the moral reasons for acting nor the reasons of self-interest against it are found to be clearly overridden:

> A man who does something for a moral reason which has roughly equal weight with his countervailing reason of self-interest has performed a supererogatory act. Such an action would not be a moral duty. . . . But such an action would nevertheless be morally good, and deserving of praise, because it is performed for a moral reason—a reason which is not overridden by an available reason of self-interest to the contrary.[6]

In outcomes of the first type, an agent has a moral duty to act, and hence acting cannot qualify as an act of supererogation. In outcomes of the second type, it would be foolish for the agent to act. Presumably, then, in outcomes of the second type an agent who acts does not deserve praise. If so, there is no possibility of performing an act of supererogation. But in outcomes of the third type things are different. Here there is the possibility of performing acts which are both praiseworthy and fulfil no moral duty, and hence there is the possibility of supererogation. (Curtis does not seem to acknowledge that an act cannot be blameworthy to omit in order to qualify as an act of supererogation, but I shall ignore this complication for the purposes of the present discussion.)

Actually, Curtis affirms the stronger principle that acting in outcomes of the third type always qualifies as supererogation. Whenever the moral reasons in favor of acting are found to be roughly equal to the reasons of self-interest in favor of not acting, acting is supererogatory. In such a situation it is praiseworthy to act, for one is acting in accordance with the moral reasons which favor action. Moreover, one's acting falls outside the realm of duty since one is not acting in outcomes of the first type. Accordingly, Curtis believes that acting in outcomes of the third type invariably qualifies as supererogation. As he sees it, supererogation begins and ends at the point where "the cost or risk deliberately incurred by the agent is roughly as significant as the moral value of the end."[7]

It might be objected that a person in an outcome of the third type can conceivably act with evil motives, and on Curtis's account the act turns out to be supererogatory. Suppose I donate money to a charity for the sole purpose of discrediting one of my adversaries who has not done so. Here there are moral reasons in favor of acting as well as reasons of self-interest in favor of not doing so (retaining possession of my funds), neither of which clearly overrides the other. By choosing to donate money, therefore, I appear to have performed an act of supererogation on Curtis's account, even though my motives for doing so are tainted.

However, in defense of Curtis, the objection fails to recognize that one's motives typically qualify as reasons of self-interest for acting or for not acting. Surely my desire to discredit my adversary is a reason of self-interest in favor of acting. Thus, in this example I have reasons of self-interest both in favor of acting and in favor of not acting. But it seems clear from the example that my reasons of self-interest in favor of donating money override my reasons of self-interest in favor of not doing so. I prefer discrediting my adversary to retaining possession of the money I donate to charity. And if this is so, my reasons of self-interest in favor of not donating money are effectively irrelevant, and the situation cannot rightly be described in terms of an outcome of the third type. Thus, this situation does not pose any obvious problems for the account Curtis offers. When there are moral reasons in favor of performing an act and a person performs the act for the wrong reasons, the situation does not qualify as an outcome of the third type. It is instead a situation in which one's moral reasons and reasons of self-interest are directed to the same course of action.

It is not always clear from Curtis's discussion whether or not the moral reasons in favor of acting are the agent's own moral reasons in favor of acting. Suppose a man whose family has recently been killed in an automobile accident desperately needs the friendship of others. Perhaps, then, there are moral reasons in favor of befriending him. But I may know nothing about the accident and befriend him just because I believe that befriending people brings them happiness. My reasons for acting (which are certainly moral reasons) are distinct from the moral reasons for befriending him which relate to his recent tragic loss.

Which set of moral reasons is relevant to the process of comparing with reasons of self-interest in the model described by Curtis? Although he does not address this issue, I will proceed on the assumption that what are relevant here are the agent's own moral reasons for acting. The perspective of wisdom is assigned the task of weighing the moral reasons for acting against the reasons of self-interest against acting, and this task can hardly be carried out with respect to moral reasons for action which are unknown to the agent and hence unavailable for examination by the perspective of wisdom. Thus, when one weighs the reasons against one another, one is presumably weighing what one believes to be the moral reasons in favor of acting against what one believes to be reasons of self-interest against acting.

The overall picture presented by Curtis can be illustrated by imagining a situation in which a woman is considering whether to risk her job by protesting a social injustice on the part of her employer. The moral reasons in favor of acting are the perceived benefits of protesting. Perhaps these perceived benefits are considerable; perhaps she knows from past experience that her employer is gravely concerned about social justice and will be highly responsive to correcting the inadvertent harm or suffering which is being caused by the present injustice. She may also know that the risk of losing her job is almost negligible. In such a case the moral reasons in favor of acting may to an overwhelming degree override the reasons of self-interest in not acting, and according to Curtis's principles she has a moral duty to protest the social injustice. Because the perceived benefits are so significant in relation to the perceived risk of losing her job, it is her moral duty to take action.

Imagine, on the other hand, that her employer is known to be highly vindictive toward those who criticize him. Further imagine that the social injustice in question is highly trivial: the labels of one of the firm's products might be mildly offensive to members of an exotic religious cult. She knows it is highly likely that she will lose her job if she protests this social injustice, and she knows that her chances of finding another job are highly questionable. In this set of circumstances her reasons of self-interest in favor of not protesting clearly outweigh the moral reasons in favor of protesting. Consequently, protesting would not qualify as an act of supererogation. It would be foolhardy of her to protest under these circumstances, and according to Curtis she ought not to do so.

Finally, imagine that there is no clear superiority of one set of reasons over against the other. She is concerned about a social injustice which is neither horrendous nor trivial. Perhaps she is concerned about a product defect which, although not hazardous to the safety or health of the product's users, is likely to impede the effective use of the product after a period of time. She is concerned that purchasers of the product get their money's worth, and she feels that she ought to voice her protest. Her employer is well aware of the defect and has made it clear that there are no plans to correct it, but she feels that protesting is still the ethical thing to do. She is not sure how her employer will react, and she feels that she may be taking a considerable risk. She has a good job and would be very unhappy to lose it.

Like many situations in real life, her moral reasons in favor of acting do not clearly override her reasons of self-interest in favor of not acting, nor do the latter clearly override the former. Curtis emphasizes that a person can frequently learn more about the situation so as to obtain clear guidance as to the wisest course of action, but sometimes additional information does not serve to break the stalemate. It may still be that no set of reasons clearly overrides the other, and Curtis believes that in these circumstances it is supererogatory to act in accord with the moral reasons supporting action. In the above example, then, it would be an act of supererogation to protest the social injustice. It is not her moral duty to protest, but it would be praiseworthy of her to do so. In general, it is for Curtis always an act of supererogation to act in accord with the moral reasons for acting when they are perceived to be of roughly equal weight with the reasons of self-interest for not acting.

2. MORAL REASONS, REASONS OF SELF-INTEREST, AND SUPEREROGATION

The model presented by Curtis is attractive in its simplicity. There are three categories, depending upon whether the moral reasons (for acting) override reasons of self-interest, are overridden by reasons of self-interest, or are roughly equal to reasons of self-interest. In the first case an agent has a moral duty to act, in the second case it is foolish to act and the agent ought to refrain, and in the third case it is supererogatory for the agent to act. The third of the categories is where Curtis feels that supererogation begins and ends, and hence it appears that for Curtis a necessary and sufficient condition for being an act of supererogation is acting in accordance with moral reasons in a situation where one's moral reasons for acting are roughly comparable to one's reasons of self-interest for not acting.

Those of an anti-supererogationist persuasion will find fault with this model on the grounds that the third of the categories should be assigned to moral duty. But among many of those who acknowledge that the category of the supererogatory is legitimate, I believe that the view defended by Curtis will strike a responsive chord. There is something intuitively appealing about the idea that the boundary between duty and supererogation is determined by the relative strength of moral reasons. When one sees that these reasons for acting are much stronger than one's reasons of self-interest for not acting, one has a moral duty to act. If the strength of the reasons is roughly equal, it is good and praiseworthy of one to act but one has no moral duty to do so. I believe that many people's ordinary intuitions about supererogation are captured by these ideas, and there is no denying that there is something plausible and appealing about the scheme Curtis defends.

Nevertheless, in this section I wish to raise some questions about this scheme. I shall begin be calling attention to acts of supererogation in which the cost to the agent is very great. In his discussion of Urmson's example in which a soldier throws himself upon a live grenade, Curtis adopts the view that the soldier is performing an act of supererogation if his act is intended to save the life of a comrade. Had the soldier thrown himself upon a live grenade for the sake of protecting government property, his act would qualify as foolhardy. In order to qualify as supererogatory his moral reasons for acting must be roughly comparable to his reasons of self-interest for not acting, and in the case at hand these reasons of self-interest are considerable.

Now imagine that the soldier falls upon a live grenade in order to save the lives of two comrades. No longer is it obvious that the costs and benefits are roughly equal, for it is now a question of sacrificing one life in order to save two lives. On the other hand, it is not obvious that the soldier's reasons of self-interest are clearly overridden by the moral reasons in favor of saving two lives. Curtis notes that there are no precise formulas available for deciding the relative importance of the reasons, and perhaps the perspective of wisdom will judge that sacrificing one's life for the sake of two comrades' lives still falls within the realm of supererogation.

However, as one increases the number of comrades' lives which can be saved by the sacrifice of one's own life, it begins to look more and more dubious that the costs and benefits are roughly equal:

> But what if a soldier lays down his life to save a dozen other lives? Or a hundred? . . . At some point, as the moral value of the end increases, such an act begins to look like a moral duty.[8]

At some point it is necessary to concede that the moral reasons in favor of sacrificing one's life clearly override one's reasons of self-interest in favor of not doing so. And when one reaches this point, Curtis's model dictates that one has a moral duty to sacrifice one's life. When it a question of saving the life of one comrade, it is morally permissible for the soldier not to fall upon the grenade; but when it is a question of saving a dozen lives, or perhaps one hundred lives, Curtis believes it is no longer an act of supererogation to fall upon the grenade. At some point the sacrifice of one's life passes from the realm of supererogation to the realm of moral duty.

Curtis emphasizes that the precise location of this point is difficult to determine, and reasonable people might arrive at differing judgments concerning it. In some cases it might be extremely difficult to know exactly where supererogation ends and moral duty begins. But if the cost or risk of an agent's act is held constant while the moral reasons in favor of acting increase, one sooner or later reaches a point at which one has a moral duty to act in situations of this type. Again, it is supererogatory for one to act when and only when the moral reasons for acting are roughly equal to the reasons of self-interest in favor of not acting; when the former become disproportionately large in relation to the latter, it is no longer morally permissible for one to refrain from acting.

Is Curtis correct in thinking of moral duty as dependent upon the relative weights of the moral reasons for acting and the reasons of self-interest in favor of refraining? One might raise questions about his justification for operating with a notion of duty which relies upon making comparisons of this nature. To some it might not be evident that whether or not the soldier has a moral duty to throw himself upon the grenade should depend upon the number of lives which can be saved. To some the question of whether the soldier has a moral duty to perform this act might be "a matter of principle" having no connection with the number of lives to be saved or any sort of comparison between the costs and benefits of acting. To some philosophers moral duty might be conceived as something which has no connection at all with the comparison between the costs and benefits of taking action.

Here it is not my aim to attack the basic conception of duty with which Curtis is operating (I am more in sympathy with his view than with the view that moral duty has no connection at all with a comparison between the costs and benefits of acting.) Instead, I shall go back to his claim that a soldier in Urmson's example can have a moral duty to sacrifice his life when the perceived number of lives which can be saved becomes large enough. Suppose, then, that the number of soldiers in the immediate vicinity of the live grenade is large enough to judge on Curtis's principles that the soldier really does have a moral duty to perform the act of self-sacrifice. By parity of reasoning the same judgment can be made with respect to other soldiers who are in a position to throw themselves upon the grenade. Perhaps each one of the soldiers is in a position to perform an act of self-sacrifice for the sake of the others. According to the view proposed by Curtis it then follows that each of the soldiers has a moral duty to fall upon the live grenade.

It is here that Curtis's model yields consequences which are highly questionable. It is one thing to discover that only one soldier is in a position to fall upon the grenade and to judge that the soldier has a moral duty to perform this act of self-sacrifice, but it is another thing altogether to discover that many soldiers are in a position to save the lives of their comrades and to judge that each has a moral duty to do so. To say that each of several soldiers has a duty to fall upon the live grenade is to say that each ought morally to fall upon the live grenade, and this is the case regardless of what each of the others does.

Thus, the conclusion seems inescapable that they all ought to do so. There is no provision for nullifying duties in the event that another soldier falls upon the grenade. If you sacrifice your life by falling upon the grenade before I do it follows that I am guilty of having failed to discharge my duty, and the same is true of other soldiers in a position to fall upon the grenade.

I conclude that in some circumstances Curtis's model assigns a role to moral duty which is unacceptably inflated. Perhaps a soldier who is the only one in a position to throw himself upon the grenade has a duty to do so if a large number of lives can be saved (of course, even this claim is debatable). But to say the same about each and every soldier who is in a position to do so seems to commit one to the conclusion that they all ought to do so, and this is a conclusion which is patently unacceptable. Falling upon the live grenade to save the lives of their comrades is not something which they can jointly do, as it is impossible for all of them to do this, and by the principle that ought implies can it follows that it is not something which they all ought to do.

To state without qualification that one has a moral duty to act whenever the moral reasons for acting override the reasons of self-interest in favor of refraining seems extravagant, and it is not simply in acts of heroic self-sacrifice that this is evident. Curtis's model seems to generate large numbers of moral duties in ordinary situations which likewise seem questionable: On my way to the hardware store I notice a nursing home. It occurs to me that it is in my power to stop and spend several hours bringing cheer to dozens of very lonely residents, and I realize that the cost to me is quite minimal (I can wait a week to repair the doorbell in my house). The moral reasons in favor of stopping and visiting with the residents significantly override the reasons of self-interest in favor of going to the hardware store and subsequently repairing my doorbell. Is it my moral duty to do so?

No doubt many, among them anti-supererogationists, will agree that it is indeed my moral duty to stop and spend time visiting the residents. And it is indisputable that moral duty is sometimes determined by whether one is able to realize great benefits to others through a small cost to oneself. But it is by no means evident that visiting the residents is a moral duty for me and not an act of supererogation. Contrary to the principles set forth by Curtis, it seems that it is sometimes possible to perform acts of supererogation even when the moral reasons for acting significantly override the reasons of self-interest in favor of refraining. To judge that it is morally forbidden of me to proceed to the hardware store instead of visiting the residents seems excessively harsh, and the same is true of many other instances in ordinary life where the benefits to others clearly outweigh the costs to oneself.

The model proposed by Curtis captures an intuition about moral duty which seems correct. Other things being equal, one is more likely to have a moral duty to perform an act as the moral reasons in favor of acting become more significant; and, other things being equal, one is more likely to have a moral duty to perform an act as the reasons of self-interest in favor of refraining from it become less significant. Moreover, other things being equal, one is especially more likely to have a duty to perform an act when the moral reasons for acting become more significant *in relation to* the reasons of self-interest in favor of refraining. But the principles which are operative in Curtis's model embody this intuition in the form of an inviolable rule, and this is where problems arise. It is unrealistic to insist that one always has a moral duty to act when the benefits of acting clearly override the costs. There are other factors to be taken into account, and the model proposed by Curtis fails to make provision for these.

Up to this point it has been my suggestion that some acts which Curtis's model assigns to moral duty are arguably acts of supererogation, and hence questions can be raised about the boundary between the realm of moral duty and the realm of supererogation which is assigned by the model. I shall now go on to suggest that questions can also be raised concerning the boundary between the realm of the supererogatory and the realm of the foolish.

Earlier it was shown that, according to Curtis's model, it is foolish to perform an act when the reasons of self-interest in favor of refraining override the moral reasons in favor of acting. Curtis employs several examples to illustrate acts which would be foolish to perform in light of the large costs or risks to the agent in comparison with the benefits realized by performing them. Thus, it is foolish to throw oneself upon a live grenade in order to protect government property. No doubt many would maintain that it is immoral to perform this act, but it is at least evident that it is highly imprudent to do so. Curtis contends that when the reasons of self-interest in favor of refraining from an act override the moral reasons in favor of performing the act, one ought not to perform the act. Perhaps in special cases one ought morally not to perform the act, but in general the 'ought' Curtis has in mind here is something along the lines of a prudential 'ought'. When one ought not perform an act in this sense, it is foolish for one to perform it.

Curtis argues that acts which fit this description cannot qualify as acts of supererogation. Some writers have emphasized that acts of this nature fail to qualify as acts of supererogation because their performance constitutes a violation of one's duties to oneself. Just as I have various duties to bring about or preserve good on behalf of others, so I have various duties (at least of the prima facie variety) aimed at bringing about or preserving my own welfare. Other things being equal, I have a duty to myself to safeguard my own life, my good health, my job, and so forth. I have a duty not to place my life, my health, or my job in jeopardy, unless I have a conflicting duty of such magnitude that my duty to myself is overridden. Hence, when my duties to myself are not overridden, it cannot possibly be an act of supererogation to act contrary to my self-interest in situations where my self-interest is protected by such duties. To do that which is morally forbidden cannot be morally praiseworthy, and hence it cannot be supererogatory.

In Curtis's discussion, however, no appeal is made to duties which moral agents have toward themselves. He simply appeals to Aristotle's belief that foolish acts of self-sacrifice are not morally good, and he observes that the performance of such foolish acts is not deserving of moral praise. We do not, he observes, praise from the moral point of view what we condemn as foolish or unwise. And if the performances of these acts are not morally praiseworthy, they obviously cannot qualify as acts of supererogation. Thus, it is never supererogatory to perform an act when the cost or risk to oneself significantly outweighs the moral benefits of acting.

There is something intuitively appealing in Aristotle's basic intuition, although the anti-supererogationist may disagree, and Curtis is correct in separating the realm of the supererogatory from the realm of the foolish. Of course, one who is concerned only with the realization of one's self-interest might have no hesitation in describing many or most acts of supererogation as foolish. To such a person it is foolish to make sacrifices for the sake of others (and this is perhaps the basis for St. Paul's advice to become foolish in I Corinthians 4:10). But in reality it is not supererogatory to do that which is genuinely foolish, for it is not deserving of praise to do so. On this point I shall not take issue with Curtis.

Nevertheless, the method by which Curtis separates the realm of the supererogatory from the realm of the foolish is open to criticism. Again, if the moral reasons in favor of acting are overridden by the reasons of self-interest in favor of not acting, Curtis's model designates acting as foolish. If the two sets of reasons are roughly comparable, his model designates acting as supererogatory. And, as before, my concern is that his model is overly simplistic.

Suppose that I pour an enormous amount of time and energy into attempting to correct a minor injustice. The black pastor of a small rural church in South Africa is described in a newspaper article as sympathetic to apartheid, and I am convinced that the article has confused the pastor of one small rural church with the pastor of another. When I contact the author of the article, I am told that the one has indeed been confused with the other. However, the newspaper does not judge that the issue is of sufficient importance to warrant a printed correction. In response, I spend hundreds of hours trying to organize a letter writing campaign aimed at changing the minds of the editors. My feeling is that an injustice has occurred, and as a matter of principle I wish to see the record set straight. In the end my massive efforts achieve nothing, for very few people care whether the record is set straight, but I rest assured that I have done everything I can in my failed attempt.

Many similar examples can be described in which a person spends a great deal of time and effort or undergoes personal insult or injury (recall the example of the political terrorists in chapter two) to achieve an end whose actual benefits are very minimal. Often it is sheer foolishness to embark upon these courses of action. However, the question is whether it is always sheer foolishness to undertake this expenditure of time and effort, for in some instances the actual benefits which accrue, whether perceived or real, are of little concern in upholding a certain ideal or principle. When a person makes considerable personal sacrifices for the sake of upholding an ideal or principle whose actual perceived benefits are minimal or nonexistent, it appears that these sacrifices will invariably be judged as foolish by the model. But is this always the correct verdict?

It might be suggested that Curtis's model does do justice to these situations, contrary to initial appearances, if it is recognized that the ideal or principle for which one is acting constitutes a powerful moral reason in favor of acting. In the example of the inaccurate newspaper article it initially appears that the moral reasons in favor of my letter writing campaign are greatly outweighed by my reasons of self-interest. However, if my intense desire is construed as one of the moral reasons in favor of my subsequent action, it is possible that my reasons of self-interest in favor of not acting no longer override these moral reasons. For there is a sense in which I regard acting for the sake of principle to be worth all of the trouble and effort which it demands of me. According to this suggestion, then, my letter writing campaign may turn out to be an act of supererogation after all. My moral reasons in favor of acting turn out to be sufficiently weighty that the act is not classified as foolhardy.

Unfortunately, one who follows this suggestion is faced with the prospect of countenancing large numbers of obviously foolhardy acts as acts of supererogation. The woman who risks losing her job in order that the members of an exotic religious cult not be offended by certain labels of her firm's products might act out of a desire to prevent injustice which is so intense as to regard the risk as worth taking. And if this intense desire is construed as a moral reason in favor of her risking her job, it follows that it is supererogatory, not foolhardy, for her to take the risk. Similarly, virtually anyone who takes great risks for the sake of some dubious principle can in like manner be portrayed as performing an act of supererogation. But surely this is not the manner in which Curtis intends the model he is proposing to be understood.

The underlying problem is that the boundary between supererogatory behavior and foolish behavior seems to be more complicated than what can be spelled out in terms of a simple formula. Sometimes it is an act of supererogation to go through a great deal of personal sacrifice for the sake of upholding a principle, even when the perceived benefits are minimal or nonexistent. Some might be inclined to doubt whether my letter writing campaign in the inaccurate newspaper article example is an act of supererogation, as opposed to an act of foolishness, but I believe there are many plausible examples of supererogatory acts in which the moral reasons in favor of acting are clearly overridden by reasons of self-interest in favor of refraining. There is no straightforward way to decide which principles or ideals for which people make personal sacrifices are foolish and which are not. Whether a personal sacrifice for the sake of a principle or ideal qualifies as an act of supererogation depends upon more factors or considerations than the mere question of whether the costs are roughly equal to the benefits.

I conclude that the boundary between acts of supererogation and acts of foolishness is more complex than Curtis's model leads one to imagine. It is reasonable to believe that the performance of an act is more likely to qualify as foolhardy as the cost or risk to the agent is increased, other things being equal. And it reasonable to believe that it is more likely to qualify as foolhardy as the perceived benefits to be realized are decreased, other things being equal. Moreover, it is quite reasonable to believe that it is more likely to qualify as foolhardy as the reasons of self-interest in favor of refraining become more significant *in relation to* the moral reasons in favor of acting. However, to embody these intuitions in a hard and fast rule generates a criterion which is unrealistic. Just as Curtis's model provides a boundary between duty and supererogation in a way which is overly simplistic, the same is true with regard to the boundary it provides between the foolhardy and the supererogatory.

There is one final respect in which Curtis's model does not seem to do justice to describing the true nature of supererogation. In an earlier chapter it was argued that the making of promises can qualify as supererogatory. When I promise to perform a future act on your behalf, my act of making the promise can fulfil the conditions required to qualify as an act of supererogation. However, my performing the promised act on a future occasion is almost certainly not an act of supererogation, for promising to perform the act creates a prima facie duty on my part to perform the act (and even if this duty is overridden by another duty, my performing the act cannot be supererogatory for the reason that it is then a violation of another duty). It is the making of the promise which is an act of supererogation, not the subsequent performance of the promised act.

Typically, the act of promising to perform a future act is something which involves very little cost or risk to the agent in and of itself. Of course, one can imagine dramatic instances to the contrary, such as the promise of marriage to a person whom one's parents find intolerable made in the presence of these parents. Occasionally the very act of making a promise will be costly, and in these cases an agent may have considerable reasons of self-interest to refrain from making the promise. But in most instances it is the promised act whose performance has the potential of involving a cost to the agent. Promising to mow your lawn while you are vacationing involves very little effort, but mowing your lawn involves considerable effort.

The criterion provided by Curtis allows an act to qualify as supererogatory when and only when the moral reasons for acting are roughly comparable to the reasons of self-interest in favor of refraining from action. And it is hard to see how this criterion can admit into the ranks of the supererogatory more than just a certain proportion of instances in which people make promises. The problem is that the perceived benefits to others which result from making a promise typically outweigh the cost to the agent. There may be considerable costs involved in performing the promised act, but it is not evident that these costs have any bearing upon whether the act of making the promise is to count as an act of supererogation. As stated, Curtis's criterion seems to yield the consequence that only certain cases of making promises turn out to qualify as acts of supererogation.

Of course, it is open for Curtis to argue that the benefits generated by the very act of making a promise are often considerably less than the benefits generated by the performance of the promised act. Suppose I promise to redecorate your house at no charge for my labor during your three month vacation abroad. Assuming that I actually discharge the promise that I make, it is obvious that the benefits accruing to you are far greater than the benefits accruing to you as the result of hearing me promise to do so. Thus, it appears that the minimal costs involved in the act of making this promise are balanced by the minimal benefits realized by your hearing me make this promise, and hence it appears that my act of making the promise qualifies as supererogatory after all.

Nevertheless, it is far from clear that the costs and benefits associated with my act of making the promise are roughly equal in examples of this type. No doubt the benefits generated by my redecorating efforts greatly overshadow the benefits generated by my act of promising. But these latter benefits should not be minimized. For the making of this promise may relieve you from the considerable trouble of making the arrangements for redecorating your house prior to your three months abroad. The actual carrying out of this promise will result in enormous benefits, but the making of this promise is likewise of great benefit to you. For suppose you go to the trouble of making these complicated arrangements, and after your departure I cancel these arrangements and do the work myself. You may be grateful for my having saved you a great deal of money by having done the work myself, but it would have been far easier for you if I had taken the slight trouble to announce my intentions in advance.

In this example my promising to redecorate your house seems to benefit you to a degree which clearly outweighs the costs to myself, and this is true in spite of these benefits being overshadowed by the benefits which the redecorating itself brings about. Thus, the point remains that certain instances of promise making fail to qualify as genuine acts of supererogation in Curtis's scheme. The costs involved in the mere act of making a promise are typically so trivial as to be easily overridden by the benefits realized by the act, and whenever this situation occurs the act cannot qualify as supererogatory.

3. CONCLUSION

The theory proposed by Curtis embodies a number of commonly accepted intuitions about duty, supererogation, and foolhardy behavior. Moral duty arises in human life when there are pressing moral reasons for performing an act (where the performance of this act may actually consist in deliberately refraining from a course of action) and correspondingly insignificant reasons of self-interest not to. This explains why people have moral duties to come to the aid of accident victims, drowning swimmers, and the like, unless doing so forces them to risk their own lives. It is often foolish, on the other hand, to perform acts in which the risks or costs to oneself are large in relation to the insignificant benefits which are perceived to result. Curtis follows Aristotle in noting that such foolish acts are not morally good, and he rightly concludes that acts of supererogation cannot be foolish in this sense. Thus, the designation of supererogation is reserved for situations in which the costs and perceived benefits are roughly equal.

In this chapter I have emphasized that whether an act qualifies as supererogatory is largely determined by the relative strength of these moral reasons for acting over against the reasons of self-interest for refraining. Here Curtis captures a key ingredient in our ordinary intuitions about supererogation. On the other hand, I have argued that there is more to the concept of supererogation than what can be captured within the confines of the model he sets forth. Whether an act qualifies as an act of supererogation cannot be totally reduced to a question of the relative strength of the costs and benefits of performing it. In particular, it is sometimes a matter of acting in accord with principle that an agent is willing to endure great personal sacrifices for the sake of an end product with few, if any, real (or even perceived) benefits. In some instances it is foolhardy to make sacrifices of this nature, but it is a mistake to judge that it is inevitably foolhardy to make such sacrifices. There are more factors which enter into the determination of whether it is supererogatory to perform an act than the mere question of costs and benefits.

At the other end of the spectrum, I have suggested that one does not inevitably have a moral duty to perform an act when the moral reasons for acting significantly outweigh the reasons of self-interest for refraining from action. Consequently, it is possible that acting in such situations is supererogatory. It sometimes happens that agents performing acts of supererogation bring enormous benefits to others at very little cost to themselves. Again, it is not strictly a matter of costs and benefits.

Perhaps the theory proposed by Curtis can best be approached as a model which allows one to make a preliminary approximation as to whether a given act qualifies as supererogatory. While the model lacks the flexibility to take into account all of the relevant factors and hence cannot plausibly be viewed as providing a totally adequate criterion for supererogation, it is useful to know that the performance of an act is a prime candidate for the status of supererogation when the perceived costs and perceived benefits are roughly equal. When the moral reasons in favor of acting override or are overridden by the reasons of self-interest in favor of refraining, it is less likely that the act qualifies as supererogatory. I have argued that it is still possible for an act to qualify when the one set of reasons overrides the other, but it is reasonable to regard Curtis's model as providing one of the key tests for determining whether it is to be classified as an act which fulfils a duty, an act of supererogation, or an act of foolishness.

Chapter 8

SUPEREROGATION AND OFFENCE

In a previous chapter acts of offence are characterized as acts whose performance is morally blameworthy, though not morally forbidden, and whose omission is not morally praiseworthy. It has sometimes been noted that supererogation and offence stand to one another in a type of symmetric or mirror image relationship. While acts of supererogation are praiseworthy to perform, acts of offence are blameworthy to perform. While one fulfils no duty by performing an act of supererogation, one fulfils no duty by refraining from an act of offence (an act is forbidden just in case one fulfils duty by refraining from it). And while it is not blameworthy to omit an act of supererogation, neither is it praiseworthy to omit an act of offence.

Chisholm describes offence as a "kind of complement" to supererogation and seems to have initially become aware of offence through its status as a logical counterpart to supererogation. The creation of a place for supererogation in a formal scheme (such as the one described in chapter five) will likely create a complementary place for offence. If it is possible for an act to satisfy the requirements to qualify as an act of supererogation, it seems reasonable to believe that the situation is no different in the case of offence.

182   Beyond the Call of Duty

Although supererogation and offence are defined as though they are mirror image counterparts of one another, the two concepts are in reality not nearly as symmetrical as they initially appear. On the basis of their respective definitions one might expect that every characteristic of supererogation is neatly reflected in a counterpart characteristic of offence. In this chapter I will argue that this is by no means the case. The one concept is by no means a perfect mirror image of the other, and the relationship between supererogation and offence is considerably more subtle than is suggested by their respective definitions. In the course of the discussion it will become evident that this asymmetry can have considerable ramifications for normative ethics.

1. The Nature of Offence

In chapter two a brief reference was made to Chisholm's characterization of supererogation in his article "Supererogation and Offence: A Conceptual Scheme for Ethics" as "That which is good but not obligatory." According to Chisholm, a person who seeks advice whether to perform an act of supererogation may appropriately be told, "You ought to, but you don't have to" (where the 'ought' in question is not understood as moral obligation). It is good for someone to perform an act of supererogation, but the person does not have to perform it. Chisholm then asks whether it would ever be appropriate to offer someone the advice, "You ought not to, but you may."[1] Is it ever appropriate to advise someone that, although a certain act is bad to perform, nevertheless the person may perform it?

In his subsequent paragraph Chisholm makes clear that he answers this question in the affirmative. There are times at which it is appropriate to advise moral agents that a bad act is nevertheless permissible.

> A system of moral concepts which provides a place for what is good but not obligatory, should also provide a place for what is bad but not forbidden. For if there is such a thing as 'nonobligatory well-doing' then it is plausible to suppose that there is also such a thing as 'permissive ill-doing'. There is no term in moral literature, so far as I know, which has been used to designate just this latter class of actions; I shall refer to them as 'offences'.[2]

Chisholm maintains that it would be a mistake to identify the offensive with deviltry or villainy. Some acts of offence may qualify as villainous or diabolical, but it is important to recognize that others are trifling or insignificant. Just as a favor or an act of courtesy can be both trifling and supererogatory, so a disfavor or act of discourtesy can be trifling and offensive.

An example of a trifling act of offence, according to Chisholm, is failing to return a handkerchief. An example of a villainous or heinous offence is described as follows:

> Suppose A knows concerning B, whom A dislikes, that the loss of B's employment would result in great tragedy for B and his family; that there is another man, C, who could do B's work but no more satisfactorily than B does it; and that B's employer, even if he knew the foregoing, would replace B by C if he thought that C were available. One might plausibly argue that, if A were deliberately to bring the availability of C to the attention of B's employer, his act would be permissible but at the same time heinous and inhuman.[3]

In this example A is in a position to cause B to be replaced by an equally competent man C by informing B's employer of C's availability. Because such an act is known by A to end up causing great tragedy for B and his family, the act is heinous and inhuman. However, according to Chisholm, it is also morally permissible; A has no moral obligation to refrain from informing B's employer of C's availability.

To some it may not be clear how to envision the precise relationship between the category of the offensive and the category of the forbidden. Chisholm describes this relationship as similar to the relationship between sins which are venial and those which are mortal. "A venial sin is, literally, a sin or misdeed which may be *pardoned*, or, as we might now say, *excused*."[4] One can be pardoned or excused for committing a venial sin, since, according to Thomas Aquinas, a person who sins venially neither does what the law forbids nor refrains from doing what the law requires. It is not contrary to the moral law to commit a venial sin, and hence it is not a mortal sin. On the other hand, it is not good to commit a venial sin. According to Thomas Aquinas, a person who commits a venial sin acts outside the law through failing to observe the mode of reason which the law intends.[5] Perhaps the idea is that the intent of the moral law is both to show us what we must not do and to point us in the direction of doing what is good. A person who commits a venial sin does not do what the law forbids, but neither does the person follow in the direction of the good toward which the law points. Hence there is a real sense in which the person has not acted in accord with the intent of the law; that person has failed to observe the intent or spirit of the moral law.

Chisholm does not hold that the relationship between the offensive and the forbidden is exactly like the relationship between venial and mortal sins, nor does he describe offenses as sins, but he does believe the analogy is helpful. To violate the strict requirements of duty is to do that which is forbidden, and it is always blameworthy to violate these requirements. However, the category of the blameworthy extends beyond the formal violation of duty. Just as Thomas Aquinas believes that sin extends beyond a strict violation of the moral law, so one can act in a morally blameworthy manner without actually violating duty. One who has perfectly observed the strict requirements of moral duty can still be deserving of moral blame.

From the foregoing discussion it may appear that Chisholm has neglected to characterize acts of offence in such a way that it can never be praiseworthy to refrain from them. His characterization of them in "Supererogation and Offence: A Conceptual Scheme for Ethics" as 'permissive ill-doing' captures only two of the three conditions, and hence he appears to conflate acts of offence with what I have called acts of quasi-offence. However, his characterization of offence in a later discussion (coauthored with Ernest Sosa), "Intrinsic Preferability and the Problem of Supererogation," remedies this difficulty. Here he emphasizes that the non-performance of an act of supererogation is not morally bad, while the non-performance of an act of offence is not morally good.[6] While it is fairly clear that being morally good and being morally praiseworthy are not precisely the same, it is safe to assume that one who refrains from an act of offence is not, in the opinion of Chisholm and Sosa, doing that which is praiseworthy. Thus, I shall assume that for all practical purposes the characterizations of supererogation and offence which Chisholm and Sosa are working with are the same as described in chapter five.

In earlier portions of the discussion I have spoken frequently of the anti-supererogationists, those who have resisted the idea that acts of supererogation are possible for human moral agents to perform. It is not hard to imagine those of an anti-supererogationist persuasion taking an equally skeptical position regarding the possibility of performing acts of offence. For if one is convinced that there can be no praiseworthy acts outside the boundaries of duty, one is likely to hold that there can be no blameworthy acts outside the boundaries of the forbidden. After all, the forbidden is the realm of what one has a duty to avoid. Hence, a person who is inclined to think of the category of duty as having boundaries so wide as to eclipse the possibility of supererogatory acts is likely to think of the category of the forbidden as having boundaries so wide as to eclipse the possibility of offensive acts. Moreover, it is possible that some who acknowledge that acts of supererogation are possible will fail to acknowledge that acts of offence are possible (more on this point in the next section). At any rate, although the concept of offence has seldom been discussed in this context, it is likely that many will find themselves skeptical that there can be acts of offence in human life.

For this reason it is possible to imagine Chisholm's examples being greeted with a spirit of skepticism. If A proceeds to inform B's employer of C's availability, then A is taking an action which he knows will result in great tragedy for B and his family. Moreover, if A performs this act, he is apparently doing so out of an evil motive (because he dislikes B). It is easy to imagine some arguing that such a course of action is a violation of A's moral duty. Perhaps the idea is that people have a moral duty to refrain from performing acts which bring great harm or hardship to others when it is motivated by sheer dislike of the victim, and hence it is morally forbidden for A to inform B's employer of C's availability. In this way it is possible to imagine one agreeing with Chisholm that A's act is morally blameworthy, disagreeing with Chisholm that A's act is not morally forbidden, and hence being unable to accept Chishom's verdict that A's act is an act of offence.

In "Intrinsic Preferability and the Problem of Supererogation" Chisholm and Sosa provide another example of an offensive act which is also villainous. In this example an industrialist, whose business is already flourishing, develops an advertising strategy which is calculated to drive a minor competitor out of business. Here the industrialist is attempting to "win without actually cheating."[7] According to Chisholm and Sosa he is acting in a manner which is morally blameworthy, but his act stops short of being wrong or morally forbidden. In the same article the authors provide an example of an offensive act in the form of a minor discourtesy: taking too long in a restaurant when others are known to be waiting. They observe that most people feel they have a right to perform such acts, but nevertheless these acts are morally offensive.

But here too it is not difficult to imagine objections arising. On the one hand, it may be felt that Chisholm and Sosa are overly harsh in their judgments. To some it might not be evident that either the industrialist or the people lingering at their tables deserve any moral condemnation. Perhaps it will be maintained that one need make no apologies for attempting to win in the game of free enterprise, even when one's goal is to drive another out of business, or forcing others to wait longer for tables. Perhaps it will even be felt that it would be supererogatory for the industrialist to cancel the advertising campaign and supererogatory for the people in the restaurant to vacate their tables for the sake of those waiting. This, in fact, seems to be the position taken by I.L. Humberstone (that it is supererogatory to omit an act which would be both permissible and blameworthy to perform).[8] A less extreme version of this position is that, while these acts are blameworthy to perform, they are nevertheless praiseworthy to refrain from performing. On this view they are acts of quasi-offence, not offence.

Nevertheless, it is easy to imagine others maintaining that Chisholm and Sosa are overly lenient in their verdicts concerning these examples. On this line of objection, a prosperous industrialist who attempts to drive his small competitor out of business is not only villainous, as the authors grant, but is violating his moral duty. It is not enough to describe this behavior as morally blameworthy; it is a sheer failure to fulfil one's moral duty to treat others with decency and respect. And the same point applies to those waiting for tables. People who linger at their tables after having completed their meal fail to treat those who are known to be waiting with decency and respect; hence they too stand in violation of their moral duty. Regarding Chisholm's example of the handkerchief, the moral duty in question might be identified as returning articles to their rightful owner. Thus, when I fail to return a handkerchief, I violate that duty.

In each of these examples the objection is that Chisholm and Sosa have failed to recognize that moral duty is violated. They have failed to recognize that the industrialist has a moral duty to refrain from an advertising campaign calculated to drive a small competitor out of business; that the people at tables have a moral duty (when their meal is finished) to allow others to be seated; and that people have a moral duty to return articles to their rightful owners. It is not hard to imagine, in fact, that this line of objection can be made with respect to any example of an offence which Chisholm and Sosa are able to propose. For whenever a moral agent engages in behavior which is truly blameworthy, it is open for one to object that the agent has a moral duty to refrain from such behavior. Just as an anti-supererogationist might maintain that there is no room for praiseworthy moral behavior outside the confines of duty, so here is the objection that there is no possibility of blameworthy behavior outside the confines of what duty forbids.

Chisholm is fully aware that some will reject the possibility of performing acts of offence for these reasons. In "The Ethics of Requirement" he describes supererogation and offence as having a place in a system of ethics which he describes as 'latitudinarian'.[9] Neither supererogation nor offence, he claims, has a place in a system of ethics such as strict utilitarianism. Very roughly, the idea is that in a system of strict utilitarianism an agent has a duty in every set of circumstances to act in such a manner as to bring about the greatest benefits (or some such thing) for the greatest number. And, as explained earlier, an agent who has a continual duty to maximize utility will have no opportunities to perform praiseworthy acts which the agent has no duty to perform; hence supererogation is ruled out in a system of strict utilitarianism. Offence is ruled out for similar reasons. If an agent at every moment has a duty to maximize utility, then every act the agent performs is either the fulfillment of duty or the violation of duty. Hence, on the assumption that it is never morally blameworthy to fulfil one's duty to maximize utility in a system of strict utilitarianism, it follows that every blameworthy act is at the same time the violation of duty. Consequently, no blameworthy act can fail to be forbidden.[10]

Thus, a system of ethics which accommodates supererogation and offence is more latitudinarian than alternative systems in which moral duty is assigned a wide expanse of the moral terrain. Chisholm illustrates the situation by imagining morality as having been laid down by a supreme lawgiver. A charitable lawgiver would create a system of ethics which accommodates supererogation and offence. It is in the power of the lawgiver to create a strict system of morality which places considerable moral demands on people at every moment. But, in what Chisholm says might itself be an act of supererogation (perhaps in some meta-system of ethics), the supreme lawgiver might fail to demand of moral agents as much as the lawgiver might. A strict lawgiver will create a system of morality which leaves no room for supererogation or offence, while a charitable lawgiver will create a relatively latitudinarian system. Given this model, it is clear that the opponents of supererogation and offence picture the lawgiver as having declined to perform an act of supererogation in the act of creating a system of morality for human moral agents, and the result is a system devoid of supererogation and offence.

2. Chisholm and Heyd on the Asymmetry of Supererogation and Offence

In the same passage where he designates systems accommodating supererogation and offence as latitudinarian, Chisholm makes the tantalizing comment that a system which accommodates offence is even more latitudinarian than one which accommodates supererogation alone. Thus, he believes that the addition of offence to a system which already accommodates supererogation results in a system even more latitudinarian than the original system.[11] Whether he believes the reverse is true (that the addition of supererogation to a system which accommodates offence results in an even more latitudinarian system) is not revealed. But surely there is something initially surprising about this claim, given Chisholm's earlier pronouncements that one who creates a place for supererogation in a formal system should also create a place for offence. These earlier pronouncements might lead one to believe that the concepts of supererogation and offence are neatly symmetrical in a way which makes it hard to see how a system can become more latitudinarian with both present than with one present and the other absent.

Regrettably, Chisholm supplies no reasons for his claim that systems accommodating offence plus supererogation are more latitudinarian than those accommodating only supererogation. Having made the claim, he gives no apparent clues as to his reasons for arriving at this belief. Nevertheless, it is a claim which has a certain degree of intuitive appeal. Suppose a supreme lawgiver, after a good deal of anguish, eventually decides to create a system of ethics which accommodates praiseworthy acts which are permissible (but not blameworthy) to omit. Will it now be a foregone conclusion that the lawgiver will likewise allow blameworthy acts which are permissible to perform (but not praiseworthy to omit), or will the decision to allow these acts strike the lawgiver as allowing still a further degree of permissibility into the system? Chisholm's suggestion is that the latter is the case, and I believe many would agree. The bounds of duty are restricted considerably by allowing acts of supererogation, but allowing for acts of offence seems to involve restricting the bounds of duty to a perceptively greater degree. On the basis of these considerations it appears that Chisholm's claim is quite plausible, but it remains to be discovered what the reasons underlying his claim might be.

Heyd observes that the idea that there is a logically neat symmetry between supererogation and offence has been a source of attraction to certain philosophers. The concept of offence has been discussed only sparingly in the literature, and where it is mentioned it is usually treated as a mirror image of supererogation (Mary Forrester is a case in point; she refers to supererogation simply as its "opposite number").[12] But just as Chisholm seems to sense that this neat symmetry is less real than it is apparent, Heyd finds that under close scrutiny this symmetry has no basis in reality.

The first argument given by Heyd for rejecting the idea that this symmetry can be maintained is that he finds it unreasonable to define acts of offence in such a way that they are not praiseworthy to omit. While acts of supererogation are not blameworthy to omit, it is not reasonable to conceive of acts of offence as not praiseworthy to omit, for, in his opinion, "Forbearance from doing evil is always a right thing to do."[13] Thus, Heyd believes that there are no acts which are both morally blameworthy to perform and not praiseworthy to omit; an act which is blameworthy to perform is inevitably praiseworthy to omit.

In effect, Heyd is expressing the desire to characterize acts of offence in the manner that acts of quasi-offence have been characterized in chapter five. Convinced that there are no blameworthy but permissible acts which are not praiseworthy to omit, he is suggesting that they be thought of as praiseworthy to omit, and hence that supererogation and offence are not perfect logical counterparts of one another.

Of course, Heyd's claim that there can be no acts which are both morally blameworthy to perform and not praiseworthy to omit can itself be challenged. His claim is based upon the argument that it is always right to forbear from what is evil, and surely it is reasonable to judge that one does that which is right when one refrains from evil acts. But it is far from evident that from this point one can conclude that it is always praiseworthy to refrain from performing a blameworthy act. Suppose a person is faced with the choice whether to return a borrowed article. The failure to do so, according to Chisholm's analysis, constitutes blameworthy behavior. But what if the person refrains from failing to do so? That is, what if the person returns the article? Is it correct to judge that the person has behaved in a praiseworthy manner? I see no reason whatever to conclude that the person has done anything worthy of moral praise. Returning borrowed articles is the right thing to do, but from this it does not follow that someone's returning a borrowed article is worthy of moral praise. In special circumstances it may be praiseworthy to return a borrowed article, as when someone overcomes a great temptation to keep or destroy the article, but in most ordinary circumstances it seems highly dubious to judge that there is anything inherently praiseworthy in one's returning it.

The second argument employed by Heyd to discredit the idea that there is a neat symmetry between supererogation and offence concerns Chisholm's claim that some offences are trifling and others are heinous or villainous. Just as acts of supererogation can range from the trivial to the heroic or saintly, Chisholm contends that acts of offence can range from the trivial to the villainous. Nevertheless, Heyd is not convinced that heinous or villainous acts of offence are possible. How, he asks, can an extremely bad or heinous act fail to be morally forbidden? It is far more difficult to find plausible examples of these acts than it is to find plausible examples of supererogatory acts which are saintly or heroic.

Chisholm's example of the informer is regarded by Heyd as particularly unconvincing. Recall the example in which A is in a position to inform B's employer of C's availability, knowing that the employer will replace B (whom A dislikes) with C and thereby bring great hardship to B's family. Heyd admits that A's informing B's employer of C's availability is not illegal; A is within his legal rights to take this course of action. But Heyd finds this course of action to be morally wrong and morally forbidden, for "A villain can never free himself from the grip of the moral law." Villainous behavior is not only morally blameworthy, it is morally forbidden. In order to fulfil his moral duty, it is necessary for A to refrain from informing B's employer of C's availability.

It might be argued that there are similar cases in which it is permissible for such an individual to be an informant, but Heyd believes that this argument is plausible only when the act of the informant is no longer villainous. Thus, even if one can alter Chisholm's example in such a way as to make the act of the informant morally permissible, this can be done only by removing the features of the example by which the act qualifies as villainous. According to Heyd, one cannot have it both ways. Either an act is morally forbidden or it is not. If it is forbidden it can qualify as villainous, and if it is not forbidden it cannot qualify as villainous. Once again, a villain can never free himself from the moral law. Thus, the neat symmetry between supererogation and offence breaks down. It is easy to find dramatic, nontrivial examples of supererogation, but the same is not true of offence. From Heyd's perspective it is dubious that one will find any clear, nontrivial examples of offence.

Heyd's third argument, in fact, raises doubts about whether one can even find clear trivial examples of permissive ill-doing. The example of taking too long in a restaurant when others are known to be waiting for tables, for instance, can be challenged as to whether it qualifies as an act of offence. Heyd observes that this act is not a grave moral sin; moreover, it is only mildly blameworthy, and one can easily be excused or forgiven for having performed it. But is it really morally permissible? Here Heyd appears to be genuinely uncertain, for there seems to be a bit of ambiguity in the meaning of the term 'permissible'. One can readily agree that there are bad acts which are morally permissible, but it is not clear to Heyd that one who affirms this claim is operating with a concept of permissibility which is the same as when one claims that acts of supererogation are permissible to omit.

> There are definitely cases in which a bad act is (morally) permissible (in the same way as there are good acts which are not obligatory), but it is doubtful whether a *morally* bad act may be permitted in the same way as a morally good act is not always obligatory.[14]

Thus, when one states that acts of offence are bad but permissible and that acts of supererogation are good but permissible to refrain from, it is doubtful that one is employing the concept of 'permissible' univocally.

In this passage Heyd is not attempting to argue that the example of taking too long in a restaurant definitely fails to qualify as an act of offence (he, in fact, seems to waver as to whether it actually qualifies). Rather, his point seems to be that one who judges this act to be morally permissible is appealing to a different sense of permissibility than one who judges that an act of supererogation is permissible to omit. Again, there initially appears to be a logical symmetry between supererogation and offence, and Heyd has now identified a third respect in which this symmetry can be challenged. The symmetry appears to rest upon an equivocation on what is permissible to do.

What is puzzling about Heyd's discussion is that he says very little about how the concept of permissibility is employed in the context of offence and how this differs from the way it is employed in the context of discussing supererogation. The only clue he appears to offer is his assertion that the proposition, 'You ought not to but you may' is consistent only if the terms 'ought' and 'may' are interpreted on "different levels," such as the moral and the legal.[15] Thus, it often makes sense to judge that one does something which one ought morally not to have done but which is legally permissible. Perhaps, then, people who affirm that acts of offence are possible have a tendency to think of permissibility in a legalistic fashion.

Here one might interpret Heyd as suggesting that the view that acts of offence are possible rests upon a confusion between what is morally permissible and what is legally permissible. But I believe he is making the subtler point that alleged examples of offence are plausible only when one is thinking of permissibility legalistically. After all, it is possible to think of the moral law in a legalistic manner, and there is something to be said for the contention that alleged examples of offence are most plausible when they are viewed as blameworthy acts which are, strictly speaking, permissible. Perhaps they violate the spirit of the moral law, but they do not violate the letter of the moral law (compare with Chisholm's analogy of venial versus mortal sins). According to this interpretation of Heyd's argument, it is different with supererogation. One need not resort to a legalistic interpretation of permissibility when one supplies alleged examples of praiseworthy acts which are permissible to omit. There are plenty of plausible examples of such acts whose omission is not only in accordance with the letter of the moral law but also with the spirit. Thus, I shall interpret Heyd as claiming that alleged examples of offence depend upon employing the concept of permissibility legalistically, while the same is not true of supererogation.

To summarize, Heyd advances three lines of reasoning to show that there is no "logically neat symmetry" between supererogation and offence. First, he believes that no acts are morally blameworthy to perform and morally praiseworthy to omit. Hence, to prevent the category of the offensive from being empty, he believes it is necessary to drop the condition that acts of offence are morally praiseworthy to omit; but dropping this condition leaves the definition of supererogation with a clause which has no counterpart in the definition of offence. Second, while there is an abundance of examples of supererogation which are dramatic and nontrivial, the situation is otherwise with the category of offence. Heyd is skeptical that there can be any nontrivial examples of offence. Third, alleged examples of offence seem to depend upon an interpretation of the concept of permissibility which is legalistic, a fact which Heyd believes is not the case with supererogation.

Heyd is not alone in maintaining that there can be no neat symmetry between supererogation and offence, for there are several philosophers who acknowledge supererogation and at the same time express grave reservations about acknowledging offence (these philosophers do not specifically address the asymmetry issue, but surely it would be awkward to maintain that there is a perfect symmetry between them if it is believed that the existence of the one is clear and the existence of the other is dubious). Knut Tranoy is highly skeptical that acts of offence are possible. He observes that it is very reasonable to hold that we have a duty "always to abstain from doing evil."[16] Moreover, he states that we are under a permanent obligation to do no wrong, for "it is tautological that to do evil is wrong and that it is our duty to abstain from it."[17] Apparently he not only believes that there are no acts of offence, but also it is his view that it is tautologically true that there are no acts of offence.

At the same time Tranoy appears willing to grant that acts of supererogation are possible. He states that we do not, generally speaking, have a duty to be benevolent. Although he believes that it is tautological that to do evil is wrong, he goes on to affirm that right action is not coextensive with dutiful action. It is possible to do good when under no duty to do so. Thus, he concludes, "the duty to avoid evil does not entail or require a similar duty to do good."[18] It is a tautological truth that there can be no acts of offence, but from this it does not follow in his opinion that there can be no acts of supererogation.

A similar sentiment is expressed by Alan Donagan in his book, *The Theory of Morality*. He asks whether it is plausible to countenance acts which are "demeritorious" or objectionable and at the same time "not impermissible" (noting that these are the acts designated by Chisholm as "offensive"). His answer is that their existence is not at all clear: " . . . offenses such as self-righteousness, sloth and want of consideration are morally impermissible; and, provided that there is no want of consideration, ill-breeding, affectation, and coarseness, while demeritorious, do not seem to be morally offensive."[19] Donagan's point seems to be that some demeritorious acts are clearly impermissible; others, associated with ill-breeding, affectation, and coarseness, are demeritorious only in a non-moral sense. But he is aware of no clear examples of permissible acts which are morally demeritorious. On the other hand, Donagan acknowledges that there can be acts of supererogation, and offers several examples throughout the course of his book (one example involves a woman who has conceived as the result of rape and subsequently gives birth).

In a related observation J.N. Findlay complains that philosophers have ignored "the close and one-sided tie-up of the obligatory with the bad, and its comparatively loose tie-up with what is good."[20] By stating that there is a comparatively loose tie-up between obligation and what is good, Findlay seems to be affirming that many good or praiseworthy acts manage to fall outside the realm of obligation (a position which accords with the analysis of his views offered in chapter four). And, although this is not a straightforward declaration that acts of supererogation are possible, it can be taken as an affirmation of the principle that acts of supererogation are not ruled out by an airtight connection between what is obligatory and what is good or praiseworthy.

On the other hand, there is in Findlay's opinion no corresponding looseness in the tie-up between what is obligatory and what is bad. Here I take Findlay to be taking the position that behavior which is morally bad or blameworthy can seldom, if ever, succeed in being separated from what is obligatory to refrain from. There is a close tie-up between the bad and the obligatory in that moral agents have an obligation to avoid morally bad behavior.

Thus, it appears to be Findlay's view that good acts can frequently be separated from what it is obligatory to do, but bad acts can seldom, if ever, be separated from what it is obligatory to refrain from. It is a "one-sided tie-up" in the sense that the close tie-up between what is bad and what is obligatory is not reflected in the tie-up between what is good and what is obligatory.

3. The Praiseworthy and the Blameworthy: More Asymmetry

Chisholm, Heyd, Tranoy, Donagan, and Findlay are correct in believing that there is no neat logical symmetry between supererogation and offence, but more needs to be said in this connection about the role which the concepts of moral praiseworthiness and blameworthiness play in the respective definitions of supererogation and offence. In this section I shall call attention to some features of the role these concepts play in an effort to shed further light upon the asymmetry issue and ultimately to see more clearly to what extent a system of ethics which accommodates offence is even more latitudinarian than a system of ethics which accommodates supererogation.

The concepts of 'praise' and 'blame' are usually treated as mutually complementary in discussions of ethics. Just as good and evil are treated as opposites of one another and right and wrong are treated as opposites of one another, so it often seems to be assumed that the same is true of praise and blame and, by extension, praiseworthiness and blameworthiness. Praiseworthy acts seen naturally to align themselves with good, and blameworthy acts seem to align themselves with evil. Thus, there seems frequently to be an implicit assumption that a type of symmetry exists: Acts can be good or bad, right or wrong, praiseworthy or blameworthy, where each member of each pair is the mirror image opposite of the other.[21]

In chapter five I argued that praiseworthiness and blameworthiness are concepts which admit of degrees. The performance of a given act can qualify as more or less praiseworthy or blameworthy, depending upon the particular circumstances of its performance. Suppose it is morally praiseworthy for me to loan you money during a difficult period in your life. Then it seems possible to imagine an increase in the praiseworthiness of this type of act by altering the circumstances. It might be more praiseworthy if I myself were in very tight financial circumstances; more praiseworthy yet if in addition I loan you money I had set aside for a long awaited vacation; or still more praiseworthy to cancel an appointment with a key client to get you the money; and so forth (here caution must be exercised to avoid the category of the foolish). Similarly, it is possible to imagine a blameworthy act becoming increasingly blameworthy as the circumstances of its performance are altered. If it is blameworthy to tell you a lie, perhaps it is more blameworthy if I know that your believing the lie will cause you to miss an important meeting; more blameworthy yet if I know it will cause you to take the wrong medication for your heart ailment; or cause you financial ruin, and so forth.

When one imagines acts becoming more and more praiseworthy, or more and more blameworthy, by altering the circumstances of their performance, a curious phenomenon comes to light. As a type of act becomes increasingly morally blameworthy to perform, it tends to become more and more likely that its performance is morally forbidden. As the known consequences of my telling you a lie become more and more severe, the performance of my act seems to become an increasingly prime candidate for qualifying as forbidden. If I tell you a lie whose only intended consequence is that you receive tea from the vending machine instead of coffee, it seems somewhat implausible to judge that I have done that which is morally forbidden. But when the intended consequences include states of affairs such as your missing an important meeting; your taking the wrong medication for your heart ailment; and your suffering financial ruin; it seems to become increasingly plausible to judge that I have violated a moral duty. Surely it is plausible to judge that it is morally forbidden to tell another a lie which causes that person to suffer financial ruin (and is intended to do just that). It is only slightly less plausible to judge the same about a lie which causes you to take the wrong medication for your heart ailment, and so on.

There might be some disagreement about the particular example I have chosen, but I believe the general principle which I am attempting to illustrate is reasonable. The more blameworthy it becomes to perform a given act, other things being equal, the more likely it becomes that the performance of the act is morally forbidden. At some point the act becomes so blameworthy to perform that its performance actually constitutes the violation of duty. Of course, those who deny that acts of offence are possible may accept this principle in its degenerate form, holding that when an act becomes blameworthy to perform, even to the slightest degree, it already constitutes the violation of duty. But in any case it seems intuitively correct to conceive of the realm of the forbidden as the final destination of acts whose performances become increasingly blameworthy. The more blameworthy it is to perform, the closer it tends toward the realm of the forbidden.

There is a remarkable contrast to this phenomenon in the relationship between morally praiseworthy acts and the realm of the obligatory. When one imagines altering the circumstances so that a given act becomes more and more praiseworthy to perform, it is not the least bit plausible to argue that its performance becomes an increasingly prime candidate for the designation of obligatory. As the performance of an act moves across the spectrum from mildly praiseworthy to exceedingly praiseworthy, it may move closer to the realm of the heroic. An act of heroism is typically praiseworthy to a very high degree. However, it does not seem to move closer to the obligatory. The realm of the obligatory is certainly not the final destination of acts whose performances become increasingly praiseworthy.

In many instances an act becomes increasingly praiseworthy as its performance requires increasingly greater personal sacrifices on the part of its agent (again, being cautious of foolhardy sacrifices). But it would be highly implausible to argue that as the level of personal sacrifice becomes greater, it is increasingly more likely that the act is obligatory to perform. Indeed, in such cases it seems more plausible to argue that the reverse is true: as the level of personal sacrifice becomes greater, it is increasingly unlikely that the act is obligatory for the agent to perform. Naturally, the anti-supererogationist will regard the entire asymmetry controversy as resting upon the mistaken supposition that an act can be praiseworthy to perform and yet not obligatory, and hence the degree to which the performance of an act is morally praiseworthy will be judged to have no bearing upon whether or not it is obligatory. But for those who believe that acts of supererogation are possible, it should seem extremely dubious that as an act requires an increasingly greater sacrifice on the part of its agent, it is increasingly likely that it qualifies as obligatory.

In other cases an act becomes increasingly praiseworthy as its benefits to others increase. If I am the owner of a video games arcade, it may be praiseworthy to give a coupon worth five free games to an underprivileged child; more praiseworthy to give the child a coupon worth ten free games; and so on. But there is no plausibility whatever in the suggestion that there is more likelihood of my act's being obligatory as the level of my generosity increases. As before, it seems more reasonable to affirm the opposite principle, that as the level of my generosity increases there is less likelihood that what I am doing is morally obligatory.

I conclude there is a striking dissimilarity between the relationship between the blameworthy and the forbidden, on the one hand, and the relationship between the praiseworthy and the obligatory on the other. The more blameworthy it is to perform a given act, other things being equal, the closer its performance tends toward the realm of the forbidden. But it is certainly not true that the more praiseworthy it is to perform a given act, other things being equal, the closer its performance tends toward the realm of the obligatory. In fact, it appears in many cases as though one is less likely to fulfil a moral duty through the performance of an act as it becomes increasingly praiseworthy. Thus, there seems to be a significant asymmetry in the manner in which the concepts of praiseworthiness and blameworthiness relate to what is morally required of one to do and to avoid, respectively.[22]

The asymmetry to which I am attempting to call attention runs deeper than the asymmetry between supererogation and offence discussed by Heyd. What I am suggesting here, in effect, is that the asymmetry between supererogation and offence may at least partially be the result of a deeper asymmetry between what is praiseworthy and what is blameworthy. If the latter concepts were perfectly symmetric, one might expect that their relation to the obligatory and forbidden, respectively, would be symmetric, and it has been shown that this is not the case. It could be objected that the source of the asymmetry lies in the concepts of the obligatory and the forbidden, not in what is praiseworthy and blameworthy. But if one employs the standard account of the interdefinability of the obligatory and forbidden from deontic logic (an act is obligatory to perform if and only if it is forbidden not to perform, and an act is forbidden to perform if and only if it is obligatory not to perform) it seems evident that these concepts can be nothing but mirror image opposites of one another. Therefore, to the extent that the asymmetry described above derives from a deeper asymmetry in one of these two pairs of conepts, it is more reasonable to identify the praiseworthy and the blameworthy as the source.

It is possible to imagine a culture which adopts a system of morality which does not have this asymmetry. In such a culture various forms of behavior are judged morally blameworthy, and it is possible for the performance of an act to be judged blameworthy to a greater or lesser degree depending upon the circumstances of its performance. But imagine that in this culture it is not the case that as an act becomes increasingly blameworthy it is more likely to become forbidden. Acts which are considered to be violations of moral duty tend to be considered modestly blameworthy, not significantly blameworthy. Acts which are extremely blameworthy to perform are judged to be villainous or roguish, and only on rare occasions are these acts considered to be morally forbidden (just as saintly or heroic acts are rarely considered to be obligatory by those who acknowledge supererogation). Thus, the realm of the forbidden is by no means regarded as the final destination of acts whose performance becomes increasingly blameworthy.

Much could be said about the ways in which the moral intuitions of the people in this culture differ from those of people in other cultures, but I believe that one feature of their moral intuitions is particularly relevant to the present discussion. Acts of supererogation and acts of offence are regarded by the people of this culture as equally plausible to acknowledge. It is possible for them to understand how someone might be skeptical as to whether acts of supererogation or acts of offence are possible, and perhaps there might be such skeptics among their own number. But it is highly difficult for them to understand how someone might acknowledge acts of supererogation and yet remain skeptical as to whether acts of offence are possible. They can imagine this puzzling moral intuition taking place only in cultures having a fundamentally different system of moral requirements. In their culture the paradigm examples of supererogation are acts whose performances are highly praiseworthy, and the paradigm examples of offence are acts whose performances are highly blameworthy. Heroic and saintly acts are paradigm examples of supererogation, and villainous acts are paradigm examples of offence.

From our own perspective it is not such an easy matter to find paradigm examples of acts of offence, and perhaps it is here that the moral intuitions from this alternative culture can shed some light upon the basis of our own moral intuitions. Given the moral intuitions about the concepts of praiseworthiness and blameworthiness with which we operate, it is far more difficult to find paradigm examples of offence than paradigm examples of supererogation. Moreover, the very recognition that acts of offence are possible is more controversial than in the case of supererogation, given these intuitions. A great many people who have no qualms about acknowledging that acts of supererogation are possible (such as Heyd, Tranoy, Donagan, and possibly Findlay) are hesitant to embrace wholeheartedly the category of offence.

An examination of an alternative culture characterized by the type of symmetry described in the preceding example makes it tempting to conclude that people have a greater reluctance to countenance offence than to countenance supererogation because (in part) of the asymmetry which pervades our own conceptual scheme. If the relation between supererogation and obligation were perfectly symmetric with the relation between offence and the forbidden, it seems likely that people would be no more reluctant to acknowledge that acts of offence are possible than that acts of supererogation are possible. Thus my suggestion is that there is an intimate connection between the presence of asymmetry in our conceptual scheme and what appears to be a common tendency to regard the reality of offence as more dubious than that of supererogation. People do tend to think of offence in such a way as to bear out the truth of Chisholm's claim that a system of ethics is more latitudinarian when the category of offence is present than when the system accommodates supererogation but not offence, and this way of thinking is intimately connected with the asymmetry which pervades our conceptual scheme.

4. The Pharisee and the Counterpart Pharisee

In this section I shall discuss what I take to be still another symptom of the asymmetry between supererogation and offence. At several points in earlier chapters I have made references to the practice of avoiding performing acts of supererogation while nevertheless making a constant effort to fulfil one's moral obligations. And I have described an individual who engages in this practice as a type of modern day Pharisee. Such an individual is eager to fulfil moral obligations while at the same time exerting a minimum effort to benefit others, thus fulfilling duty while not going beyond the call of duty.

Regarding such individuals I have already argued that their behavior is open to moral criticism in spite of the fact that an act of supererogation is never blameworthy to omit. First, the Pharisee who sets out to avoid performing praiseworthy acts which fulfil no moral obligations is deliberately setting out to avoid acts of both quasi-supererogation and supererogation. But since acts of quasi-supererogation are blameworthy to omit, the Pharisee can rightly be criticized for omitting them. Second, following Trianosky, I argued that a person who sets out to refrain from praiseworthy acts which fulfil no moral obligations can be criticized on aretaic grounds, even if the person cannot be criticized on deontic grounds. In addition, following Kant and Mill, I argued that persons can have "imperfect" obligations to perform good works on at least an occasional basis. Thus, good works which are optional on a specific occasion may be obligatory to perform at some time or other. And hence the Pharisee might be actually violating some moral obligations after all. Thus, there is a sense in which the approach of the Pharisee may be self-defeating in the long run.

Imagine next the counterpart of the Pharisee who is determined to avoid performing acts which are morally forbidden while nevertheless remaining eager to perform acts of offence. Just as the Pharisee avoids performing acts of supererogation, so the counterpart Pharisee avoids passing up opportunities to perform acts of offence. Each is concerned to avoid the violation of what is morally required, but beyond this limitation each is concerned to take full advantage of what is morally permissible. The Pharisee takes advantage of what is morally permissible by refraining from acts of supererogation, and the counterpart Pharisee takes advantage of what is morally permissible by performing acts of offence.

It might initially be thought that people do not actually exemplify the type of person characterized here as a counterpart Pharisee. But a bit of reflection will reveal that the approach of the counterpart Pharisee may be fairly common in economic and political life among those who will not hesitate to stoop to any type of behavior as long as it is not strictly forbidden. In an atmosphere of cutthroat competition there will always be some who will aggressively pursue every possible advantage they can secure for their own interests, short of that fine line which separates the offensive from the forbidden, and regardless of the ill effects their behavior may have for others. It is the idea that anything goes, as long as it is strictly permissible. In a society such as ours there is no shortage of persons for whom this idea is the operative principle in their business and professional lives. (And, unfortunately, there are still others for which the realm of the forbidden is not even a deterrent).

It might also initially be thought that the two positions I have described are mutually exclusive. But surely it is possible for the same individual simultaneously to adopt the characteristic practice of the Pharisee and of the counterpart Pharisee (with a slight qualification to be introduced momentarily). On the one hand, such a person avoids doing the good which is not required, and on the other hand that person avoids refraining from the bad which is not forbidden. There is no incompatibility between the two. Indeed, the practices are similar enough that it is not difficult to imagine a person simultaneously seeking out opportunities to perform blameworthy acts which are permissible and avoiding opportunities to perform praiseworthy acts which are permissible to omit.

Here again, however, one must resist the temptation to think of these two practices as symmetrical to one another. It is true that the Pharisee and counterpart Pharisee have in common the commitment not to run afoul of their moral obligations. Moreover, they have in common the commitment to exploit the category of the permissible to their own advantage as far as they are capable. But there are other respects in which the symmetry breaks down.

First, I have argued that the Pharisee is open to moral criticism on aretaic grounds but not deontic grounds, except when refraining from acts of quasi-supererogation. The counterpart Pharisee, however, is open to moral criticism on both aretaic and deontic grounds. A person who adopts the practice of seizing opportunities to perform bad but permissible acts can certainly be criticized for a failure to cultivate and practice moral virtue. But such a person can in addition be criticized on deontic grounds. By the very nature of offence, a person who performs acts of offence is doing that which can be criticized on deontic grounds. Thus, while the strategy of the Pharisee is to avoid moral criticism on deontic grounds, the counterpart Pharisee has no parallel strategy. The latter is perfectly willing to perform acts which can be criticized on moral grounds. Neither the Pharisee nor counterpart Pharisee can tolerate being criticized with the violation of moral duty, but the counterpart Pharisee has no qualms about performing acts which invite the charge of engaging in behavior which is morally blameworthy (from which it does not follow, however, that the counterpart Pharisee welcomes this criticism).

As a corollary to this point, a second symptom of the asymmetry I wish to call attention to concerns the manner in which each regards the practice of the other. Since the Pharisee wishes to avoid being charged with having done that which is morally blameworthy, the Pharisee will not be attracted to counterpart Phariseeism. Adopting the practice of the counterpart Pharisee will defeat the Pharisee's strategy of avoiding moral blame (at least on deontic grounds). On the other hand, there seems to be no particular reason why the counterpart Pharisee will not find the practice of the Pharisee attractive. A person who seeks out opportunities to do that which is blameworthy but permissible will find nothing unattractive in the idea of refraining from that which is praiseworthy. In fact, it would be somewhat surprising to find a serious counterpart Pharisee who makes a point of avoiding the practice of the Pharisee. The practice of avoiding praiseworthy but permissible acts seems a natural extension of the practice of performing blameworthy but permissible acts. The reverse is not true, however, and it is here that another symptom of the asymmetry reveals itself.

Earlier I claimed that Phariseeism and counterpart Phariseeism are not mutually exclusive. Nevertheless, in the light of what has just been shown about the asymmetry of the two positions, it is evident that a slight qualification needs to be made. If the Pharisee deplores doing that which is morally blameworthy (with suitable qualifications), and if the counterpart Pharisee makes a practice of doing that which is morally blameworthy, it is not possible to be both a Pharisee and counterpart Pharisee. However, it is clearly possible for a counterpart Pharisee to adopt the Pharisee's practice of refraining from that which is praiseworthy without at the same time adopting the Pharisee's negative attitude toward doing that which is morally blameworthy. It is in this sense that one can simultaneously adopt the practice of the Pharisee and the practice of the counterpart Pharisee without actually functioning as both a Pharisee and counterpart Pharisee.

A major difference between the Pharisee and counterpart Pharisee, then, is that the former wishes to avoid being made worthy of moral blame, and the latter actively seeks to do that which turns out to be worthy of moral blame. On the basis of this difference it might be argued that in a very real sense what the counterpart Pharisee does is doubly wrong. On the one hand, that agent actively resolves to do that which is morally blameworthy, and, on the other hand, follows through on this resolve and does that which is morally blameworthy. It is one thing to perform a series of offensive acts, but it quite another thing to do so after having deliberately set out to take advantage of opportunities to perform acts of offence. It is one thing to linger at one's table in a crowded restaurant, but it is another thing to do so as the result of having resolved to perform acts of offence whenever the opportunity presents itself.

It might be argued that what the counterpart Pharisee does is so bad, morally speaking, that it actually constitutes a violation of moral duty. Of course, it is never a violation of moral duty to perform acts of offence; by its very definition, no act of offence can be forbidden to perform. But the very resolve to take advantage of opportunities to perform blameworthy but permissible acts might strike some as a form of moral perversity which is itself morally forbidden. Perhaps the idea is that it is one's moral obligation to exert at least a minimum of effort to avoid the regular practice of blameworthy behavior. People do from time to time allow themselves to act in a blameworthy manner, and, if one agrees that acts of offence are possible, this is not a violation of moral duty. But if one deliberately makes a regular practice of performing such acts, then one is failing to fulfil an important moral obligation.

On this line of reasoning, the counterpart Pharisee is setting out to take full advantage of what is morally permissible without crossing over into the realm of the forbidden. Yet the act of setting out to take full advantage of what is morally permissible is itself morally forbidden, for it involves the deliberate resolve to do that which is blameworthy but permissible. Thus, ironically, the counterpart Pharisee's aim to avoid performing forbidden acts itself turns out to be morally forbidden. There is something self-defeating in making the resolve which the counterpart Pharisee makes.

It is at least arguable, given these considerations, that the counterpart Pharisee does that which is morally forbidden in resolving to take full advantage of what is morally permissible. Nothing comparable is true of the Pharisee's situation, however. The Pharisee resolves to avoid performing acts of supererogation while fulfilling all moral obligations. While one can certainly judge that it is blameworthy to make such a resolve, it does not seem at all plausible to charge the Pharisee with a violation of moral duty in having made this resolve. Nor, of course, does it seem plausible to judge that the Pharisee fulfils a moral duty through making this resolve. The truth of the matter seems to be that the making of this resolve comes nowhere near either the violation of moral duty or the fulfillment of moral duty. Whether it is morally permissible to make the resolve of the counterpart Pharisee is highly debatable, but it seems clear that it is morally permissible to make the resolve of the Pharisee.

I conclude that there are several ways in which one can attack the hypothesis that the situations of the Pharisee and counterpart Pharisee are symmetrical. And since the positions of each are defined with respect to the categories of the praiseworthy and the blameworthy and their relationship, in turn, with the obligatory and the forbidden, I take these asymmetrical phenomena to be symptoms of the deeper asymmetry described earlier. Given the discussion of the previous two sections, it should come as no surprise that the situations of the Pharisee and counterpart Pharisee do not conform to a neat logical symmetry.

5. Conclusion

A system of ethics which accommodates the categories of supererogation and offence has the appearance of providing a neat logical symmetry between these categories. However, already in Chisholm's "The Ethics of Requirement" one is warned that such a system is more latitudinarian than a system which accommodates supererogation alone. I have suggested that this observation provides an important clue for the conclusion that supererogation and offence are not as neatly symmetrical as they might appear. This hypothesis of asymmetry receives considerable elaboration at the hands of Heyd. Although one need not agree with all of the details of Heyd's discussion, his arguments make it abundantly clear that a hypothesis to the effect that they are neatly symmetrical is doomed to failure.

One important point which emerges from Heyd's discussion is that the category of offence is more controversial than the category of supererogation. As Heyd points out, this is most evident in the case of acts which are praiseworthy or blameworthy to a significant degree. Many paradigm examples of supererogatory acts, such as acts of heroism or saintliness, are praiseworthy to a high degree. However, it is difficult to find clear examples of offensive acts which are blameworthy to that same degree. Chisholm believes that there can be villainous acts of this sort which are not morally forbidden, but Heyd argues with some plausibility that Chisholm's examples are quite unconvincing. If an act is truly villainous, there seems to be a strong presumption in favor of believing that it cannot reasonably be judged morally permissible.

Nevertheless, even among so-called trifling acts of offence there is room for a certain amount of skepticism. On the one hand, it might be argued that many such acts are sufficiently trifling as not to merit the designation of morally blameworthy. On the other hand, it might be argued that those which merit the designation of being morally blameworthy can no longer be defended as genuinely permissible. Heyd, of course, argues that trifling acts of offence can be defended as permissible only by employing a different notion of permissibility than one employs by asserting that acts of supererogation are praiseworthy to perform but permissible to omit. But whether or not one agrees with Heyd on this point, it is clear that there is no inconsistency or incoherence in the position that there can be acts of supererogation in human life but not acts of offence. Like Heyd, Tranoy, Donagan, and perhaps Findlay, there are probably many who are inclined to adopt a position of this sort. And I suspect that few if any anti-supererogationists would be inclined to acknowledge that acts of offence are possible.

It is hard to say precisely why people appear more reluctant to embrace the possibility of offensive acts than the possibility of supererogatory acts. Certainly one relevant factor is that it is far more controversial that there can be offensive acts which are highly blameworthy than that there can be supererogatory acts which are highly praiseworthy. But even among acts which are praiseworthy or blameworthy to perform to a relatively small degree, people tend to be more suspicious of offensive acts than they are of supererogatory acts.

Perhaps part of the reason is that people may assume that a greater threat to society is posed by those whose behavior resembles that of the counterpart Pharisee than those whose behavior is modelled after that of the Pharisee. In the case of the Pharisee there is the possibility that certain acts which would be praiseworthy to perform will be omitted because they are considered optional, and this situation results in fewer benefits to society. But in the case of the counterpart Pharisee there is the possibility that certain acts which are blameworthy to perform will be performed (rather than omitted) because they are considered optional, and this situation tends to bring about greater harms to society. Thus, following the example of the Pharisee suggests the possibility of fewer benefits to society, while following the example of the counterpart Pharisee suggests the possibility of greater harms to society. And I suspect many are inclined to feel that the presence of fewer positive benefits is to be preferred to the presence of harms or negative benefits.

Of course, not everyone will see that there is any reason to prefer the absence of that which is beneficial to society to the presence of that which is harmful to society. Some may feel that, other things being equal, the two are equally unfortunate. Thus, the counterpart Pharisee is capable of causing harm to society by performing acts of offence (even if there is no such thing as a villainous act of offence). But it is perhaps no less unfortunate to society when the Pharisee withholds performing acts of supererogation, for society is being deprived of the significant benefits which acts of selfless sacrifice bring about. In fact, if someone is of the opinion that performing acts of personal sacrifice is itself an intrinsic good of considerable significance, it might be that a greater overall misfortune is caused to society by someone's withholding potential acts of supererogation than by performing acts of offence.

Still, I believe that most people will feel that the counterpart Pharisee is a more alarming prospect than that of the Pharisee. It is more alarming to imagine a person actually causing harm to society than to imagine a person withholding potential benefits to society. Naturally, the harm caused by a person performing an act of offence is more noticeable than the potential benefits which are withheld by a person refusing to perform an act of supererogation. Hence it may appear to be slightly preferable that society be populated by Pharisees than by counterpart Pharisees.

My suggestion here is that some elements of the asymmetry described earlier may function in people's intuitions concerning what is best for society at large. Supererogation is not the perfect mirror image of offence, and hence it is not be be expected that people will think about the performance of acts of supererogation and offence and their respective effects upon society in a precisely symmetrical fashion. For a variety of reasons philosophers have embraced positions which are anti-supererogationist, and some of these reasons have been surveyed in chapters three and four. And, although there is little in the literature concerning the concept of offence and reasons for being skeptical that there can be acts of offence in human life, most people to whom the concept is explained seem to have the tendency to regard offence with more skepticism than supererogation. Again, there seems to be a strong tendency among people to assume that if one's behavior is truly worthy of moral blame, it must at the same time be a violation of one's duty. One has a moral duty to refrain from whatever behavior turns out to be truly worthy of moral blame.

Anti-supererogationism is based in large measure upon the idea that one ought to do whatever is morally good or praiseworthy, and many people find this idea intuitively correct. And one who finds this idea intuitively correct will no doubt feel the same about the idea that one ought never do that which is morally bad or blameworthy. But given the asymmetry thesis defended in this chapter, it should come as no surprise if people find these ideas intuitively correct to slightly different degrees. And my belief is that most people will be likely to find the second idea slightly more intuitively convincing than the first. People will be more likely to affirm the principle that one ought never do that which is morally bad or blameworthy than the principle that one ought to do whatever is morally good or praiseworthy. I do not pretend to have given more than a few scattered remarks in the general direction of explaining this phenomenon. But, once again, this phenomenon is not altogether surprising in the light of the asymmetry which has been shown to characterize systems of ethics accommodating both supererogation and offence.

This discussion began with a plea for understanding by Kurt Waldheim: "Yes, I admit I wanted to survive by following orders. . . .

I have the deepest respect for all those who resisted. But I ask understanding for all the hundreds of thousands who didn't do that, but nevertheless did not become personally guilty."

No doubt it is highly controversial whether Waldheim's failure to resist can be identified as the failure to perform an act of supererogation. Nevertheless, he is clearly of the opinion that this is the case, and there is a sense in which all of us tend to think about our failures in this manner. There are higher courses of action in life which we might have pursued, noble sacrifices we might have made, significant benefits to others we might have brought about. In many diverse ways we have failed to realize the good that is within our power, and to the extent that others are aware of these failures it is our desire that they be understanding. We cannot realistically expect others to be understanding of everything we have done or failed to have done in life (such as our failure to have fulfilled our duties), but these particular failures seem to us worthy of understanding. It seems to us understandable that we have failed to do all the good we are capable of doing.

In this essay it has not been my concern to present an outright refutation of the anti-supererogationist's position; surely it is highly uncertain whether the supererogationist is in a position to formulate arguments capable of convincing the anti-supererogationist that acts of supererogation are possible. Instead, I have attempted to arrive at an understanding of the various reasons why people are attracted to the anti-supererogationist point of view and to suggest that some of the reasons why people have formed a negative or distasteful view of supererogation are based upon misunderstandings of various sorts. The literature on supererogation is filled with discussions of anti-supererogationists, principally Kantians and utilitarians, as well as people's reasons for rejecting supererogation as a separate category of human action. But these discussions typically stop short of diagnosing possible misunderstandings which creep into the picture of supererogation with which these anti-supererogationists operate. In chapters five and six I hope to have made a beginning in addressing this issue, and in doing so I hope to have laid some of the groundwork for convincing anti-supererogationists that they ought to at least reexamine their reasons for rejecting supererogation as a separate category of human action.

In the final chapter I have discussed acts of offence and their relationship with acts of supererogation. Like acts of supererogation, I believe that acts of offence are possible in human life, and, as with acts of supererogation, there are many who would disagree. I suspect those who would reject acts of offence as a legitimate category of human acts would do so for reasons growing out of negative or distasteful attitudes toward such a category similar in nature to the negative or distasteful attitudes toward supererogation. Here too there is room for asking whether these attitudes are based upon mistaken perceptions, and here too it does not seem unreasonable to ask others to be understanding. When I have done that which is worthy of moral blame but still within the bounds of the morally permissible, such as lingering at my table when others are known to be waiting, I can admit that I have failed to live up to the highest expectations others might have for me and yet perhaps feel worthy of their understanding (maybe not as worthy, however, as those who have declined to perform acts of supererogation and have therefore done nothing blameworthy; perhaps this is still another symptom of the asymmetry already discussed at inordinate length).

In the end the proponent of supererogation and offence can perhaps do little more than admit that one could have done a great deal more in life of that which is praiseworthy or avoided a great deal more of that which is blameworthy (but permissible) and hope that others will be understanding. It would be highly disconcerting to think that these failures are inevitably the failure to fulfil duty, as opponents of supererogation and offence would maintain, for surely it is far more difficult to ask others to be understanding of shortcomings when they constitute the violation of duty. But it is my opinion that these failures are not inevitably the violation of duty, and hence I believe that, given the way human beings are constituted, it is reasonable to expect others to be understanding of these failures, whether they are the failure to throw oneself upon a live grenade, the failure to live a life of saintly virtue, or simply the failure to perform a minor courtesy.

NOTES

CHAPTER ONE

1. As reported in *Time*, 22 February 1988, p. 38.

2. "In retrospect, while I was not involved in the decision to conduct the [Watergate] break-in, I should have set a higher standard for the conduct of the people who participated in my campaign and Administration. I should have established a moral tone that would have made such actions unthinkable. I did not. . . . Not taking a higher road than my predecessors and my adversaries was my central mistake." From Richard Nixon's *In the Arena* (New York: Simon and Schuster, 1990), p. 41.

3. J.O. Urmson, "Saints and Heroes," *Moral Concepts*, ed. Joel Feinberg (London: Oxford University Press, 1969), p. 63.

4. Ibid.

5. David Heyd, *Supererogation* (Cambridge: Cambridge University Press, 1982), p. 142.

CHAPTER TWO

1. My account is intended to be neutral with respect to whether acts are fine-grained or course-grained, repeatable or non-repeatable, and so forth. Accordingly, I will regard the performances or omissions of acts, not acts themselves, as what can be praiseworthy, blameworthy, obligatory, or forbidden. If on occasion I lapse into speaking of an act as having one of these

properties, this is not an indication of having changed my position. Thus, it is the performance of an act on a particular occasion which is praiseworthy or blameworthy, and circumstances such as the agent's frame of mind will be regarded as relevant to judging whether it is praiseworthy or blameworthy.

2. As quoted in "Supererogation: Artistry in Conduct," Daniel R. DeNicola, *Foundations in Ethics*, ed. Leroy S. Rouner (Notre Dame, IN: Notre Dame University Press, 1983), p. 151.

3. Lucian, *Works*, Volume 6, trans. K. Kilburn (Cambridge: Harvard University Press, 1968).

4. Sheldon Peterfreund, "On the Relation between Supererogation and Basic Duty," *The Personalist* LIX (1978), p. 54.

5. Ibid.

6. Robin Attfield, "Supererogation and Double Standards," *Mind*, LXXXVIII (1979), p. 486. See also his recent book, *A Theory of Value and Obligation* (London: Croon Helm, 1987), p. 115.

7. David Heyd, *Supererogation* (Cambridge: Cambridge University Press, 1982), p. 115.

8. Ibid., p. 131.

9. Ibid., p. 133.

10. Ibid., p. 137. Millard Schumaker similarly requires that acts of supererogation be performed primarily for the sake of someone else, but immediately after offering his definition he makes the commendable confession that it may not capture all instances of supererogation. See his book, *Supererogation: An Analysis and Bibliography* (Edmonton: St. Stephen's College, 1977), p. 11).

11. Roderick Chisholm, "Supererogation and Offence: A Conceptual Scheme for Ethics," *Ratio*, V (1963), p. 5.

12. Roderick Chisholm, "The Ethics of Requirement," *American Philosophical Quarterly*, I (1964), p. 152.

13. Roderick Chisholm and Ernest Sosa, "Intrinsic Preferability and the Problem of Supererogation," *Synthese*, XVI (1966), p. 326. It might be thought that Chisholm is laying down requirements which are impossible to satisfy, since acts of supererogation are said to be not obligatory and yet such that one ought to perform them. Obligation is often described in terms of what one ought to do; how, then, can there be acts which one ought to perform which are at the same time not obligatory? The problem is resolved in an earlier section of "The Ethics of Requirement" in which Chisholm makes clear

that he is employing the 'ought' locution (in terms of requirements which have not been overridden) in a way which is much weaker than what is customarily understood as moral obligation. According to this usage, even little acts of kindness and small favors are acts we ought to perform. To say that one ought to perform a certain act, according to Chisholm's usage, by no means implies that one has any moral duty to perform it. Accordingly, one can say of an act of supererogation that one ought to perform it with no risk of inconsistency.

14. Heyd, *Op. Cit.*, p. 6.

15. Ibid., pp. 5–6.

16. Ibid., p. 31.

17. Michael Stocker, "Acts, Perfect Duties, and Imperfect Duties," *Review of Metaphysics*, XX (1967), p. 507.

18. Michael Stocker, "Supererogation and Duties," *Studies in Moral Philosophy*, ed. N. Rescher (Liverpool: Basil Blackwell, 1968), p. 61.

19. John Stuart Mill, *Utilitarianism* (London: Longmans, Green, and Co., 1907), p. 74.

20. Millard Schumaker makes this observation: " . . . the doctrine of imperfect obligation has very often been employed as an *ad hoc* device used to force recalcitrant facts into a Procrustean theory of duty and thereby obviate the need to introduce a doctrine of supererogatory behavior," *Op. Cit.*, p. 35.

CHAPTER THREE

1. Thomas Aquinas, *Summa Theologiae*, Ia IIae, Question 108, Article 4.

2. Ibid.

3. Ibid.

4. Martin Luther, "Treatise on Good Works," *Works of Martin Luther* (Philadelphia: Muhlenberg Press, 1943) 1:187, as quoted in Joseph Allen, *Love and Conflict* (Nashville: Abingdon Press, 1984), p. 116).

5. John Calvin, *Institutes of the Christian Religion*, ed. John T. McNeill, trans. Ford Lewis Battles (Philadelphia: The Westminster Press, 1960), Volume I, p. 419 (II, viii, 56).

6. Ibid., p. 420.

7. Ibid., p. 421.

8. Martin Luther, "Explanation of the Ninety-Five Theses," Thesis 58, *Works of Martin Luther*, ed. H.T. Grimm (Philadelphia: Muhlenberg Press, 1955), Volume 31, p. 213.

9. Philip Melanchthon, *Loci Communes Theologici*, ed. Wilhelm Pauck, (Philadelphia: The Westminster Press, 1969), p. 57.

10. Ibid., p. 59.

11. Karl Rahner, "The Theology of the Religious Life," in *Religious Orders in the Modern World*, ed. Gerard Huyghe et al. (Westminster, Maryland: The Newman Press, 1965), pp. 48–49.

12. Allen, *Op. Cit.*, p. 127.

13. Ibid., p. 128.

14. Ibid., p. 130.

15. It is still conceivable that Allen is willing to leave room for acts of supererogation if he thinks there are some which do not involve going beyond the call of duty.

16. Louis Berkhof, *Systematic Theology* (Grand Rapids, MI: Eerdmans Publishing, 1960), pp. 537–538. Perhaps Rahner himself is of the opinion that perfection is attainable for some, since he speaks (in the passage quoted earlier) of God giving people the power to obey.

17. Reinhold Neibuhr, "Love and Law in Protestantism and Catholicism," in *The Essential Reinhold Niebuhr: Selected Essays and Addresses*, ed. Robert McAfee Brown (New Haven and London: Yale University Press, 1986), p. 159.

18. Ibid., p. 144.

19. Ibid., p. 150.

Chapter Four

1. Here I paraphrase Heyd's characterization of Kant's ethics in his book, *Supererogation* (Cambridge: Cambridge University Press, 1982), p. 53.

2. C.D. Ross, *The Right and the Good* (London: Oxford University Press, 1973), p. 24.

3. Paul Eisenberg, "From the Forbidden to the Supererogatory: The Basic Categories in Kant's *Tugendlehre*," *American Philosophical Quarterly*, III (1966), pp. 267–268.

4. J.N. Findlay, *Values and Intentions* (New York: Macmillan, 1961), p. 339.

5. Ibid., p. 341.

6. Ibid.

7. Ibid., p. 382.

8. Ibid., pp. 341–344.

9. J.N. Findlay, "The Structure of the Kingdom of Ends," *Proceedings of the British Academy*, 1957, p. 104.

10. Ibid.

11. Fred Feldman, "Obligations—Absolute, Conditioned, and Conditional," *Philosophia* XII (1983), p. 257.

12. Ibid., pp. 259–260.

13. Fred Feldman, *Doing the Best We Can* (Dordrecht: D. Reidel, 1986), p. 49.

14. Ibid.

15. This point was conveyed to me by Feldman through correspondence.

16. Elizabeth Pybus, "Saints and Heroes," *Philosophy*, LVII (1982), p. 195.

17. Ibid., pp. 195–196.

18. Patricia McGoldrick, "Saints and Heroes: A Plea for the Supererogatory," *Philosophy*, LIX (1984), pp. 524–525.

19. Russell Jacobs, "Obligation, Supererogation, and Self-Sacrifice," *Philosophy*, LXII (1987), p. 99.

20. McGoldrick, *Op. Cit.*, p. 525.

21. Elizabeth Pybus, "A Plea for the Supererogatory: A Reply," *Philosophy*, LXI (1986), p. 527.

22. For a discussion of John Ladd's claim that morality in institutional decision making can be compared to a game of chess, see my *Individuals, Groups, and Shared Moral Responsibility* (Bern: Peter Lang, Inc., 1988), pp. 28–37.

23. Christopher New, "Saints, Heroes, and Utilitarians," *Philosophy*, XLIX (1974), p. 183.

24. Heyd, *Op. Cit.*, p. 79.

25. Ibid.

26. Ibid.

27. Ibid., p. 77.

28. G.E. Moore, *Principia Ethica* (Cambridge: Cambridge University Press, 1968), p. 148. See also *Ethics* (London: Oxford University Press, 1966), pp. 14–15.

Chapter Five

1. With the exception of my own paper, "Quasi-Supererogation," *Philosophical Studies*, LII (1987), 141–150, which forms the basis of some of the present discussion.

2. The acknowledgement that being praiseworthy or blameworthy admits of degrees is widely recognized. See, for example, Harry Frankfurt's *The Importance of What We Care About* (Cambridge: Cambridge University Press, 1988), p. 56.

3. John Stuart Mill, *Utilitarianism* (London: Longmans, Green, and Co., 1907), p. 74.

4. Marcia Baron, "Kantian Ethics and Supererogation," *Journal of Philosophy*, LXXXIV (1987), p. 247.

Chapter Six

1. Gregory Trianosky, "Supererogation, Wrongdoing, and Vice: On the Autonomy of the Ethics of Virtue," *Journal of Philosophy*, LXXXIII (1986), p. 26. As stated, this definition is somewhat redundant. If the performance of an act is not required, its omission is automatically permitted.

2. Ibid., p. 27.

3. Ibid., p. 28.

4. Ibid., p. 29.

5. Immanuel Kant, *The Doctrine of Virtue,* trans. Mary J. Gregor (Philadelphia: University of Pennsylvania Press, 1964), p. 129.

6. Of course, one may not know the motives of another well enough to be in a position to criticize. As Trianosky observes, the conditions under which one is in a position to express blame is a distinct moral question (Ibid., p. 27, note 2.)

7. Marcia Baron, "Kantian Ethics and Supererogation," *Journal of Philosophy,* LXXXIV (1987), p. 249.

8. A slight qualification: there may be cases in which one's unique expertise within the scope of one's vocation actually opens up possibilities of supererogatory behavior where they would not otherwise exist, as in Urmson's example of the physician who volunteers to work in a plague-ridden city.

9. See Gustav Wingren, *Luther on Vocation* (Philadelphia: Muhlenberg Press, 1957).

10. Robert M. Adams, "Vocation," *Faith and Philosophy,* IV (1987), p. 454.

11. R.M. Hare, *Moral Thinking* (Oxford: Clarendon Press, 1981), p. 200.

CHAPTER SEVEN

1. Henry Sidgwick, *The Methods of Ethics,* Seventh Edition (Chicago: University of Chicago Press, 1962), p. 253, as quoted in *Friendship, Altruism, and Morality,* Lawrence A. Blum (London: Routledge and Kegan Paul, 1980), p. 45.

2. Barry Curtis, "The Supererogatory, the Foolish and Morally Required," *Journal of Value Inquiry,* XV (1981), p. 313.

3. Ibid.

4. Knut Erik Tranoy, "Asymmetries in Ethics," *Inquiry,* X (1967), p. 361.

5. Curtis, *Op. Cit.,* p. 314.

6. Ibid., p. 315.

7. Ibid., p. 311.

8. Ibid., p. 317.

Chapter Eight

1. Roderick Chisholm, "Supererogation and Offence: A Conceptual Scheme for Ethics," *Ratio*, V (1963), p. 5.

2. Ibid.

3. Ibid.

4. Ibid., pp. 5–6.

5. Thomas Aquinas, *Summa Theologiae*, Ia IIae Question 88, Article 1.

6. Roderick Chisholm and Ernest Sosa, "Intrinsic Preferability and the Problem of Supererogation," *Synthese*, XVI (1966), p. 327.

7. Ibid., p. 326.

8. I.L. Humberstone, "Logic for Saints and Heroes," *Ratio*, XVI (1974), pp. 112–113.

9. Roderick Chisholm, "The Ethics of Requirement," *American Philosophical Quarterly*, I (1964), p. 153.

10. Terrance McConnell has shown that systems of strict utilitarianism not only classify certain supererogatory acts as obligatory, but in some cases they are classified as forbidden ("Utilitarianism and Supererogatory Acts," *Ratio*, XXII (1980), p. 37).

11. Chisholm, *The Ethics of Requirement*, p. 153. One might instead interpret Chisholm to mean that a system containing offence but not supererogation is more latitudinarian than one containing supererogation but not offence. Nothing of significance in the ensuing discussion is affected by one's choice of interpretation.

12. Mary Forrester, "Some Remarks on Obligation, Permission, and Supererogation," *Ethics*, LXXXV (1975), p. 225.

13. David Heyd, *Supererogation* (Cambridge: Cambridge University Press, 1982), p. 128.

14. Ibid., p. 129.

15. Ibid.

16. Knut Tranoy, "Asymmetries in Ethics," *Inquiry*, X (1967), p. 351.

17. Ibid., p. 363.

18. Ibid., p. 351.

19. Alan Donagan, *The Theory of Morality* (Chicago: University of Chicago Press, 1977), p. 56.

20. J.N. Findlay, "The Structure of the Kingdom of Ends," *Proceedings of the British Academy*, 1957, p. 103.

21. Thomas Reid, however, seems to have been aware that praise and blame are not perfectly symmetric, at least as they relate to justice and injustice: " . . . justice is entitled to a small degree of praise, but injustice to a high degree of blame." See his *Essays on the Active Powers of the Human Mind* (Cambridge, Massachusetts: MIT Press, 1969), p. 258.

22. This point is closely related to a phenomenon noted in chapter five: A disjunctive act, all of whose disjuncts are potential acts of supererogation, can at times be obligatory to perform, but the complementary phenomenon does not seem true of offence. A disjunctive act, all of whose disjuncts are potential acts of offence, seems never to be obligatory to refrain from.

INDEX

A

Act utilitarianism. *See* Utilitarianism, act
Adams, Robert, 154
Allen, Joseph, 57–64, 67, 214
Alms. *See* Charity
Altruism, 8
Anti-supererogationism, 9–11, 13, 43–44, 51, 61–67, 69–79, 99–104, 118–125, 147–160, 205–208
Approbation, 22
Aquinas, St. Thomas, 46–48, 50, 53, 57, 66, 183–184
Aretaic judgments, 135–137, 139–143, 145, 147–148, 154, 159, 202
Aristotle, 131, 164, 174, 179
Aspiration, moral 88, 90–93
Atonement, 61
Atrocities, 1–2, 6, 9
Attfield, Robin 17–18

B

Badness, 23–24, 76, 135, 182, 191, 194, 203, 207. *See also* Evil; Sin; Wrong

Baier, Kurt, 83–87
Baron, Marcia, 121, 147, 159
Beneficence, 7, 33, 163
Benefits, moral, 11, 13, 18, 22, 46, 66, 69, 161, 170–180, 187, 206, 208
Benevolence, 193
Berkhof, Louis, 63
Best, doing one's, 79, 81–85, 87, 100, 102
Blame, 2, 4–7, 18, 57, 122, 124, 142, 160, 184, 217
Blameworthy acts, 17–18, 194–204
Blum, Lawrence, 217
Bravery, 21

C

Calling. *See* Vocation
Calvin, John, 9, 44, 49–50, 52–55, 61, 121
Carnal pleasures, 46–49, 53
Catholicism. *See* Holy Catholic Church; Roman Catholic
Celebacy, 53–54. *See also* Virginity
Charity, 7, 33, 47, 83, 92, 115–116, 187
Chastity, 46–48, 60

221

Cheating, 185
Chisholm, Roderick, 11, 22–25, 111, 181–194, 200, 204, 212–213, 218
Chopra, Yogendra, 101
Christ, Jesus. *See* Jesus Christ
Christianity, 49, 55, 65
Chrysostom, 50
Commandments, 44, 46–54, 56, 59–60, 64–67
Commendation, 88–93, 96, 100, 102–103, 115
Concupiscence, 46
Condemnation, 2–4, 7, 90, 92, 118, 186
Conscience, 20
Consequences, 8, 13, 18–22, 25, 29, 79
Consequentialism, 10. *See also* Utilitarianism, act
Costs, 10, 14–15, 161, 166, 169–174, 176–180
Counsels, 46–50, 52–54, 57, 59–60, 64
Courtesy, 111, 183, 209
Courage, 29, 90
Cronus, 15–16
Culpability, 135
Curtis, Barry, 10, 161–180

D

Deontic, ethics, 138, 142, 155; judgments, 135–137, 139, 141–145, 148, 154, 159, 202; logic, 198
Deviltry, 183
Divorce, 53
Disjunctive acts, 113–117, 219
Donagan, Alan, 193–194, 199, 205
Duty, all-things-considered, 71, 73, 165; beyond, 9, 26, 34–37, 82, 83, 86–87, 96, 121–122, 154, 156, 200; continuity with, 9, 13–14, 16, 22, 24–30, 37–38; fulfilling, 17, 29–40; hortatory, 74–79; imperfect, 33–36, 115–116, 120, 134–135, 200; institutional, 58; minatory, 74–78; prima facie, 70–73, 78, 163, 174, 177; violating, 40, 96, 115–116, 120, 186–187, 196, 203–204, 207, 209. *See also* Obligation; Requirements, moral

E

Eisenberg, Paul, 71, 73, 75–78, 102
Encouragement, 97–99
Etymology, 14
Evaluation, moral, 89–90, 92, 94–95
Evil, 28, 45, 80, 89, 148–149, 166, 189, 193, 195. *See also* Badness; Sin; Wrong
Excuses, 133–135, 137–139, 142–147
Exhortation, 50, 56, 65
Expectations, moral, 17, 122, 124, 150–153, 155, 158–159, 209
Expediency, 47–48

F

Faith, 51, 52, 54
Favors, 7, 213
Fault, 135
Feldman, Fred, 70, 79–87, 102–103
Findlay, J.N., 70, 73–79, 101, 103, 194, 199, 205
Foolishness, 164–165, 169, 173–177, 179–180, 197
Forbearance, 7–8, 189
Forbidden acts, 11, 18, 23, 106–107, 110, 115–116, 120, 123–127, 181–182, 185, 190, 196–200, 203–204, 218
Forgiveness, 8
Forrester, Mary, 189
Frankfurt, Harry, 216
Friendship, 19

G

Generosity, 7, 28, 34, 37–38, 197
Gifts, 7
God, 44–46, 48–50, 54–56, 58, 60, 64–67, 77, 104, 148–150, 152–153, 155–157
Good Samaritan, 14–15
Good, 2–4, 13, 18–26, 28–29, 51, 54–55, 60–61, 64; intrinsic, 70–73, 78, 102–103, 206. *See also* Praiseworthy; Meritorious
Goods, 7, 47, 86
Grace, 49, 55, 65
Gratitude, 28, 58, 131
Guilt, 1–2

H

Happiness, 19, 47, 95–97
Hare, R.M., 157–158
Heaven, 48
Heroism, 4–8, 19–20, 57, 84, 88–91, 93, 95–98, 100–103, 111, 138, 190, 196, 199, 205
Heyd, David, 7–9, 18–19, 21–22, 24–27, 29, 39–40, 97–100, 111, 131, 189–194, 198–199, 205
Heinous acts, 183, 190
Holiness, 56
Holy Catholic Church, 9, 44–46, 48, 53–54. *See also* Roman Catholic
Honesty, 97
Honor, 46, 53
Humberstone, I.L., 186

I

Ideals, 26–27, 88–89, 91–93, 95, 175–176
Illegality, 190
Impermissible acts. *See* Forbidden acts

Indifferent acts, 23, 75–78, 136
Indulgences, 44–46, 48, 51, 53–54
Inhuman acts, 183
Injustice, 167–168, 175
Insensitivity, moral, 123, 140–141, 147
Intentions, 18–20, 22, 29. *See also* Motives

J

Jacobs, Russell, 92
Jesus Christ, 44–46, 48–49, 51, 54–57, 61, 65
Judaism, 49
Judgments, moral, 162. *See also* Aretaic judgments; Deontic judgments
Justice, 72–73, 103–104, 219. *See also* Social Justice
Justification, 51–52

K

Kant, Immanuel, 33–34, 70–71, 73, 77–78, 121, 137, 200
Kantian ethics, 10, 69–70, 104, 208
Kierkegaard, Soren, 10, 154
Kindness, 111, 213
Knowledge, 71–73

L

Labadists, 63
Ladd, John, 215
Law, moral, 46, 49–52, 54, 60, 65–67, 183–184
Lawgiver, moral, 187–188
Legalism, 120–121, 123, 192–193
Liberty, 46
Love, 50, 55, 57, 59–60, 63–66
Lucian, 15–16

Luther, Martin, 9, 44, 49–55, 61, 66, 121, 153
Luxury, 16

M

McConnell, Terrance, 218
McGoldrick, Patricia, 90–94
MacIntyre, Alasdair, 131
Marriage, 53–54
Martyrdom, 51, 61, 66
Melanchthon, Philip, 9, 44, 52–54, 60, 121
Mercy, 8
Merit, 8; treasury of, 45, 48, 51, 54, 59
Meritorious acts, 3–5, 17–18, 22, 45, 48–49, 51, 53, 55, 60, 72, 78, 104, 107, 118, 132, 193. *See also* Good; Praiseworthy acts
Mill, John Stuart, 33–34, 115–116, 120, 200
Moore, G.E., 70, 99, 100, 101, 103
Mortal Sins. *See* Sin
Motives, 28, 135, 137, 140–141, 143–146, 164, 166. *See also* Intentions

N

Neglect, 8
Neutral acts, 106–107, 109, 111, 116–117, 124, 126–128, 133
New, Christopher, 70, 95–101, 103
Niebuhr, Reinhold, 65–66
Nietzschean morality, 25
Nixon, Richard, 4, 211
Noble acts, 164
Non-obligatory acts, 7, 23–24, 39, 122–123, 126, 140, 160. *See also* Permissible acts

O

Obedience, 47–49, 51, 65, 69–70
Obligation, 196–207; conditional, 81; group, 27. *See also* Duty; Requirements, moral
Offence, 11, 23, 106–112, 114–117, 125–128, 181–209
Optimality, 83, 100–101, 103
Optional acts, 46, 48–52, 57–58, 69, 120–121, 140, 147, 152, 159, 206
Ought implies can, 62, 64–65, 67, 97, 101, 149, 172
Overspending. *See* Spending
Owing, 26–28

P

Paul, Saint, 48, 53, 174
Pardoning, 8
Pelagians, 63
Penalties. *See* Punishment
Perfection, 48–50, 55–57, 60–61, 63–65
Permissible acts, 87, 90, 95, 102, 110–111, 182, 191–193, 201–204. *See also* Non-obligatory acts
Persecution, 50
Peterfreund, Sheldon, 17–18
Phariseeism, 120, 200–204, 206–207. *See also* Legalism
Pleasure, 19, 71–73, 120. *See also* Carnal pleasures
Possible worlds, 79–81, 83–87, 102, 109
Poverty, 46–48
Praise, 4–5, 22, 90–91, 165, 174
Praiseworthy acts, 2–3, 17–18, 194–204. *See also* Goodness; Meritorious acts
Prayer, 47
Prescriptivism, 70, 88, 94
Pride, 46–49

Principle, 20, 22, 171, 175–176
Principles, moral, 157–158
Promising, 7, 38, 177–178
Protestantism, 44, 55, 60, 65, 132, 148–149, 153, 155–156, 158
Purposeful acts, 8
Punishment, 44–45, 54, 74
Purgatory, 44
Pybus, Elizabeth, 70, 88–95, 97, 100, 102, 103

Q

Quasi-supererogation, 10, 105–115, 117, 122–125, 127, 129, 140, 149, 152, 160, 200, 202
Quasi-offence, 106–107, 111–112, 114–117, 124–125, 127, 140, 149, 184, 186, 189
Quakers, 63
Quietists, 63

R

Rahner, Karl, 55–57, 60–63, 67, 214
Rashdall, Hastings, 101
Reasons, moral, 162–177, 179–180; of self-interest, 162–177, 179–180
Reformation, 9
Reformers, 60, 66, 122. *See also* Luther; Calvin; Melanchthon
Reid, L.A., 101
Reid, Thomas, 219
Relativism, 65
Relaxation, 83, 85, 87
Resistance, 1–4, 6, 9, 207; of temptation, 108–112, 117, 123
Requirements, moral, 3, 7, 17, 23, 37, 44–46, 54, 59, 66–67, 82, 119–121, 124, 132–134, 139, 159, 184. *See also* Duty; Obligation
Riches. *See* Wealth

Right, 3, 6, 20, 70, 131–132, 138, 147, 189, 193, 195. *See also* Goodness; Merit
Rights, 7–8, 77, 190
Risk, 3–4, 10, 138, 166, 170, 173–174, 176–177, 179
Roguish acts, 198
Roman Catholic, 55, 65. *See also* Holy Catholic Church
Ross, C.D., 70–73, 75, 77–78, 102–103, 162

S

Sacrificing, 6, 11, 28, 89–90, 98–99, 174–176, 179, 197, 208. *See also* Self-sacrifice
Saints, 4, 6–8, 44–46, 51, 54, 60–61, 84, 88–91, 95–98, 100–103, 111, 138–139, 144–146, 190, 199, 205
Schumaker, Millard, 212–213
Schweitzer, Albert, 158
Second-mile acts, 37, 57–61, 63–66, 122–123, 134, 153, 156. *See also* Duty, beyond
Self-interest, 46. *See also* Reasons of self-interest
Self-sacrifice, 7, 57–58, 60–61, 63, 66, 111, 138, 145–146, 161, 164, 170–172, 206
Self-righteousness, 193
Service, 7, 149–152, 154–157, 159, 163
Sidgwick, Henry, 163
Sin, 44, 56–57, 184; mortal, 183–184, 192; venial, 183–184, 192. *See also* Badness; Evil; Wrong
Skepticism, 11, 199, 207
Sloth, 193
Smugness, 121–122
Social Justice, 167–168
Society, 21–22, 64, 121, 206
Sosa, Ernest, 11, 23–24, 184–186

T

Spending, 14–16, 45
Stocker, Michael, 30–34, 37
Superiority, 121
Survival, 15

T

Temptation. *See* Resistance to Temptation
Ten Commandments, 45
Teresa, Mother, 158
Theism, 44, 55, 57, 61–62, 65, 67, 69, 77, 79, 101, 104, 121, 132, 148–153, 155, 158
Theologians, 55, 63
Theological ethics, 9, 104, 118, 148–149
Thomas Aquinas, Saint. *See* Aquinas, Saint Thomas
Treasury of works, 44–45, 48, 51, 53–54, 60, 65–66. *See also* Merit
Tranoy, Knut, 165, 193–194, 199, 205
Trianosky, Gregory, 10, 131–147, 200, 217

U

Understanding, 1–3, 11, 208–209
Urmson, J.O., 4–6, 57, 88–91, 93, 95–96, 100, 102–103, 169, 171, 217
Utilitarianism, act, 69–70, 77, 79, 82–83, 85, 97, 99, 101–104, 187, 208, 218. *See also* Consequentialism

V

Value, 9, 13, 18–19, 24–29, 121, 166
Venial Sins. *See* Sin
Vice, 131–132, 135–137, 141, 147, 154
Victims, 14–15
Villainy, 183, 185–186, 190–191, 198–199, 205
Virginity, 48. *See also* Celebacy; Chastity
Virtue, 10, 36, 38, 70–73, 89–91, 93, 95–97, 125, 131–132, 136–141, 143–148, 154, 159–160, 202. *See also* Aretaic judgments
Vocation, 10, 125, 132, 148–160, 217
Voluntary acts, 18, 21–22, 54
Volunteering, 7, 24, 27–28, 120
Vows, 47
Vulgate, 14

W

Waldheim, Kurt, 1–4, 6, 207
Wealth, 46–49, 53. *See also* Goods
Welfare, 19, 77, 174
Well being, 28
Wisdom, 162–163, 165, 167, 170
Work, 149, 156. *See also* Vocation
World War II, 6
Wrong, 17–18, 39–40, 131, 135, 139, 143, 193, 195. *See also* Badness; Evil; Sin